'STODDY':
ENGLAND'S
FINEST
SPORTSMAN

◆◆◆◆◆◆◆◆◆◆◆◆◆◆

David Frith

Von Krumm Publishing

First published in Great Britain by
VON KRUMM PUBLISHING
21 Sackville Rd
Hove BN3 3WA
www.vonkrummpublishing.co.uk

Copyright 2015 David Frith

A CIP record of this book is available from the British Library.

Cover and all interior graphic design by Lottie Warren

Printed and Bound in Great Britain by
CPI Group (UK) Croydon

ISBN 978-0-9567321-3-2

Contents

◆◆◆

PREFACE

THREE great cricketers died in 1915, intensifying the widespread sadness which arose daily from the overwhelming lists of Great War casualties.

The mighty Dr W.G.Grace, aged 67, succumbed to a stroke in October.

In Sydney, Victor Trumper's death in June at the age of 36 generated national grief.

And on Easter Saturday, in London, less than a mile from Lord's cricket ground, where he had once enchanted big crowds many times over, Andrew Ernest Stoddart, England's captain in the first great Ashes series (1894-95), lay on his bed and shot himself.

The tragedy struck profoundly at cricket's heart, because it was a life wasted: a life, moreover, which had been filled with sporting glories such as even Grace and Trumper never knew. For Drewy Stoddart had led England at rugby as well as at cricket (Lancashire's A.N.Hornby remains the only other Englishman to have achieved this, albeit in only one rugby match and three cricket Tests). Stoddart had been in turn the finest rugby footballer as well as the best batsman in the world. He had topped the records list with a supreme innings of 485 for his club, Hampstead, the highest score ever made in any form of organised cricket, bettered only seven times since, most notably by young Arthur Collins, who compiled 628 not out in a junior house match at Clifton College in 1899 – and who was killed in the Great War.

Whenever Stoddart batted with W.G.Grace, he was junior only by definition. The younger man was often the more watchable.

The fact is that even as long ago as 1912 "Stoddy's" romantic sporting life seemed to be misting over. The magazine *Cricket*, in musing over his matchless achievements, logged a shrewd assessment: "But this will be regarded in these days of rush and scramble as ancient history. It is strange how seldom one sees Stoddart's name mentioned when heroes of the past are descanted upon nowadays. Yet he was one of the very greatest, a far finer bat than some of those who are named more often."

Days of rush and scramble? What would the writer have thought of the frantic, vapid lifestyle of people in the 21st Century?

Forty-seven years ago I was drawn to investigate the life and career of this extraordinary Englishman. How could his name have faded, while those of the WGs and MacLarens and Jessops and Ranjitsinhjis lived on? The answer was partly that writers, principally Neville Cardus, had continued to sing the praises of certain cricketers (but not others) over the decades. Further, there was, and always has been, a stigma about suicide. It sometimes frightens people, and generates feelings far beyond simple sadness. It is often tinged with shame, yet the twilighting of his name is not only baffling: it is shameful.

In a mood bordering on indignation, I set about trying to retrieve "Stoddy" from this strange and unwarranted obscurity, to display his unique contemporary popularity, even to recreate his identity in its full charm and revive the splendour of his sporting achievements over all those late-Victorian summers and winters. There were no domestic computers in the late 1960s, but there were plenty of trips to the Newspaper Library at Colindale. And one uniquely valuable contact all those years ago was a man who was close to 100 years of age and had actually known the young Stoddart at school. Then came acquisition of Stoddart's large scrapbooks from his two tours of Australia as captain in the 1890s. Alongside some items in the scrapbooks he had written "For book". There never was a book by him, whatever his intentions might have been. But I was very glad to have written one for him.

That book – *"My Dear Victorious Stod"* (an expression taken, for better or worse, from Queen Victoria's imagined utterance in *Melbourne Punch* following England's wondrous victory in the 1894-95 Ashes series) – was accepted by a major London publishing house. Months later, perhaps having mislaid the typescript, when asked about progress they stated that they had changed their minds.

It was a desperate time for a young author who had devoted three years to the research and writing of what he considered to be a significant offering midst the inconsequential "autobiographies" and other unaccountable junk hitting the market. (Little has changed.) So, with the help of the wealthy young collector Anthony Baer, I published it myself.

It was decided to print only 400 copies, numbered and signed. Some enthusiastic reviews, notably by John Arlott and Ian Wooldridge, boosted sales upon the book's completion in 1970. And then, to cap it all, the Cricket Society bestowed upon the Stoddart biography its first-ever Book of the Year award.

Seven years later, Lutterworth Press published an enhanced edition, with some footnotes added to the original story. John Arlott wrote in his foreword: "This story of a life of privilege, splendid sporting achievements, the strange late marriage, and the tragic end, give this biography greater profundity than the average 'sporting life'." He ventured the thought that Stoddart could readily have provided the material for a novel (as indeed it subsequently did: in Anthony Quinn's 2012 work *Half of the Human Race*).

Since the 1977 edition of Stoddart's story an enormous quantity of additional material has been unearthed from countless sources, creating a need – indeed, a responsibilty – to produce a greatly enhanced volume. The author rues the amount of material he was not able to find and access all those years ago. However, with every newly-discovered detail safely filed over these many years, we now have something which can be regarded as a complete biography, as complete as it will ever be. Not for the first time, I thank Patrick Ferriday of Von Krumm Publishing for having faith in me and my subject.

With this publication comes fresh hope that "Stoddy's" name will be restored to the pinnacle which it once occupied, for he was a sporting god, England's greatest sportsman in what has become known as sport's Golden Age – or ever since.

DAVID FRITH
Guildford
February 2015

CHAPTER 1

A Geordie Comes South

THE manner of his death was consistent with his life. The pistol shot had not been sufficiently audible to frighten others in the house, and there was little blood about his face. It was as if, considerate and courteous to the end, although he had grown uncharacteristically irritable, he had not wished to disturb anyone. For Drewy Stoddart, all hope had gone. The glories of his rugby and cricket careers seemed to have faded. He had withdrawn from society as his breakdown took hold. Money worries were a key factor as the Great War dragged fearfully on. His application to MCC to reactivate his membership, which had lapsed probably because of his straitened circumstances, was denied. That must have hurt.

His fame should have been assured in perpetuity. Quite apart from his glorious rugby career, his cricket deeds were top-shelf. His world record innings of 485 was one thing. In county cricket for Middlesex he drew the crowds to Lord's and elsewhere, but in Test cricket, where men are judged to the finest degree, he made a spectacular mark by leading England to victory in the thrilling 1894-95 Australian season in what was the first great Ashes series. His 173 at Melbourne in the second Test that summer remained the highest score by an England captain in an Ashes Test for a further 80 years.

An unidentified writer was among those who attempted to place Stoddart in cricket's pantheon after news of his death on April 3, 1915 had come through. He recalled the MCC Centenary match at Lord's in 1887, when veteran Arthur Shrewsbury (rated the best batsman in the world by Dr W.G.Grace, aside from himself) together with his 24-year-old batting partner A.E.Stoddart charmed the crowd with a first-wicket stand of 266 against a testing bowling line-up. "I spoke to both of these classic batsmen in the evening of that day," wrote this admirer. "Arthur Shrewsbury said, 'He'll be the best bat in the world.' Stoddart a few minutes later said, 'I never knew what batting meant till I watched Arthur Shrewsbury today.' Remember they had been face to face with each other for over four hours.

That evening Stoddart was elected a member of MCC."

There follows recollection of A.E.Stoddart the bowler (although understandably regarded principally as a batsman, he bowled nearly 15,000 balls in first-class cricket, taking 278 wickets at 23.63): "I remember once at Lord's, when Middlesex were playing Notts. Shrewsbury had collected his usual century and seemed unmovable. Stoddart was put on to bowl at the Nursery end. The wicket was 'plumb'. I got over the ropes and lay down on the off side of the screen, almost exactly behind Stoddart's arm. Shrewsbury 'barn-doored' the first four balls, played forward – as he rarely did – at the fifth, which pitched six inches outside the off stump, missed the ball, and in the same action turned to walk back to the pavilion – as it seemed before the ball actually hit the wicket." This had been in late May 1890, and the mighty little Notts batsman had scored only 11.

What anguish lies in the fact that the lives of both these top-flight cricketers would come to an end with self-inflicted gunshot.

The anonymous admirer also recalled Stoddart's supreme reputation as a rugby footballer. And he also clarified the way in which he was addressed: he was universally known as Drewy in the earlier days of his sporting triumphs, and later as "Stoddy". He was seldom if ever referred to as Andrew (one imagines his parents may sometimes have used that form), and this was confirmed by the son of Hampstead Cricket Club historian F.R.D'O.Monro soon after the 1970 edition of the Stoddart biography was published.

The unsigned memoir closes with a telling appraisal of A.E.Stoddart's pleasant personality: "He created a popularity among his friends, his sporting foes, and an enormous public in England and Australia beyond precedent and without reproach. The world knew him as a sportsman, and that in the best sense. His friends knew him as a kindly comrade – to them this tragic ending is a real and personal sorrow.

"He had a proper ambition in sport – he had a great sense of loyalty to his friends. His tastes were simple, and he seemed happily content with his surroundings, with little ambition to court a greater position or to use his success for his own benefit. And if he felt that life, with all its present-day difficulties, did not provide him with a scope for his undoubted powers, if that keen regret – which we of his age share – at his inability to be in the fighting line in this hour of the nation's need weighed upon him and depressed him, still we can cherish a remembrance of many happy hours in the company of one who captained England in our two great national games." The vision of a middle-aged Stoddart in officer's uniform on the Western Front is tantalising.

In the late 1960s, when I found A.E.Stoddart's final residence, 115 Clifton Hill, just a short walk from Lord's, there was no-one at home when I called. I knocked on the front door of the house next to it, and a diminutive gentleman responded. He was Edward Hutton (1875-1969), a distinguished scholar, whose house had once been occupied by the artist William Powell Frith. (A commemorative plaque has been affixed. But no such plaque has marked Stoddart's last home, in spite of the author's two applications to English Heritage: an illogical and inexplicable response.)

Mr Hutton mentioned that his own house was home to a poltergeist, a phantom figure which appeared by the fireplace reading a newspaper. He recalled often seeing Stoddart standing by his drawing-room window and gazing down the road.

Did they ever speak to each other? They didn't, for it was an age when people first required a formal introduction. He seemed truly regretful now that he had not opened a conversation with the great sportsman, but he went to Italy shortly afterwards, and was never to see Stoddart again.

Captain Philip Trevor wrote in 1901 that aggregates and averages interested Stoddart appreciably less than they did cricket's recorders. "Mr Stoddart was wont to strike the bowler hard when the latter was fierce. What would he do with him, one may well ask, now that he has become tame?

"Years hence," he continued, "when cricket literature, historical or otherwise, takes the form of mere statistical reports, the name of Andrew Ernest Stoddart may not perchance appear in big print, but such of us who insist on inquiring not only what a man did but also how he did it will refuse to regard the size of type used as our means of measurement. Mr Stoddart was not in the habit of getting 2000 runs per cricket season, but he was very much in the habit of taking the bowler by the scruff of the neck when he had become troublesome; and it is as a winner of matches chiefly that his fame will live."

The advent of the 20th Century and the death of Queen Victoria shut tight a period of history, while the game's evolution nudged forward. Cricket's Golden Age was carried by a colourful bevy of glamorous figures: G.L."Croucher" Jessop, R.E."Tip" Foster, Ranjitsinhji, Archie MacLaren,

F.S.Jackson, Johnny Tyldesley, C.B.Fry, Hirst and Rhodes, and Victor Trumper from Australia. There seems to be something mean about a new century. It was noticeable that the 20th Century's passing (actually on New Year's Day 2001, not a year earlier) seemed to condemn the previous decades suddenly to a kind of obscurity.

Stoddart became secretary of The Queen's Club, West London, in 1906, and faced the hardest phase in any sportsman's life: the decline into almost total inactivity. He and his new bride maintained social contact for a time, entertaining at their home at 20 St John's Wood Road (since demolished), close to Lord's, the cricket ground he had graced for much of his adult life. A good deal heavier, greying, but still radiating an unmistakable and genial presence, he whiled away his time at Queen's, enjoying whisky and conversation with the members, his innate modesty cramping any temptation to plunge into reminiscence. His Stock Exchange activity scarcely provided relief from any sense of boredom.

The years shuffled past, and some months after the world had lowered itself into the mire of the Kaiser's War, his finances in jeopardy, suffering the depression of incipient pneumonia, locked into a crumbling marriage, and unable to face up to his lonely existence any longer, this much-loved man who had once had the English sporting world at his feet set about ending it all. He had just turned 52.

Since that gunshot, A.E.Stoddart, double international, has been consigned to the dimly-lit gallery of England's sadly and undeservedly half-forgotten heroes. It remains incomprehensible.

On March 10, 1863, the United Kingdom was lit up in celebration of the marriage of the Prince of Wales (later King Edward VII) to Princess Alexandra. Jenny Lind's sweet voice added lustre to the ceremony at Windsor Castle, and William Powell Frith, then in his heyday as an artist, sketched frantically into his drawing pad for the benefit of posterity. (Strangely, some years later the artist was to live in a house in St John's Wood next to one shortly to be occupied by Andrew Ernest Stoddart.)

North, beyond many bonfires and much illumination, Mrs Elizabeth Stoddart awaited the emergence of the gentle son she was to bear the following day, March 11. To place this into some further time context, Lloyd George was born on January 17, 1863 and boxing champion Bob Fitzsimmons on May 26. And propitiously for the new-born in South

Shields, that summer was to be beautifully warm and sunny.

Andrew Ernest Stoddart's birthplace

The Stoddart family lived at 10 Wellington Terrace, which now forms part of Beach Road, Westoe, South Shields, County Durham. Now numbered 51, it is a substantial terrace house in what was a select part of the town. The street runs down to a stretch of the sands lapped by the North Sea (known in Stoddart's youth as the German Ocean). A century later the property was occupied by the Bader Boys' Club. By 1979 this had given way to an organisation which supplied goods and services to nightclubs. Today a roller-shutter company occupies the premises.

The 1871 Census lists the Stoddart family at No.10: father aged 46, mother 38, three daughters in their teens, and the two sons, Henry Lawson (Harry), 12, and Andrew E. aged eight. There were two servants, Mary and Frances, both local girls. In the Census ten years earlier there had been three servants: whether this points to a slight diminution in George Stoddart's finances is open to conjecture.

The property was of three storeys, 52 steps from basement to the top (one for each year of A.E.Stoddart's life, as it happened). The rooms were large, and the domestics slept on the top floor. There were coal and wine cellars, and two spacious kitchens, soft water being drawn from rainwater tanks at low level. All the main rooms had ornate ceilings and fireplaces, and there was a bay window to the drawing-room. Each bedroom had a wash-basin, and speaking tubes connected the main rooms to the servants' quarters below. The servants regularly (before dawn) took the family washing to a public laundry. There was no shortage of bright flowers around the property when summer came.

A few doors away, at No.6, lived young Ernest Seton Thompson, who became an author, artist, naturalist and pioneer of scouting in Canada. He was two or three years older than A.E.Stoddart. They may have become acquainted as children, although Thompson went to Canada in 1866. It seems that they might have been fortunate to miss contagion when cholera hit the area that year (followed by smallpox in 1870), carried into this sea-port by unwitting seamen.

Drewy Stoddart's parents

A century later the opening scene of the popular television series *Whatever Happened to the Likely Lads?* was filmed among some ruined buildings in Wellington Street. And the record shows that a number of eminent people apart from Stoddart and Thompson have lived in South Shields: goalkeeper Sam Bartram, novelist Catherine Cookson, New Zealand prime minister Sir William Fox, comedian Eric Idle, film director Ridley Scott, and footballer Stan Mortenson.

Stoddart's father, George Best Stoddart (the middle name was his own mother's maiden name), was a wine, spirit and porter merchant, a bonded store dealer, a land agent in King Street, South Shields, and he was also the one-time owner of Bedlington Colliery. He was one of the founders, in 1850, of the Borough of South Shields Cricket Club, and his own father, Andrew Stoddart, was for 40 years agent to the Dean and Chapter of Durham in the 19th Century. This Andrew Stoddart was to die on April 3, 1869, 46 years to the day before his sporting grandson. Stoddart Street, in Tyne Dock, should keep the family name forever part of the town.

When Drewy was still a boy, and the coal industry was in the throes of major reform, the Stoddarts and their five children moved from Tyneside down to a village – almost certainly Radford, near Coventry – and then two years later to London. They took up residence in Ormonde Terrace, by Primrose Hill, with its enchanting surrounds, facing Regent's Park Zoo. It was, for any boy of nine and upwards with time on his hands, irresistibly close to Lord's cricket ground.

It is known that he had played the game at Wood Terrace, South Shields. Years later, South Shields Cricket Club were to make him an honorary life member, which pleased him greatly.

The young Stoddart was enrolled at St John's Wood School, often known as Oliver's, in Acacia Road, which runs eastwards from St John's Wood tube station. It was an establishment modest in size, serving as a prep school or, if the boy was not to have a public school education, where he could continue until 18 or 19. Drewy Stoddart was one of these. E.H.Shepard, the Winnie-the-Pooh artist, also went to Oliver's as a boy, and hated the discipline. The actor-director Bernard Miles lived in the building in later years. The death of the school's founder, the Reverend H.A.G.Oliver, led eventually to the school's decline.

There were about 120 boys at Oliver's, which had a large playground that was conducive to sports, rendering it as successful on that count as any private school in London. Although he suffered from rheumatism as a boy, there is record of young Drewy playing cricket for the school in 1876, when he was 13. The solemn little chap went in low in the order and was bowled for 2 by future Hampstead club colleague "Skipper" Pawling. Drewy's lifetime friend George Jeffery was also a low-order novice.

Westoe, South Shields, where a lad might enjoy a crisp snowy winter

At the age of 16 Drewy took a fancy to a girl who knew a boy at the junior school adjoining Oliver's, and would pass love notes through a gap in the fence to the boy, Francis B.Cooke, who duly delivered them to Stoddart's fancy. The starry-eyed youth from South Shields probably hit the ball even harder after receiving her replies via little Francis behind the tool-shed at the end of the garden playground.

Carrying his 95 years lightly, Mr Cooke, a writer on yachting who had responded to my letter of appeal in a national newspaper, recalled his schoolyard duties with wistful joy not all that far short of a century later. And as the last witness on earth, he gave a priceless reply to the question "How did Stoddy speak?" He spoke, said Mr Cooke (who died in 1974 aged 102), "with the faintest Geordie accent."

Another nonagenarian witness to the early years of Stoddart was Cecil Turner, who recalled the immense pride in his household when a brother bowled the high-scoring adolescent Stoddart in a playground game.

AGE 3.
From a Photo. by J. H. Haggitt, South Shields.

A. E. STODDART.
BORN 1863.

R. ANDREW ERNEST STOD-
DART is a native of Durham.
His cricket career, which is most
brilliant, practically commenced
when he joined the Hampstead
Club in 1885. He made no fewer than five

AGE 13.
From a Photo. by R. L. Graham, Leamington.

centuries for that club in July and August of
that year. In the following year he hit up

the highest individual innings (485) for
Hampstead *v.* Stoics, and three days later
made 207 for the same club. As a batsman
he has great strength, and plays very hard.
He is also a fair change bowler, and an
excellent field anywhere. He has gained
the highest honours on the football field, and
made his first appearance in International

AGE 21.
From a Photo. by Geo. F. Dew, Coventry.

football in the season of 1884–85. Mr.
Stoddart went to Australia with Lord
Sheffield's cricketers 1891–92, for whom he
did brilliant work. Last year he became one
of the holders of the rare record of two
hundreds in a match.

PRESENT DAY.
From a Photo. by Bradshaw, Newgate Street.

Early stages in a future hero's life (from the Strand Magazine)

Stoddart's cricket was developing significantly in parallel with his rugby prowess, even though the winter game left him with an early side injury that bothered him for years to come. It was played uncompromisingly, and he once had his shirt torn so violently that major repairs were needed. He asked a classmate's sister to do it for him for fear of alarming his mother.

Oliver's School, as seen by another eminent former pupil Ernest Shepard

Francis Cooke, closing in on 100 years in age

At fourteen he joined the Harlequins Rugby Club, and a photograph of the 1880-81 team shows him with chest out, upper lip hairless, standing behind darker, heavier brother Harry, who bore the same Stoddart handsomeness. Drewy was to play 46 times for the 'Quins between September 1880 and March 1886.

They were both making lots of runs for Blenheim Cricket Club, and Drewy's first recorded century came in 1880, when he was seventeen, for Blenheim against Eton Park. In school and neighbourhood circles he had become the object of admiration that would one day soon swell to national hero-worship.

His father died in the spring of 1882, at his residence 1 Ormonde

Terrace, after long suffering from the dreaded consumption (tuberculosis), and about this time he lost an uncle, John Broughton, who had been a mayor of South Shields. It was the momentous year in cricket history when the Australian "colonials", with Fred Spofforth as bushranger in chief, rocked England with their seven-run victory at The Oval which led to the body of English cricket being tearfully cremated, the Ashes urn becoming the eternal symbol of Anglo-Australian cricket combat.

The young man living in St John's Wood was now around five-feet-ten in height and weighed 12 stone 9 pounds, with strong limbs and torso unmistakably marking out an athlete. In the years to follow a great deal of his energy would be expended in battles for these newly-created Ashes.

After leaving Oliver's, where the Reverend Mr Oliver and Mr Bird had given him his grooming, Stoddart, who seemed to be blessed with a gift for drawing, became articled to a firm of architects in London and entered the Royal Academy School. The absence of records suggests that he failed to survive the probation term.

The seventeen-year-old Drewy Stoddart (standing right) holds a fringe place in the Harlequins Rugby Club team group 1880-81, the flowing moustache not yet part of his facial décor. Brother Harry sits in front, left arm across thigh

Blenheim CC, like Oliver's School and Merchant Taylors' too, used the Eton and Middlesex ground (north of Primrose Hill, where Elsworthy

Road and Wadham Gardens now lie), and here week after week Drewy played alongside brother Harry and others who were to become firm friends over the years: Jack Trotman as well as George Jeffery, fine footballers both, and the Whinneys, related to the Stoddarts by marriage. In 1880 Harry Stoddart and C.R.Poulter put on 212 for Blenheim's first wicket against Eton Park, the innings amounting to 517 for 11 wickets. In 1882 a man named Cooke took seven Blenheim wickets for 0, leaving Drewy and his companions gasping at 13 for seven. But 1883 was a good year. He took a stack of wickets for Blenheim and recorded two centuries, one (108) against his old school and 123 against Willesden, when mighty Harry Stoddart hit 90 and the brothers reduced the field to chaos.

Net practice was keen and amusing, and often young Cooke would hurry along in time to bowl to his idol, who sometimes set a piece of paper on a length and challenged him to pitch the ball on it. The sessions were usually concluded with a full-blooded drive across the ground, and by the time Francis Cooke had retrieved the ball the net would be empty and he would have no alternative but to return home and face up to his homework.

That autumn, controversially and to the chagrin of 'Quins, Drewy Stoddart joined Blackheath Rugby Football Club, starting an association that was to last through his career at the top in rugby. Billy Williams, full back, Middlesex wicketkeeper, and later responsible for siting Twickenham rugby ground ("Billy's cabbage patch"), brought him down to Blackheath, and that winter he swept and swerved his way to nine tries (an impressive three in his first match), second to the immortal Wilfred Bolton, who recorded 28. By the time his body gave up, "Stoddy" had played 190 matches for "The Heathens".

In 1884 Stoddart crossed paths once more with Francis Cooke, who was on holiday in Bournemouth, fishing from the pier, pulling in smelts as fast as he could drop his line back in the water.

"Hello, young Cooke!"

It was a soft voice, still faintly North-East. Cooke turned to see Drewy Stoddart, who attached some string to his fashionable cane and joined Francis in his aspirations. At the end of an absorbing hour they left the pier, Cooke with almost sufficient provision for the rest of his holiday and "Stoddy" with some unexpected bounty for his landlady.

He scored two centuries for Bournemouth that August. But the coming year was to be the important one: in 1885 he joined Hampstead

Cricket Club, for whom his performances entitle him to rank as the greatest club cricketer of them all.

CHAPTER 2

A World Record

"FOOTBALL is my game," he was once heard to say (meaning Rugby Union, for Rugby League, the professional bastard son, had not yet been devised). And it certainly seemed Stoddart's game in the winter of 1884-85. He touched down 16 times for Blackheath and was top try-scorer for the season. Gaining representative honours for South v North, he seemed to play better the higher the company he kept, despite an injury to his side which for ever more caused him pain. He had been spotted an hour or more before a game rolling in agony on the dressing-room floor in an endeavour to free himself from pain. So considerate of his parents' feelings was he that when his jersey was ripped he found a school friend's sister to repair it for him rather than cause alarm at home.

Five other Blackheathens lined up with him for the South on his home ground, the Rectory Field, five days before Christmas, and amidst the finest players in England, Stoddart acquitted himself well in the boisterous conditions. With Gregory Wade, an Australian (and future premier of New South Wales), he continually menaced the North line, and his kicking was especially penetrative. The South managed to cling to a one try to nil advantage, and even if, as the crowd broke up, there was a feeling that the South had had all the luck, for A.E.Stoddart it had been a satisfying introduction into representative football.

On January 3 came the ultimate honour: he was awarded his first England cap for the Wales match at St Helens, Swansea and, with the large red rose on his breast pocket, he partook of an extremely fast match, won by England after some misgivings by one goal and four tries to one goal and one try. The 5000 spectators witnessed an interesting contest, with the Welsh forwards having put up some stout opposition.

A month later Stoddart again took up his wing three-quarter position for his country against Ireland at the Whalley Range ground in Manchester, and his brilliancy coupled with that of club-mate Bolton and

J.J.Hawcridge along the back line and Alan Rotherham (who committed suicide in August 1898) at half-back more than evened the balance in a match in which England's forwards were "palpably worsted by the Irishmen in the scrimmage" - notwithstanding the fact that most of the visitors were suffering still from seasickness.

His black and red jersey, copious knickerbockers and international jumper lovingly placed away in a drawer, and with a fresh set of white cricket gear out of mothballs, he commenced his career with Hampstead. Elder brother Harry had left England after a serious romance had foundered, now aiming to set himself up as a rancher in the Wild West of Colorado. The mighty fraternal batting partnership was dissolved forever. Drewy was never again to be overshadowed by Harry.

He made his mark with Hampstead instantly by opening and top-scoring with 16 out of 58 and taking seven wickets against Blackheath Morden. Three days later, at Kensington Park's pleasant ground at Wormwood Scrubs, he topped the innings again with 65, and repeated his dominance at the end of June with 26 against Crystal Palace. Yet vastly more substantial things lay ahead.

Against Granville he carried his bat for 185. A fortnight later there was another century against Hendon, then an important 100 for Hampstead against an MCC combination. Next week it was seven Richmond wickets, and in the return with Blackheath Morden he cracked 108 runs and took six wickets. On the following Saturday he powered his way to 126, and *Cricket,* the twopenny weekly journal, stepped in: "Mr Stoddart, whom I take to be the well-known Rugby International footballer, has completed as many as four centuries for the Hampstead Club. As, in addition, Mr Stoddart is a particularly good bowler as well as a brilliant field, I should fancy the executive of the Middlesex County Cricket Club, for which I believe he is qualified, would do well to seriously entertain the advisability of giving him a good trial."

How proud he must have been to show this to the family.

The attention of Bob Thoms, the kindly umpire and talent scout, had already been drawn towards the high-scoring youngster by Smith-Turberville of the Hampstead club, and Thoms' recommendation carried significant weight in gaining the county club's interest. In later years he often greeted Smith-Turberville with a hopeful "Got any more Stoddarts knocking about Hampstead way?"

The invitation to play for the county duly arrived. He was staying with a brother-in-law in Coventry when a wire was forwarded from home asking him to play for Middlesex against Yorkshire.

"Here's a how-d'ye-do!" he exclaimed, for it had never occurred to him that he might be good enough to join the swells he had watched emerging from the pavilion at Lord's. There was the added difficulty that his cricket gear was in London, while the match was to start in Bradford next day. His brother-in-law lent him some flannels, which were rather too large, and the coachman lent him an old green carpet-bag, prehistoric pads and superannuated bat. Some tennis shoes completed his kit, and off went "Stoddy" to Bradford, longing still for his own carefully-selected bat and neat clothes.

As the bags came out of the van, the green carpet article appeared among the smart leather ones, and one of the dandy Middlesex amateurs remarked to the porter: "All except that one!" But Stoddart unashamedly claimed it.

On August 17, 1885, opening with E.H.Buckland, he was yorked by "Shoey" Harrison for 3. Perhaps the old bat and irregular clothing were impediments. In due course he had a bowl and took 0 for 7, and caught Bobby Peel, whose 71 kept Yorkshire at Middlesex's throat (and who would one day play a famous part in Stoddart's Test match triumphs).

Stoddart made 21 at the second attempt, caught off a drive against Test slow left-armer Ted Peate, having looked a batsman who might be of considerable value to a county still smarting from the indignity of 25 all out against Surrey. Certainly captain A.J.Webbe was satisfied with his young recruit as Middlesex went on to secure a cheering victory.

Immediately afterwards Middlesex opposed one of the greatest arrays of county cricket strength ever assembled into one field: Nottinghamshire, then enjoying the fourth of their five consecutive County Championships. There was the supreme Arthur Shrewsbury; brooding, plodding Will Scotton; the massive exhibitionist Modecai Sherwin behind the stumps; Billy Barnes, the allrounder with the Mephistopheles smile; Wilfred Flowers, well fed on Nottingham nourishment; "Dick" Attewell, penetrative or tight, as conditions required; and the towering, eagle-nosed William Gunn, finest cutter and driver when in-built caution made way: all of them current or coming Test match cricketers.

Stoddart opened with Buckland and had 102 on the board for

Middlesex in just over an hour and a half against this menacing attack. Stoddart went on to 79, "the feature of the match", stroking all around the pleasant Trent Bridge ground, sounding a fanfare to the cricket world with every elegant stroke.

In the twilight of his career he averred that what with the old cricket bag and the crummy pads, had he not made this score he would never have been heard of again outside Hampstead – which, as that other great allrounder C.B.Fry once wrote, you may or may not believe.

During an interval, Stoddart went for a stroll around the ground with A.J.Webbe, and they were gently accosted by a London boy who had taken time out from his holiday in Derbyshire to see the county match. It was Francis Cooke who had popped up again. Stoddart, now a county batsman, seemed very pleased to find him there. Francis walked with the two cricketers, and when they invited him into the privileged environs of the pavilion, his cup of joy was full.

Nottinghamshire went on to squeeze a first-innings lead and dispatch their visitors for a mere 144 second time round (Stoddart 15), but a draw ensued.

The next stop was Clifton, Bristol, and the opposition was Gloucestershire. For the tyro Andrew Ernest Stoddart it was an occasion of some moment: a first encounter with the illustrious Doctor William Gilbert Grace, who was due for a score.

And the Doctor, having been up all night attending a patient, gave a generous sample of the sort of cricket which had elevated him to such matchless levels of glory. He won the toss and opened the batting, and just over a day later, when the innings wound up for 348, he was 221 not out, his highest for eight years.

By close of play Tuesday, the Doctor and Woof had disposed of Middlesex once and half again, bowling unchanged through the first innings of 110 (WG 6 for 45) and finally bringing others in on the act as Middlesex slipped away to a peaceful innings defeat. WG snared five more wickets in the last innings, and young "Stoddy", having made only 2 in the first innings, was bowled by him for a duck in the second.

It must have been an overwhelming experience. And how could "Stoddy" ever have foreseen the great friendship that would develop with the "Grand Old Man" in the years to follow, when they would bat together and tour together?

There was one more county match for the 1885 season, against Kent at Maidstone, and Stoddart made 21 out of 187 on a moist pitch. Again Stoddart the bowler was overlooked, and when Middlesex batted again his final important innings of the summer amounted to a paltry 8, with ruin all around him.

It seems unlikely that Stoddart was finding complete bliss as a county cricketer. Cliques existed among the amateurs, many of whom had distinguished family and educational backgrounds, leaving the Durham man at this stage something of a loner. A.J.Webbe was kind to him, saw his potential, helped and advised him. But confusion clouded his mind as he considered the future.

For the first time his name appeared in *Wisden Cricketers' Almanack,* tantalisingly listing him as an allrounder "likely to be of great service to the county".

In the rugby world he was now revered and unanimously regarded as the finest wing three-quarter there had ever been. What a spectacle it must have been as the ball was fed out to him and he set sail for the line, sweeping and swerving past opponents until only the full back blocked his way. Here he often waited until the last split-second before leaping high over the lunging defender and sprinting in to score.

The high-jump tactic more than once landed him in trouble, and one head injury sustained when a desperate opponent grabbed his boot meant a spell in hospital. Twice during his career he suffered concussion of the brain.

He could drop-kick beautifully with either foot, and it was a phenomenal kick into a howling gale for Middlesex against Yorkshire that brought his county victory by one all-important goal to four then-insignificant tries. It was an historic kick in that it persuaded the Rugby Union to review and then amend the scoring system.

The pattern of the rugby game then was very different to that of today – quite apart from being strictly amateur. Scrimmages went on for an age, forwards kicking and thrashing about while the three-quarters waited patiently. When their turn came they had the chance to work some sparkling moves, as when Stoddart at Manchester zigzagged through the ranks of the opposing backs from within his own half on a very wet ground to score the *three* tries of the match.

One of his most interesting and unusual exploits was passed on by A.A.Thomson: "Once, playing for Harlequins against West Kent on Chislehurst Common, Stoddart dashed towards the enemy line in his usual steam-engine fashion, only to find that the area behind goal was deep – not inches but feet – in water. Without an instant's hesitation he dived in, head first, like a tufted duck, and was an unconscionable time in coming up again. The referee had almost decided to have the pond dragged, when Stoddart reappeared, smiling, having scored what was probably the first submarine try in rugger history."

He was again Blackheath's top try-scorer in 1885-86, with 11 touchdowns, and played in all three internationals. At the Rectory Field, Wales showed improved form, and perceptive judges were reading sagely into their display. They went down by a try to two tries and a goal, despite superiority in the scrimmages and some determined tackling. Stoddart, playing with his good friend George Jeffery under the famous C.J.B.Marriott, Blackheath's captain, landed a place-kick after the English forward Charles Elliot had surprised everyone by calling for a mark after catching a Welsh miskick, disregarding what had seemed to be a clear run in for a try. Elliot's mark at least 40 yards out, it was said, might have won applause in Durham,

The Scotland v England rugby match, Edinburgh 1886: a battle for tough men; Stoddart was in the thick of it

his county of origin, "but it met with emphatic and forcible expressions of disapproval from the English captain and the 'finished' players of the South". Stoddart's kick ensured that "the laugh at the finish was on Elliot's side".

This was the match in which, as recorded by Huw Richards in *The Red and White*, just before that decisive kick Stoddart's shorts had slipped down as he sprinted along the right wing. Embarrassed, he left the field for repairs.

At Lansdowne Road, Dublin, before a very large audience, Marriott kicked off, and the Stoddart-Rotherham magic was soon evident, the ball swinging its way along the back line and Stoddart bringing off several bewitching runs. He took the penalties, though not to any great advantage, and the match developed into a grim tussle, with the lighter Irishmen gradually giving ground. Wilkinson went over for England but Stoddart's place-kick failed. Nevertheless the Englishmen took the result and felt justifiably pleased with themselves as they splashed in the bath afterwards.

Foul weather delayed the Scotland match at Raeburn Place, Inverleith, Edinburgh from March 6 to March 13, 1886, when a tough, determined contest ended without any score. Stoddart was described as being "indisposed", and for one reason or another it was to be his last Home International for four years. This might have been the match when he was concussed and was so keen not to be ruled out of the evening's convivialities that he bought an evening paper, discovered that he had played well, and confidently joined his team-mates.

He enjoyed most sports, and according to Herbert Chipp he could have attained a very high standard at lawn tennis: "It was truly refreshing to hear a cricketer of Stoddart's rank and achievements speak with admiration of a game for which in those days most followers of cricket had no epithet contemptuous enough."

In middle age, while employed at The Queen's Club, he embarked upon tennis with tremendous zeal, receiving his first lessons from the esteemed coach Andre, who had him mystified in the beginning: "I don't understand *this* game," Stoddart exclaimed to a friend. "The fellow kept on saying 'Keep the head up, sir, keep the head up!' till I was looking at the skylight and couldn't see the blessed ball at all. All I've got out of my first lesson is a crick in the back of the neck."

Of course, Andre had meant that the head of the *racquet,* not the player, should be kept up, as recommended by the great Peter Latham.

Tennis elbow was to contribute to Stoddart's withdrawal from active sport around 1907. He had refused to rest the injured arm and it had become really bad, forcing him to give up golf too just as he had developed a strong taste for it. The jar of cricket ball on bat also became unbearable, and so a man who had lived for sport and prided himself in his physical condition actually grew ill from lack of that same exercise.

At least in his prime, while the chance was there, he had ridden horse and excelled at real tennis as well as hockey (playing skilfully as wing forward for Hampstead). He was also a first-class billiards player, and without being a Charlie Mitchell, he was sometimes a force to be reckoned with in the boxing ring, despite his innately gentle nature. He was truly a sporting man of leisure born into the appropriate era.

The summer of 1886 saw his establishment as a Middlesex opening batsman, under the captaincy of G.F.Vernon, with J.G.Walker occupying the other opening berth until later that summer. Then Alexander Josiah Webbe (Harrow, Oxford, gentleman, reliable, experienced, 31 years of age) came back after the death of his brother to form with Stoddart one of the very best opening duets.

It was a year of destiny for Drewy Stoddart. In July the magazine Cricket (edited by C.W.Alcock) featured him as its front-page celebrity, and then later in the month announced that he intended to settle in Colorado in the autumn. Perhaps brother Harry's letters had excited him.

"I should fancy," opined the editor, "so keen an athlete will find it very difficult to tear himself away from cricket and [rugby] football, in both of which he has made his mark, and I should not be surprised after all to hear that at least he has deferred the parting, which is said to be such sweet sorrow. Personally I hope to see him yet in the attainment of the highest honours of amateur cricket."

The writer's hopes were fulfilled beyond expectation in the exciting years to come, but at the time of writing "Stoddy" was experiencing grievous disappointment with Middlesex, averaging 19 over sixteen innings and finding the Lohmanns, Peates and Emmetts on rain-affected pitches several degrees more difficult than the average club bowler.

George Lohmann, the tall, blond and charming ladies' man, was to prove a recurring problem. Stoddart liked to hit the medium-pace and fast bowlers hard, and this impetuosity often brought his downfall against England's greatest – Tom Richardson, Bill Lockwood and later George Hirst, with his left-arm late swingers. But if these were to become his betes noires, there were four who were more noire than the others: Dick Attewell, Arthur Mold, Bobby Peel, and the Australian C.T.B. "Terror" Turner.

Attewell, the admirable and kindly Notts professional, took his wicket more than anyone else did, and in so sensitive a man one wonders to what degree he worried himself out as the Attewell dismissals piled up. The bowler, for his part, played down his own powers, and paid tribute many years later by saying that on a good wicket you could not bowl a ball to Stoddart which he could not hit for four if he really desired.

Mold, of the dubious delivery action, was deadly and destructive on pitches giving the slightest assistance – and there were plenty like that in the 1880s and early 1890s. Wilfred Rhodes, in his 91st year, patted his thigh tenderly and recalled vividly the feeling that a knife was being turned in your flesh after Mold had beaten the bat and hit you.

Charlie Turner, the terror with protruding ears, was to capture Stoddart's increasingly desirable wicket 19 times in all (nine times in Test matches). But then "The Terror", touching five feet eight in height and whose head resembled that of Emperor Claudius, caused more than just one England batsman troubled sleep.

Drewy Stoddart warmed up for this phenomenal club season of 1886 with several attractive innings for Hampstead, including 127 against the long-suffering Granville side off whom he was to carve another hundred in July.

The county campaign commenced with a two-day innings defeat by Surrey (Stoddart 3 and 4) and on the Monday morning he made his way to Lord's for his first contest on the historic strip. He may have stroked his moustache pensively that evening after twice having been dismissed cheaply by the Kent bowlers in one day's play. Rain had dampened the pitch, helping 22 batsmen back to the pavilion before sunset.

He spent practically the entire month of June at Lord's, witnessing at close quarters a five-hour 91 by the notorious plumb-bob from Yorkshire, Louis Hall, and a stirring innings by George Ulyett. He had reason to feel satisfied with a 29 against Yorkshire, and, given a bowl at last, pocketed a distinguished first victim, the Honourable M.B.Hawke, soon to be Lord

Hawke.

Stoddart made 42 against Gloucestershire before WG got a roundarmer through him, and a six-wicket Middlesex victory was gratefully chalked up. Then, without any sense of disgrace, Middlesex gave ground to Nottinghamshire, who were now winning their fifth title in a row, always to be acknowledged as one of the strongest combinations ever to dominate a county cricket field.

He next made 36 against Surrey on a firm surface, all four innings in the mid 200s, the finest balance for the taste of the majority of spectators.

Now, on June 24, he came face to face with Australian bowling for the first time. "Tup" Scott's men had a disastrous time in 1886, losing the three Test matches and many of the other contests. Here at Lord's, they almost threw away victory over Middlesex. Stoddart made only 3 and 16, falling twice to the mystic "Joey" Palmer. With the Australians needing a mere 123 to win, the 100 came up with only three down and it seemed as good as over, but George Burton kept taking wickets and soon amazingly part-time tourist Rowley Pope and wicketkeeper Jack Blackham found themselves in the last ditch with eight runs still required.

For the great 'keeper it was a strange pre-enactment of a similar situation in years to come, when a Test match at Sydney rested just as delicately on the determined shoulders of his bat. Now, at Lord's, he saw his team home, and the spectators congratulated themselves on being present at a cricket match truly worth the name.

At Chiswick Park a week later the Australians' 345 was sufficient for an innings win, Stoddart making 8 down at No.8 in the order before Garrett of the sinister beard caught-and-bowled him, then seeing out the second innings on that hot afternoon with 27 not out.

Focussing between cricket matches as best he could on stocks and shares, he made two centuries for Hampstead and sensationally took seven wickets for three runs against Crystal Palace. (In reply to an enquiry from the author in 1967, Middlesex cricketer R.H.Twining wrote that it was "quite probably that he would have been associated with Gregor MacGregor – but not a partner of his or a member of the Stock Exchange.")

The most telling of "Stoddy's" first-class innings was an extraordinarily patient 32 against that summer's county champions Nottinghamshire, Middlesex's final county fixture of the summer. He batted for 200 minutes for 32 against the best county attack in the land:

Wilfred Flowers, "Dick" Attewell, Alfred Shaw, Billy Barnes and Bill Lockwood (who would later move to Surrey). It served as useful preparation for one of the most famous innings the game has ever known.

In the Hampstead Cricket Club pavilion next day, August 22, 1886, A.Russell Parker was presented with a gold watch to mark his 20 years with the club. He expressed his thanks and his pride in "the best club, the best ground, and one of the best men in Middlesex" – referring unmistakably to A.E.Stoddart.

Drewy Stoddart - "The Masher" and a new world record-holder

A match against Stoics was programmed for that Wednesday, August 26, upon the Hampstead ground so heartily praised by Russell Parker in his speech. And on Tuesday night Stoddart and some of his friends went dancing and afterwards got to playing poker "just for half an hour". It was after midnight when they began, and when the well-dressed young stockbroker's assistant – now sometimes known as "The Masher" for his sartorial elegance – found himself winning substantial amounts of money he played on, perhaps mesmerised by the pattern of play but also a touch reluctant to leave the table with his friends' losses. He gave them generous time to recover. One round of jackpots followed another, and his play became wilder with each hand. But he kept winning. Then, as dawn broke, they decided that stumps ought to be drawn.

There seemed little point in going to bed this fine summer morning, so it was warm baths all round then a hansom cab to the swimming baths to freshen up. Stoddart usually rose early, except on the day of a big match, when he often saved himself by getting up when the time was fast approaching to take the field, but this was bordering on absurdity. He was known to be slow and meticulous about his morning toilet and he always ate a late breakfast. On this great day, after a hearty meal, he ambled down to the ground, where the wickets were pitched in the centre of the expanse.

"Stoddy" padded up and took Marshall with him to the wicket at 11.30. Marshall was soon bowled, and "Daddy" Besch walked out to join the erstwhile gambler. After an hour of murderous assault Hampstead were 150 for one wicket, and after Besch had gone at 242, two short of his century and Smith-Turberville had been bowled for five, Swift came in and helped to thump the total to an amazing 370 at lunch after two and a half hours of play.

Lunch lasted an hour, then Stoddart and Swift resumed their tempestuous fun and finally achieved 383 runs together as the fourth wicket went at 652. Russell Parker came in and, possibly mindful of the security of his gold watch, was caught for only four and returned to the pavilion. Doyle and then Dollar supported Stoddart in his furious but never inelegant rampage. His "Magic" brand bat (or was it a Warsop Conqueror, as stated in the 1903 *Wisden*?) was sending the ball singing to the edges of the ground with power drives born of muscular forearms and a middleweight's shoulders. The afternoon sun blazed down as he hurtled through the 300s and, around 5 o'clock, reached 400. Everybody was wide-eyed with excitement.

The highest score ever recorded at that time (419 not out, made a year previously by J.S.Carrick at Chichester) was now just a few strokes away. The Stoics bowlers stuck bravely to their task, but the Hampstead champion took the world record – and immediately gave the sole semblance of a chance: on 421 he hit a screaming drive to mid-on, who failed to hold it. Two more runs were taken.

On past 450, and the umpire, probably as amused as fatigued, urged him to make sure of his half-thousand. At 485, when the stoical trundlers and fielders must have been looking desperately towards their only salvation, the clock, Stoddart miscued a hit to leg off Renny and sent the ball swirling high into the breeze. It was said that the batsmen ran almost three, "Stoddy" calling out 100-1 on the ball, before it plummeted into the hands of F.F.Kelly, the tall and inexhaustible left-arm fast bowler who had been grazing at deep point. Hampstead were now 813 for seven, and the remaining three wickets fell without addition.

That final tally of 813 (not a wide bowled throughout) was, unsurprisingly, the highest total ever in any one-day match, and one report stated academically that Stoics did not bat. There was no declaration law then, and although many may have wondered down the years why the Hampstead men didn't throw their wickets away around, say, 400, the innings did at least make a fruity talking point. And more pertinently it gave a huge fillip to the career and reputation of A.E.Stoddart (who was later – 1896 to 1905 – to serve as president of the Stoics, a sympathetic gesture). Close study of the entry of all those runs, as preserved in *Lillywhite's Annual* for 1887, is one of cricket's stranger pleasures.

It was later suggested that this must have left him feeling very anxious to get some sleep; to which he replied: "Well, perhaps I was, but we had a lawn tennis match – a four – on that evening, so I had to play that. Then I had another tub, and had to hurry too, because we had a box at the theatre and a supper party afterwards. But after that I got to bed all right – and it wasn't nearly three!"

His 64 hits for four (plus three over the top and an overthrow eight) in his 370 minutes at the crease had not drained his energy or enthusiasm. Three days later he was entertaining the local Saturday crowd again. This time it was with an innings of 207 in even time off Blackheath. Again the visitors had no time to bat against the 459 for four, and the hospitality of the Hampstead cricketers might logically have been queried. (A 4¼ inch gauge, incidentally, was kept in the pavilion to ensure that no bat exceeded the regulation width.)

Come Monday and Stoddart was in Gloucester, no doubt receiving congratulations all round, and capitalising on his wonderful form with three hours at the wicket, putting on 90 with captain Webbe and seeming certain to reach his first first-class century. W.G.Grace, bowling monotonously on and cunning as ever, sensed the young man's eagerness and said, "I think you won't be long in getting your hundred." He served up his notorious long-hop and Stoddart (98) obligingly hit it to Woof.

Now to the Bat and Ball ground in Gravesend, to field out to Kent. Across at The Oval, WG was busy making 170 against Australia in the Test match, his opening partner, Will Scotton, scoreless for 67 minutes, contributing a phlegmatic 34 to their stand of 170 and driving *Punch* to pen the immortal "Wail of the Weary".

At the end of this day Webbe and Stoddart had posted an unfinished 106, carried on Friday the 13th to 205, when the captain left for 103. Stoddart soon happily reached his maiden first-class century, a chanceless effort of 116 eventually cut short by an agile throw from Alec Hearne.

Astoundingly, in four innings over 10 days, "Stoddy" had compiled 906 runs. Well might F.B.Wilson have written that "he was probably one of the most tireless men who ever lived".

Middlesex were happily placed that evening, but their bowling lacked the penetration to win on such a perfect pitch. It lacked the ability to dismiss a team of solid batsmen on a soft surface too, as was shown in the next match.

They met Yorkshire at Bradford, and the situation at lunch gave little indication of what was to come. It seldom does. On a slow pitch Stoddart and Webbe had put on 54 before Stoddart was bowled by Merritt Preston, whose bowling had killed a batsman in a Yorkshire club match. Yorkshire now made 401, then Tom Emmett pushed Middlesex aside again for 82, doubtless enjoying a jocular running commentary to his mid-off fielder throughout.

At Trent Bridge, Stoddart displayed an unexpected ability to stay and grind it out. The Notts trundlers sent down 165 four-ball overs and 92 of them were maidens, left virgin by Middlesex bats ambitious to show their equality with the champions. Stoddart's surprisingly gritty 32 against Shaw, Attewell, Fowers and Barnes was the highest innings of the match, lasting 200 minutes.

There was only one more match for him that season, a sensational game at Scarborough between the Gentlemen of England and I Zingari, when he topped the first innings with 23 against the unchanged attack of A.G.Steel, nostrils flaring, spinning his leg-breaks two feet, and H.W.Forster.

The Gentlemen batted again with a deficit of over 200, and at 113 for 4 C.I.Thornton strode in to play an innings which has excited statisticians and connoisseurs of big hitting ever since. His 107 not out in 29 scoring strokes – something scarcely ever seen in a first-class match even though it has probably been known in modern-day Twenty/20 cricket – quite naturally overshadowed Stoddart's 57, and Thornton's seven hits out of the ground included the immortal smack into Trafalgar Square, Scarborough.

It was while in Scarborough one summer that, as the rain dripped down and the cricketers were confined to barracks, WG overheard "Stoddy" in song with H.V.Page. "Stoddy" had a pleasant singing voice and often crooned at family gatherings. Often too he used to knock out a melody on the banjo. On this occasion, WG appreciated the harmony so much that he implored: "Now, Stoddy, let's have another of those little dittoes!" The Old Man was as capable of the malapropism as the cover drive.

Cricket magazine now assured its readers that "Mr Stoddart has found it difficult to tear himself from cricket and football here. I have it, in fact, on the best authority that he has decided after all to remain in England."

So keen was he that his Hampstead cricket chum A.S.Johnston once found himself virtually commanded to join Blackheath Rugby Club.

The 1886 season had been glittering: joint leader of the Middlesex batting with 506 runs at 28 and over 1600 for Hampstead at 83, with 72 wickets added for flavour. (E.H.D.Sewell was to write that Stoddart had the massive aggregate of 3067 runs in 60 innings in all matches this season, an estimate recorded in the September 1893 edition of *Baily's Magazine*.) A record of some oddness also came his way in the autumn: he made the highest score ever recorded with a broomstick: 110 not out.

There can be little doubt that after his sensational 485 for Hampstead he will have been perceived somewhat differently, with a sense of awe which might even have been shared by some of the public school and university products who played as amateurs alongside him and against him, some of them of a snooty disposition.

Now for the winter game once more, where a few drops of rain are not always unwelcome.

CHAPTER 3

♦♦♦

Runs Galore

STODDART scored 11 tries for "The Club" (Blackheath) in 1886-87, heading the honours list but sustaining a sprained ankle in the South v North match. He took part in none of the internationals but he did play for Middlesex against Lancashire in the Jubilee Festival match at The Oval before the Prince of Wales (later King Edward VII, whose marriage had taken place the day before "Stoddy's" birth), Prince Christian and Prince Christian Victor (a grandson of Queen Victoria whom Stoddart bowled first ball later that year in a match at Scarborough).

As early as February of 1887 he had indicated his willingness to tour Australia in the autumn with an English combination to be led by W.G.Grace. It was the sort of promise to buoy him through the gloomiest passages, and, as in 1886, he began the season with a marked lack of success after starting off with 173 for the Football Club against the Cricket Club at Blackheath.

It was only a brief stroll from his accommodation to Lord's, where groundsman Percy Pearce and his staff adored him and addressed him uninhibitedly as "Stod". Yet for four matches running he traced over those steps and only once could he smile with feeling, after a 42 that sealed victory over Yorkshire.

WG made 113 for Gloucestershire, following up with a cluster of wickets, including Stoddart, for whom he, as well, was developing a soft spot. (WG had obtained his FRCS from Durham). In the final innings Stoddart's early dismissal by the cunning brothers Grace deprived his side instantly of much of its attacking function.

F.S.Ashley-Cooper was there and noted in his scholarly manner that Stoddart, "like all young'uns, was induced to believe that there was more in it than met the eye. He began with the obvious intention of sticking to back-drill until he got one he could jump at. Whether the Old Man signalled to Teddy [brother EM] or not, I don't know. What happened was that he dropped one just short of a length on the leg stump. It reared a bit, and Stoddart climbed up well on top of it, meaning to drop it at his feet. He played the stroke perfectly, but Teddy had crawled in under his nose; he caught the ball in his right hand, transferred it to his left, and handed it to Frizzy Bush, who was keeping wicket, without either of them moving a foot.

"I reminded Stoddart of the incident shortly before he died, and found that it still rankled, although he quite appreciated the humour of it."

There was a solitary Sunday between this duck and the next, and 1 and 3 in an innings defeat by Nottinghamshire was hardly offset by the opportunity to study Arthur Shrewsbury from mid-off for over four hours while he scored 119. Yet within a week Stoddart was to join him in a famous first-wicket stand (as referred to at the beginning of this book) that would erase all the early disappointments of 1887.

> When Stoddart makes her hum,
> Up at Lord's,
> Till the bowler bites his thumb,
> Up at Lord's,
> How the Middlesex supporters
> Turn vociferous exhorters
> As he jumps on Lockwood's snorters,
> Up at Lord's!

> *(Norman Gale)*

They never wrote stuff like that about that other Middlesex and England Andrew S. (Strauss). At last the sun shone and batsmen everywhere flexed their shoulders and promised vengeance upon the trundlers who had been having their own way since Spring had first flaunted her ankles. An illustrious band of cricketers arrived at Lord's under a blue sky to partake of the MCC Centenary match.

After the Marylebone side had made 175, Shrewsbury and Stoddart, so unalike yet often identified as similar by later generations, began "England's" reply. If the sun hadn't dazzled a fieldsman when Stoddart was 13 the bowlers would probably have been spared a good deal of bother over the next few hours. The Notts pro and the Middlesex amateur faced them all and sent the ball scudding to all parts of the St John's Wood turf until the MCC total seemed meaningless. They passed it that evening, when Stoddart, 111 not out, will have slept sweetly as any cricketer after his maiden hundred at Lord's. Shrewsbury, who had been through it all before, was 70.

They resumed, with Barnes, Rawlin and Flowers, all with a little flesh to spare, bearing the brunt of the hard labour. Stoddart, full of joy and confidence, displayed his strength in front of the wicket, and his hooking was powerful. He may even have indulged his "dog stroke" occasionally, left leg raised *a la* W.L.Murdoch, the ball flying away fine or square to leg. It was his only departure from orthodoxy or elegance in an imposing array of explosive but graceful attacking strokes radiating from a sure defence which matured annually. He stood with his chest square to point. Not for him the pernicious "two-eyed" stance.

Sensitive Shrewsbury went meticulously on his way, knowing that his own precious bed was far away and he would again have to put up with a strange mattress and something less than a full night's sleep.

The opening stand threatened the 283 of W.G.Grace and B.B.Cooper, but when the partnership had reached 266, Stoddart fell. He had hit 19 fours in his 151, and the crowd with whom he was now so popular gave him a heart-felt reception as he walked off.

Johnny Briggs, the popular little Lancashire slow left-armer, again did the damage when MCC batted, in league this time with Billy Bates, whose time was fast running out. The match would have been something of a travesty if WG hadn't made *some* runs, and he obliged in a minor key with 45 and his team slid to an innings defeat – and all before the gaze of diminutive schoolboy Pelham Warner, sitting engrossed by the sightscreen.

> Or, in a shiny hansom cab,
> With bells that clinked a careless life,
> Cutting the corners like a knife,
> We'd helter-skelter to the ground,
> And eyes would glisten, pulses pound,
> To read the posters as we galloped past:
> 'Stoddart Still Going Strong' or 'Shrewsbury Out At Last'.

(*Herbert Farjeon*)

Hampstead folk had another treat on the following Saturday as Stoddart took the Willesden attack apart with a knock of 238. His side's 399 for 6 suggested a programme of two-day matches might be preferable in future.

At the Hampstead Sports there was further evidence annually of his amazing muscular co-ordination. One year he won eight events in the afternoon – and always he was a classic exponent of the egg-and-spoon race.

Back with Middlesex, he made 78 against Kent at Lord's ("not one of his best efforts" - *Wisden*), and the latter half of the week was spent at Chiswick, suffering humiliation at the hands of the young men of Oxford University: the burly Kingsmill Key made 281, the erudite and talented Hylton Philipson 150. A.E.Stoddart's stunted performance amounted to 1 and 10 in the reply.

The lapse was only momentary. At The Oval, Surrey, after pardoning him before he had scored, felt the force of his bat as June burned itself out. He slammed 85 in 100 minutes, his best display of the summer.

Now, in his first Gentlemen v Players engagement, he fielded out to another Arthur Shrewsbury century. WG captured five of the best wickets then escorted Stoddart to the centre to chase 396. They made 38, and by lunch Billy Barnes had 6 for 7 off 16 overs. The Gentlemen folded up for 102 and in the follow-on made 171. Stoddart's sober introduction to the showpiece match was 15 and 13.

They jousted again straight afterwards at The Oval, but it was almost a repeat enactment. The professionals once again topped 300 and the amateurs were ingloriously bundled out for 161 and 162, Stoddart heading the first innings with 40 and making a fast 25 in the second.

Now came an astonishing Cricket Week at Hampstead during which he scored 900 runs in six innings, half of them not out. He also found the strength to take 17 wickets. "Stoddy" made 205 against Ne'er-do-Weels, carried his bat against London Scottish for 275, following with 55 and a mini-century (114 not out) preceding a final flourish of 230 not out off the Old Finchleians' so-called attack.

Three double-centuries in one week had everybody wondering . . . .

Back in the county game, A.J.Webbe caused a further stir in August by carrying his bat twice: for 192 against Kent at Canterbury (Stoddart 46) and for 243 in a superb recovery against Yorkshire at Huddersfield. There, when the cricket was done with, they all had a game of football.

There was a fine batting surface at Trent Bridge as well, and Shrewsbury kept the Middlesex men running around for over ten hours while he accumulated 267 runs, the joint-highest of his 59 first-class hundreds. Billy Barnes also made a century, and Will Scotton was there in all his molluscan glory to scrape out 51 runs. At a time when the over consisted of only four balls, Middlesex sent down 414 overs, 27 of them by "Stoddy" (0 for 64). Later he fell for only 17, and 15 in the follow-on. The match was drawn.

A thrilling win over Gloucestershire at Clifton came next, with Timothy O'Brien, who usually disdained a protective box and sired ten children, making 83 excellent runs in the fourth innings as Middlesex edged towards a one-wicket victory that even W.G.Grace couldn't prevent. F.G.J.(Francis) Ford, the tall, slender forerunner of Frank Woolley, stroked 38. On the opening day "Stoddy" had caught WG, who returned the compliment in due course. In the second Middlesex innings Stoddart was bowled for a duck by the Reverend Edward Peake, a fast bowler who had been capped by Wales at rugby in 1881.

The season had embraced only 10 County Championship matches for Middlesex in an uneven programme which saw champions Surrey playing 16. And Drewy Stoddart's figures had been unspectacular all this month. Perhaps with thoughts on the trip to Australia, to which he had been invited, and a reaction to his orgy of recent run-making at Hampstead, his grey eyes recently were not always as intent on the swinging ball as they might have been.

For the Gentlemen against I Zingari at Scarborough he did give onlookers something to remember, stroking 116 (caught-and-bowled by H.W.Forster, a young man who would soon become Member of Parliament for Sevenoaks and later president of MCC and of Kent, as well as Governor-General of Australia). Then, handed the ball, "Stoddy" bowled over (first ball) the blue-blooded wicket of Prince Christian Victor, grandson of Queen Victoria. The young man from the North-East was moving in a new, exalted sphere.

He further showed his usefulness with the ball on Scarborough's happy and breezy ground with 6 for 33 for MCC against Yorkshire, deflowering the obstinate Louis Hall for 0 and also dismissing Bobby Peel, one of his bowling bogeys. These performances reminded everyone that he was something more than a specialist batsman. He broke the ball back nippily from the off, usually pitched a good length, flight sometimes deceptive, although his virile attempts to put big spin on the ball did sometimes cause comment.

Having played for MCC (captained by the fabled I.D.Walker) against the Gentlemen of Canada, in his final match of that extraordinary 1887 season, South v North at Scarborough in the first week of September, Stoddart opened (29 and 7) with WG (a duck and 8), had a bowl (1 for 27) and on September 15 sailed out of Tilbury on the steamship *Iberia*, bound for Australia.

CHAPTER 4

Australia the First Time

"AMONGST all the English cricketers who have visited Australia in my time I did not know one whom I 'cottoned' to more than I did A.E.Stoddart. Urbane, kind and courteous, he was a 'man' to his fingertips." So wrote "Felix" (former Australian Test cricketer Tom Horan) in 1915.

This 1887-88 venture was financed by Melbourne Cricket Club and led by the Honourable Martin Bladen Hawke, who was, had he but known it, to succeed to his father's title inconveniently soon after sailing. Hawke declared upon arrival in Australia: "We have come here just to enjoy ourselves and we mean to do it. But the great point is that it does not matter to us whether we win or lose, though, of course, we should like to win for the sake of England. I mean by this that our men are likely to hit out and play with dash and freedom." Not quite the sort of remarks a modern-day touring captain (let alone Jardine or Hutton) would have been likely to make.

Bizarrely, there was a second English touring party in Australia at the same time, got together by Alfred Shaw, Arthur Shrewsbury and Jim Lillywhite (who had captained England in the very first Test match, at Melbourne ten years earlier). This team toured under the auspices of Sydney's cricket authority and was captained by C.Aubrey Smith, a stage actor who later became famous in Hollywood screen roles.

There was plenty of good cricket for Australians to watch during that sweltering summer despite the fact that W.G.Grace had declined to tour and despite the cumbersome and profitless arrangement of having two rival touring parties. In a way it foreshadowed Australia's two confused summers in the 1970s when Kerry Packer's World Series Cricket ran alongside traditional Test series.

Stoddart's panache appealed to the people of this young country as well as to exiled fellow countrymen who had sought a new life while remaining susceptible to the reminders of home. He found Australia's faster cricket pitches generally to his liking, and when the tour was over he stood at the head of the batting table with 1188 runs at 38 – hot work in brown boots. Altham and Swanton's history has marked this point in time: "Perhaps the most notable feature from an historical standpoint was the introduction to Australia of A.E.Stoddart, destined as a batsman to play a very great part in the international cricket of the future, and as a man to win the heart of every sportsman in Australia."

The two teams went about their travels across the sunburnt country, feted wherever they went and enjoying an outdoor life such as England's tame green fields seldom afforded. Stoddart, responded well from the start with a "dashing" 64 in Adelaide and reaching the nineties against "Demon" Spofforth, Hugh Trumble and Harry Boyle, big names all, in Melbourne. He also caught Horan brilliantly, running backwards in the outfield. And again a week later he just missed a hundred at the goldfield town of Ballarat, where the team had to down gallons of champagne at two civic receptions.

On the way he had taken 8 for 27 against Castlemaine, where the tourists had strawberries each morning. He had also joined Martin Hawke and Timothy O'Brien in a Government House Victoria match against Bohemians at Melbourne Church of England Grammar School, making 45 in a game with an aristocratic feel to it. Up in Sydney they suffered their only reversal of the tour. George Vernon, who had fallen down a companionway on the voyage out, played his first match here, his head injury now knitted up. But high scores from Percy McDonnell, Harry Moses and the handsome Sammy Jones, and a collapse by the English team, gave New South Wales a nine-wicket victory. The "terror" pair Turner and Ferris opposed English batsmen for the first time, but "Stoddy" during his 55 played "all round the wicket in hard, clean and graceful style". Reminiscing years later, Lord Hawke referred to him as "the British Victor Trumper", supreme praise.

There were drawn matches against odds at historic Parramatta and Richmond (where news of the death of Hawke's father came through, and Vernon took over the leadership), and at Manly, the picturesque seafront suburb across from a bridgeless Sydney Harbour, where Stoddart used the coconut matting strip well to take 7 for 34.

Now under the leadership of double-international G.F.Vernon, the Englishmen returned to Victoria, now adopting the caps and sashes of their sponsors, the Melbourne club (Stoddart and four other amateurs had been given honorary life membership by Melbourne CC). About this time too the umpires were creating a stir with their white coats. Hitherto the code had lent itself to dress of the most offhand and informal nature.

But now a certain sophistication had reached the cricket grounds and was starting to unpack its bag. Mercifully it would be another century or so before cricketers became walking billboards and the grounds smothered by commercial hoardings.

Stoddart hit the headlines again in the match against Eighteen Melbourne Juniors by batting over six hours on matting for 285 runs, the highest score made by a touring Englishman until R.E.Foster's enchanting 287 in a Sydney Test match in 1903-04. Against fourteen bowlers and unabashed by six missed chances, "Stoddy" placed 24 fours through the thick maze of fielders. Then the local lads, strong as they might have been physically and psychologically, wilted to 70 for fifteen wickets in front of a mere hundred or so onlookers.

The Englishmen drew with Maryborough, shot some game, and beat Sale by an innings, both matches against Twenty-twos, a fair sliver of the local population. Then, four days before Christmas, while practising on the Melbourne ground, Billy Bates was struck the dreadful blow which effectively finished his cricket life, a popular Yorkshire yeoman lost to the game, impoverished and soon to attempt suicide, but with his Test match hat-trick a shining mark in the voluminous records of Anglo-Australian encounters.

It had become a sad tour, Martin Hawke and Billy Bates having had to return home, and the sensation in the South Australia match did little to lessen the distraction. With the Englishmen 239 ahead, someone flooded the pitch and cut chunks of turf out of it during the night. The omnipotent George Giffen was horrified and embarrassed, and countered Vernon's suggestion to abandon the match by urging the rolling of a fresh pitch. In the end they resumed on the damaged strip. Giffen amazed everyone with an innings of 203, and South Australia salvaged an astonishing draw.

Drewy Stoddart seems to have fallen in love with Australia by now – and also, in all probability, with a girl of tender age. This association would unfold as years and tours went by. *The Referee* ran a report hereabouts that he had intentions of taking up residence in New South Wales: the restless soul susceptible to the enticements. Arthur Shrewsbury's migration was also rumoured.

A side tantalisingly billed as Combined Australia now took on Vernon's team at Melbourne, and Harry Trott, in an opening spell of medium-pace leg-breaks, had Stoddart (stumped for 10 by Jack Blackham),

Abel, Peel and O'Brien all out with the total 16. But the last four wickets added 241 (A.E.Newton 77, Vernon 50, J.T.Rawlin 78 not out, "Dick" Attewell 43) and by stumps the Combined XI were in trouble.

It was 1888 when the contest was resumed on the Monday, and the new year brought the Englishmen success. After a thunderstorm the opposition fell away for 136 and 78, giving Vernon's side a victory of some prestige.

In the minor matches which came next Stoddart indulged himself: 8 for 36 at Yarra Bend, 91 off the bowling of Northern Tasmania, six wickets and 40 runs at Latrobe. Then he caught a cold and could not play against Cootamundra, where little Bobby Abel carried his bat for 92 to emphasise that physical appearance should not count for everything. After all, the Surrey man had recently lifted a loaded rifle for the first time and made a kill first shot.

At this point was arranged what was billed as the greatest match yet staged (considering the relative strengths of the teams) between an English and an Australian combination. Financial rivalry was forgotten as the two touring teams pooled resources, selecting what was considered the strongest combined team available under the captaincy of Walter Read of Surrey. Disappointingly many of Australia's front-rank cricketers were not

Turner: a terror to "Stoddy"

available, for one reason or another. The low-scoring match at the modest Sydney venue from which only the exquisite pavilion (1886) survives today, went to England by 126 runs on the fifth day, rain having prevented play on the second and third days (Saturday and Monday). What mattered here was that this was Andrew Ernest Stoddart's first Test match. Closing in on his 25th birthday, he had now become a double international sportsman. Charlie "Terror" Turner, the medium-pace off-spinner from Bathurst, NSW, was a phenomenal wicket-taker through much of his career, particularly on tours of England, where the damp surfaces played into his hands, especially when he had Jack Ferris, left-arm, operating from the other end and providing nasty footmark damage to the pitch. Turner took 12 wickets in this Test match, including Stoddart's in both innings. "Stoddy" scored 16 and 17, having opened with Shrewsbury, whose 44 on the first day was to be the highest innings of the match. On the three days of actual play (out of five scheduled), the total attendance at the SCG was a dismal two thousand souls, a record low.

Percy McDonnell had put England in to bat, the ground being still sodden, but Shrewsbury and Stoddart soon had the runs ticking up, the older pro taking care of Turner while Stoddart hit Ferris hard and often. He would have been caught on the boundary had a drain not impeded Harry Moses as he ran round the pickets after the catch. Soon, though, a big hit off Turner was caught by McShane.

Shrewsbury fought on while wickets fell to Turner and Ferris, padding away anything which hadn't pitched straight, as the lbw law then allowed. But England managed no more than 113.

Yet by that evening Australia lay in ruins: 35 for 8. George Lohmann and Bobby Peel had been unanswerable. The only wicket not attributable to the "sticky" was that of Burton, who lashed what seemed a certain five (over the boundary but not out of the ground for six: the six over the fence came a few years later). Stoddart, running back very fast, took a high-class catch.

A Saturday wash-out, with no scheduled play on Sundays in those days, and another wash-out on the Monday proved very frustrating, but the match continued on the Tuesday, when Australia were shot out for 42, a deficit of 71.

"Stoddy" hit Ferris hard in the second innings, though the left-armer got Shrewsbury cheaply and then George Ulyett. Turner now trapped Stoddart again, caught behind by Blackham for 17, and the bowler went on to secure 7 for 43.

Australia's target of 209 might as well have been 709 in the conditions. And that evening they lay mortally wounded at 47 for five, Lohmann, Peel and Attewell having thrust deeply into the Australian batting order.

The weather was dull as the last rites were performed, England winning by 126 runs. Mission accomplished, the two touring parties split up and went their separate ways, G.F.Vernon's to prepare for the return with

New South Wales.

The ubiquitous Charlie Turner stood at the start of his run-up; Stoddart tapped his bat. The first ball fizzed down and he hit it for four. The next one spat through and disturbed the stumps.

The tourists didn't falter, however, but reached 337 (Walter Read 119), against which New South Wales, having batted first, mustered only 445 in two innings on a good surface. An oddity was Stoddart's reciprocal dismissal of Turner twice, only for the Englishman to be bowled by Turner for a duck as the English XI set about making the 109 to win, Read and Peel saw them home.

Humiliation lay ahead. They went to Goulburn, wool country, and after dismissing the local Twenty-two for 124 (Peel 13 for 43, Stoddart 5 for 40) the Englishmen crashed for 31, the lowest ever by an English team in Australia. "Stoddy's" 6 was equal top score, and the tourists did better second time round as the two-day match drifted to a face-saving draw.

The final match against odds was at Wagga Wagga at the end of February. The Englishmen drew lots for the batting order, and "Stoddy" (11) went in last for possibly the only time in his life. The tourists won by an innings, as was expected of them.

The penultimate fixture was at the MCG against the "Sixth Australian Team", the 1888 side which was about to sail for England (although Tom Horan and Ken Burn were not to tour). Vernon's Englishmen won by 87 runs after rain had made batting next to impossible against Dick Attewell's artful medium-pace. Dispatching the Australians for a blush-making 32, the Notts man took 7 for 15 to go with his 5 for 33 in the first innings. "Stoddy" had made 28 and 6, Turner getting him again in the second innings, during which seven frustrated batsmen fell to him as they lofted him, edged him or missed altogether as the pitch got nastier by the minute.

The final match, against Victoria, was won resoundingly by the Englishmen, Walter Read hitting another fine hundred (Stoddart a "brilliant" 75, with the field setting sometimes all on the off side), and Attewell taking 11 for 58 in the match. It was a happy note on which to end.

There was a farewell dinner in a room beneath the grandstand, compliments flying thick and fast, and it was remarked with feeling that "if the public did not come to see them play, the public were the sufferers by it." George Vernon thanked the club for its hospitality and for having provided Jim Phillips as touring umpire, little knowing what mileage and headlines lay ahead for the tough, ginger-haired Australian.

Young Stoddart on the first of his four tours of Australia.
Back row: "Turkey" Rawlin, Monty Bowden,George Vernon,
Timothy O'Brien, John Beaumont;
Seated: Arthur Newton, Billy Bates, Martin Hawke,
"Dick" Attewell, Bobby Peel;
Front: Bobby Abel, Walter Read, AES

Next day a match was played against the Melbourne club in aid of the seriously injured Billy Bates, whose eye injury had already forced his repatriation to Yorkshire. Hardly a hundred people showed up, and the absent beneficiary failed to benefit.

The English players sailed for home on the Orient steamer *Austral*, without four players who had sailed from England: Lord Hawke and the injured Billy Bates (both returned on compassionate grounds), George

Vernon (who went home later), and the batsman who, together with Walter Read, the Australian crowds of locally-born and immigrants had most enjoyed watching: Andrew Ernest Stoddart.

While the cricket tour had been in progress, the shrewd promotional duo of Alfred Shaw and Arthur Shrewsbury, left with a massive loss of £2400 from the cricket tour, had been busily organising a rugby football tour of Australasia which they hoped would balance the books, and their prime signing had been the box-office rugby player "Stoddy". His county cricket club Middlesex were greatly to regret his absence during the 1888 season, for they slumped to seventh place in the Championship (which then consisted of only eight counties, and was won that summer by reigning champions Surrey).

When the Shaw-Shrewsbury rugby players reached Australia, their star player "Stoddy", suntanned from his cricket tour, was there to greet them.

CHAPTER 5

Rugby Missionary

WHILE England suffered an extremely wet 1888 summer, and the home cricket Test matches for the Ashes went 2-1 in England's favour (the average for every wicket that fell being a ludicrous 11 runs), Jack the Ripper was indulging in his blood-splattering frenzies in the gloomy alleyways of East London while in faraway New Zealand and Australia, A.E.Stoddart became a sensation not only at his familiar rugby game but also at Victorian Rules football, which he and his team-mates were obliged to learn in an alarmingly short time.

Remarkably, by playing in these matches under the Australian code, "Stoddy" became a *triple* sporting international.

The Englishmen played it fairly tough at both codes of football, more so as they encountered some brutal play by the locals, so disturbing that an indignant Arthur Shrewsbury, accompanying the tour, wrote home about it. To test the Englishmen's manhood further, it was a very long tour: opening match (rugby) at the Caledonian ground, Dunedin, New Zealand on April 28; final match (rugby) in Wanganui on October 3. In total there were 35 rugby matches (mostly in New Zealand, two fixtures at the Basin Reserve, Wellington), with 27 won, two lost and six drawn.

The 19 Aussie Rules matches (all in Australia, of course, as the middle sector of the tour undertaking) resulted in 12 losses, a draw and only six victories. Nor were the Melbourne authorities generous in covering expenses.

The tourists were, as proclaimed in the title of modern author Sean Fagan's intensively-researched 2013 book, *The First Lions of Rugby*. Playing in long knickerbockers and with shirts showing red, white and blue horizontal bars, the touring team were soon without Stoddart for a few days. He was seen as a marked man, and was badly knocked about in an early match at Lancaster Park, Christchurch.

Crossing to Australia after nine matches in a month in New

Zealand, the bruised footballers listened to their revered star "Stoddy" as he encouraged them with the assurance that they could now master the Australian (Victorian) Rules code "in half-an-hour". He had witnessed a match between Geelong and Melbourne during his recent cricket tour, and had called in a few locals to help the Englishmen understand the rules and tactics. But while Stoddart, thanks to his footballing genius, was often able to bedazzle the opposition and the crowds alike at this strange football code, his remark was to prove over-optimistic. Some of the refereeing was beyond the Englishmen's comprehension too.

Recovering from injury, he won plaudits again and again, especially in the rugby matches, kicking beautifully (with either foot), often from sharp angles to score, and running fast and deceptively, twisting, swerving, side-stepping, never better than in Otago and Canterbury. (It was in the Otago match that the brilliant local, Keogh, scored a try, sat on the ball, and put his thumb to his nose.)

"Stoddy's" leaping evasion inspired youngsters to copy him when they got onto a rugby field themselves. Maybe it is not altogether surprising that he once told Australian batsman John Barrett that rugby was more enjoyable than cricket in that it allowed each player a chance to distinguish himself in trying for goal. This probably was with the horror and shame of the contrasting sudden first-ball dismissal in cricket in mind.

To demonstrate his all-round sporting genius further, he even came second in the skating race on the ice in Dunedin. It might have compensated slightly for the anguish generated by the physical punishment he had to absorb in most of the matches, and even for being cheated by a bent referee in the Taranaki game. Arthur Shrewsbury, tour promoter and helpless onlooker, felt the defeat against Auckland was the result of something else: "Too much whisky and women." Later, in Australia, three players (Anderton, Smith and Brooks, the last two doctors), were seen to have taken the field against Essendon while drunk.

"Stoddy" was in the process of creating yet another unique niche for himself in sporting history by playing the local football code on Melbourne, Sydney and Adelaide cricket grounds, upon all of which he would end up also playing Test cricket. The first match, played at the MCG, was a tough one, for the opposition was Carlton, current champions. The tourists went down by 14 goals 17 behinds to three goals eight behinds, noticeably tired in the final quarter.

The 1888 British Lions battle it out on the Sydney Cricket Ground

It was on Adelaide Oval that Stoddart had one of his very best matches, taking difficult marks, kicking a spectacular goal, then another to clinch the match. It must still have seemed very strange, with 20 players a side (two more than today), after the 15 in Rugby Union.

On July 16, 1888, following four Australian Rules matches on Adelaide Oval (one won, three lost) the Englishmen played there at rugby, beating an inexperienced Twenty of South Australia 28-3, a heartening victory nonetheless. Through August and September and into October they reverted to their own code across Australia's eastern states before returning to New Zealand for the final two matches in October, occasionally employing local Australian Rules players (and two rugby footballers) who happened to be within reach to help out. Stoddart continued match after match to attract praise for his kicking and his speed and agility across the turf.

None put it better than a writer in *Town & Country*, as quoted by latterday author Sean Fagan: "Stoddart was simply immense, his performance eclipsing anything we have yet seen here under the Rugby rules. The way he gets through his opponents is wonderful. He appears to hang fire for a second or so, whenever a man is approaching him; and before his would-be collarer is aware of it, a sudden turn of the body gets him clear of the intended grasp; and off he bounds once more at a great pace, either to score or to improve the position of his team on the field. In nearly all the runs that he made on Saturday he generally passed three or four men in the manner alluded to above before he was overcome by numbers."

This was at the Sydney Cricket Ground, where he had so recently made his debut in Test cricket and enjoyed an England cricket victory.

The tour captain, R.L.(Bob) Seddon's surviving letters provide a priceless insight into events on and off the field. At dawn after their match in Bathurst, a large party of footballers and locals set out on a kangaroo and hare hunt. Soon fires were lit and the meat cooked. Seddon unwisely wandered off, and suddenly took some pellets in his back. The injury wasn't serious, but the accident was soon to be seen as a grim omen.

Following the August 14 match in Maitland, where "Stoddy" had missed several shots at goal in the Australian Rules match, the Englishmen went down to the river next morning before packing for the journey to Newcastle. Stoddart and fellow three-quarter Jack Anderton remained by the river with skipper Seddon, planning to relax a little longer before catching a later train.

Hours later the shock inflicted on the team when news came through that Bob Seddon had drowned was utterly profound and rendered the continuation of the tour doubtful. Shrewsbury wrote that he had never met a more straightforward, honourable and honest young fellow. He described how Seddon's feet had been strapped to the floor of the outrigger as he rowed on the Hunter River, and he was trapped when it overturned.

Sean Fagan has recreated the passage of events that day: the three (Seddon, Stoddart and Anderton) took to the water in a pleasure boat, and soon Seddon saw the outrigger and fancied going solo. Stoddart and Anderton rowed off and were out of sight when Seddon got into difficulties. The first two rowed to the riverbank and sat watching as Seddon rowed past and around the bend, out of sight. About 25 minutes later a boy approached Stoddart and Anderton and told them that a man had capsized his boat and gone under.

The two rowed frantically up to the bend and beyond, and saw the upturned skiff, Seddon's cap in the water, but no sign of Seddon himself. Two men had witnessed the accident and watched helplessly as the footballer swam agonisingly on his back about 15 yards before going under, his feet still trapped in the straps of the boat.

It took half-an-hour to recover the body, and it was Drewy Stoddart and Jack Anderton who dragged their captain onto the riverbank. For almost an hour frantic, futile attempts were made by the local doctor to revive him. "The shock of that sight will forever remain with me," said Anderton. As for the ultra-sensitive Stoddart, who had tried to avoid journalists throughout the tour, he was traumatised to such an extent that it was thought he was unable to speak of the tragedy ever again.

The two English rugby footballers had to give evidence at a hastily-convened inquest before leaving Maitland, and hundreds of local people paid tribute by the coffin at the Royal Hotel. Soon the football fraternity from far and wide descended on Maitland to pay respects, including the English rugby footballers, all of whom broke down when the reality of Seddon's death hit them. The team sent a collective message of condolence to Seddon's family.

There were two to three thousand at the funeral, and several of Seddon's tough team-mates wept unashamedly. Then, contractually committed, they were faced with the task of continuing the tour. A.E.Stoddart was made captain, and there was a job to be done.

In time, a fine large white-granite memorial was erected over Seddon's grave in the churchyard of St Paul's Church of England, Maitland, with a memorial tablet inside the church. Back home, no-one mourned more deeply than Seddon's fiancee, his later letters continuing to arrive some time after his death.

The footballers were now in Queensland, and Stoddart had to respond to the Mayor of Brisbane's speech of welcome and sympathy. He did his duty with some difficulty. "It is very trying to speak on such an occasion, knowing well that I would not be doing so if our late lamented captain had still been alive."

That afternoon, at the Exhibition Ground (where young Don Bradman was to make his Test match debut 40 years later), the visitors sat for a team photograph, with an empty seat in the front row in honour of their late beloved skipper.

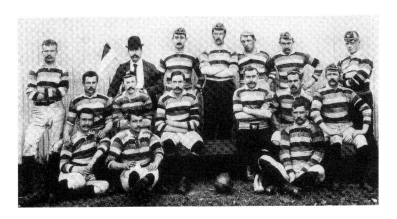

The stunned British rugby footballers leave a space for their recently drowned captain, Stoddart now taking over the mantle

The Englishmen wore black armbands, which they continued to display for the rest of the tour, on and off the field.

Before a gathering of about 10,000, the visitors secured an easy victory, with Stoddart playing at his brilliant best. It must have been a relief to be doing something he loved and so often had done so well. The rounds of entertainment and distractions were resumed, and to a man the footballers were relieved for the distractions. On to Ipswich they went, 20 or so miles inland from Brisbane, a stop made memorable when Stoddart had his pants torn off in a tackle (he battled on to register the try). At the civic reception, he had acknowledged the "sporting spirit" displayed to them since coming to Queensland.

Back in Brisbane, he played with a damaged shoulder and went to full back for a while. Then, returning to centre three-quarter, he stood out with his tackles, made really with just one arm.

Soon they were back in New Zealand, much relieved to return to softer ground, though Stoddart's shoulder was still bothering him, persuading him that full back might be preferable to his usual position. Maoris were beginning to take an interest in rugby, and one of them, Jack Taiaroa, learned something vital in the Hawke's Bay match in Napier. He doubted the tactic of bouncing the ball back in and collecting it. "What trick is this, Englishman?" he called indignantly. "Stoddy" took the trouble to explain to him. The Maori nodded gravely, and soon worked the trick himself and scored, summarising the situation by saying, "My word, that's the best trick I ever learned!" Stoddart's reaction was almost certainly congratulatory.

And other nations have been paying for Maori strength and skill ever since.

At Lancaster Park, Christchurch, "Stoddy" was back to his best, posting two tries and a conversion. But in the last few matches of this long tour there were signs of impatience among the players, most of whom were probably longing for home now. Author Sean Fagan found references to "little dodges on the line-out, off-side play and various other smart practices". They'd had enough.

In Dunedin, Stoddart and Shrewsbury and a few of the footballers from both sides had some cricket practice on the Caledonian ground. There must have been a yearning for the summer game, which would distance them from the discomforts of both codes of football and from the ongoing grief.

The following day there was almost another tragedy as a horse-drawn coach carrying many of the party, including promoter Jim Lillywhite, suffered a brake failure and capsized. Most had jumped clear, but some bounced with the carriage and were very lucky to escape serious injury or worse.

Four thousand watched South Island play the British team, the visitors winning narrowly. The tributes were of a familiar type: "Stoddart was the hero of the match. He has played well heretofore but never such a game as today's. He was everywhere and once he got started on a run it was impossible to stop him till he was grassed with two or three sitting on him." Another report stated that "he was ubiquitous. One second he would be on the wing of a scrum and then he would be back in a favourable position to get a pass, after which he would be seen careering away towards the goal. It seemed impossible to stop him unless he was fairly grassed, as with even three players hanging to him he still kept moving."

Late that afternoon crowds of sports-lovers gathered outside the Lions' hotel calling for Stoddart, who eventually and hesitantly appeared and took a bow.

Another informal cricket match followed at Lancaster Park (or possibly Hagley Oval), Shrewsbury (32 and 46) in fine form and Stoddart showing well too (16 and 13, and 4 for 16, falling to the father of Tony Wilding, the great tennis player who was to die in the Great War, a month after "Stoddy" had died). A third Test cricketer on show was Jim Lillywhite, England's first captain back in 1877, eleven years earlier. Full back Arthur Paul, who had been a close friend and neighbour of the late skipper's, was soon to become a first-class cricketer too, with Lancashire. In this age of the all-round sportsman, Paul also kept goal for Blackburn Rovers.

Fatigued they may have been, but the Lions showed courage right to the end: Tom Kent, who had nursed injuries almost throughout the tour, played full back against Wanganui in the final match with an arm in a sling. Harry Eagles, the resilient Salford forward, alone played in all 54 matches, and must have needed some relief at the end of this historic tour more than most.

They sailed for England (without Harry Speakman, "Stoddy's" fellow three-quarter, who remained in Queensland) on the steamship *Kaikoura*, the same coal-fuelled vessel (with sails as back-up) which had brought them out to the "colonies", their memory banks now brimming with countless images, some touched by grief. Some may even have been aware of their own significance in sporting history. Their steamship landed them safely home on November 11, 1888.

A.E.Stoddart had been away for fourteen months. He was still nursing his bruises and still coping with grief as he faced an English winter and some more rugby, while the sporting world continued to buzz with the controversy over possible illicit payments to the ostensibly amateur rugby footballers (even though they had all signed affidavits to the effect that no extra money had come their way).

"Stoddy" at least seemed in the clear, for he was chosen by the Rugby Football Union to play for a combined team from London clubs against Oxford and Cambridge early in the 1888-89 winter. Late that season a Seddon Memorial match was staged at his old club, Swinton, with Stoddart leading the touring team, and thrilling the crowd with a run that led to a try. At the end, a brass band played *God Save the Queen*, which may have brought some kind of closure.

Controversy and suspicion continued to rumble on. It was understood that the ruling body wanted each member of the touring party to sign an affidavit to the effect that he had received nothing beyond his hotel and travelling expenses throughout the Australasian venture.

A.E.Stoddart was a privileged exception. The RFU had no desire to upset or perhaps even lose their prime asset by harrying him. Stoddart had joined the venture for a sizable payment of "at least £200" (plus all expenses), with £50 up front, no questions apparently asked, and seemingly no refund requested later. Any indication of money beyond expenses at that time would have consigned him into the sporting wilderness. Even as the tour of Australasia had started many weeks before, Halifax forward Jack Clowes was under suspicion by the RFU on account of some perceived cash payment, and absurdly became a non-playing passenger on the tour, even though Shrewsbury told partner Shaw that in Stoddart's opinion the RFU back in England exercised no control at all over the touring players.

Seven years later, in August 1895, in the George Hotel in Huddersfield, Rugby League was formally created, and players (initially almost all in the North) could now openly and honestly play for money. When, less than a century later, Rugby Union was forced to pay its participants openly, as in Rugby League, how "Stoddy's" ghost must have smiled.

Till '88 we played a kind
Of ancient game of scrum and maul,
Where muscle triumphed over mind,
And heavy feet chased tortured ball -
Indeed a very stupid game
Till '88 when Stoddart came.

(An Australian tribute)

CHAPTER 6

Maoris and Bobby Peel

STODDART'S close friend George Jeffery, a Cambridge blue, captained Blackheath during the 1888-89 rugby season, which was a quiet one for "Stoddy", apart from the international fixture at the Rectory Field against the touring Maoris, who were led by Joe Warbrick. These good-natured giants played an amazing total of 107 matches in New Zealand, Australia and Great Britain during their travels, and went home a tired, battered band, wiser in many ways and having given a lot of pleasure to those who had watched with curiosity.

The deep-throated "Ake, Ake, Kia, Kaha!" had startled many an inoffensive Englishmen looking on, and at times their vigorous methods had sparked resentment on the touchlines and in the stands. The unpleasantness reached a peak during the match against England, when some of the Maoris demonstrated against the referee, the eminent Rowland Hill, by walking off the field.

One of the New Zealanders, T.R.Ellison, later recorded the incident which had finally snapped their patience: "Mr Stoddart made a fine, dodgy run and, after beating several of our men, I lured him into my arms by applying the feign dodge. By a quick wriggle, however, he escaped but left a portion of his knickers in my possession. He dashed along and the crowd roared; then suddenly discovering what was the matter he stopped, threw down the ball and, in an instant, we had the vulgar gaze shut off by forming the usual ring around him."

England forward Evershed then seized the ball while repairs were under way and went over for a try which the Maoris hotly disputed. Those who strode off the field were persuaded to go back, and the match continued, but the Rugby Union afterwards exacted an apology.

Stoddart scored a try for England, who won by one goal and four tries (then seven points) to their opponents' nil.

His imaginative play was yet again setting the rugby world a-chatter. In one game he caught the ball only two yards from an opponent and instead of running on he took a few steps backwards, nonplussing the opposition, who could only stand and gape as he dropped a perfect goal.

*The Blackheath rugby footballers of 1888-89, their
captain, Stoddart, wearing his England cap, holding the ball*

In February 1889 he starred in a match between the Rest of England and Yorkshire when the champion county surprisingly went down by three goals to nil. Alderson at centre and Stoddart on the wing for The Rest stole most of the glory.

Then the daffodils began to raise their heads and the winds of March whispered of the joys to come with spring.

Cricket took two steps closer to the game we know when the over was increased from four to five balls, and declarations were permitted on the third (and final) day of a county match.

The prolonged over apparently suited Stoddart, for one: his 30 wickets for Middlesex constituted his best annual tally.

"Stoddy's" rented home in Rothwell Street

He was due to play for South v North at The Oval in May, but withdrew "in consequence of business" on the morning of the match. He was now lodging at 2 Rothwell Street (and was still there three years later), a handsome avenue of terrace houses on the opposite side of Primrose Hill from Ormonde Terrace. (His mother had moved to Quarry Close, Coventry, to live with daughter Cissie, who had married Monty, son of Sir Samuel Wilks, physician to Queen Victoria – an eminent brother-in-law for England's top rugby player to have.)

During May 1889 Stoddart had scores for Hampstead of 79 and 97, then against Marlow, who had Hampstead seven down for 2, he salvaged the innings with 15 not out. The joys of club cricket on dodgy pitches.

His first county match for Middlesex had barely started before it was ended. Nottinghamshire won on a rain-affected surface.

Good opening stands with A.J.Webbe helped towards a victory over Gloucestershire. A win against WG was always especially gratifying, although The Doctor, 40 years old, with many seasons still left in him, reached 101 before Stoddart caught him at mid-off. Stoddart steered Middlesex to victory with 78 not out, hitting in a style that was repeatedly categorised as "brilliant" for want of better adjectives, and using some of that precious element – luck. This innings remained his highest in a rather drab first-class season.

At Old Trafford, Middlesex had another win, again sparked by Stoddart's free and powerful 71. He added to his select list of dismissals those of the poetic pair Hornby and Barlow.

Large attendances at Lord's saw Surrey win the local derby, Stoddart making 64 in his very best style, as so often making about two-thirds of the runs added while he batted.

Now came a historic match at Lord's against Yorkshire when the stars were several: Louis Hall carried his bat for the *fifteenth* time for Yorkshire; fine hands for T.C.O'Brien and G.F.Vernon; and "Stoddy's" 46 in 40 minutes; then Bobby Peel (158) played what was then said to have been the finest innings ever by a left-hander at Lord's.

This contest, which most of us would give a year's beer money (at least) to see played over again on television – with edited highlights only of Louis Hall's effort – now moved to its white-hot conclusion. Needing 280 to win in less than even time (no minimum overs in those days), Middlesex had a rapid 129 up when Timothy Carew O'Brien entered. Ninety minutes to get 151 runs off Yorkshire's tight bowling posed no problem if he could get his bat swinging. And he did.

The Irishman slammed the ball high and ran daring singles with Vernon and snicked and cut his way to the unlikely target. When the dust had subsided and the crowd, flushed and fidgety, raised its voice for the final hoarse chorus, Middlesex had won by four wickets and O'Brien was 100 not out. It followed a trifle of 92 in the first innings.

> Father, dear father, DO take me to Lord's;
> The clock on the stairs has struck one:
> The tape says that Stoddart the smiter is in;
> 'Tis a pity to miss all the fun.
>   Father, dear father, I'll ring for your boots;
>   The clock on the stairs has struck two:
>   The crowd will examine the pitch during lunch,
>   And leave a seat vacant for you.
> Father, dear father, don't write any more;
> The clock on the stairs has struck three,
> And Stoddart has just cut a ball to the ropes;
> 'Tis a sight every girl ought to see.
>   Father, dear father, I've brought you your hat;
>   The clock on the stairs has struck four:
>   The bowlers are both of them well on the spot,
>   But Stoddart continues to score.

Father, dear father, oh! Why don't you start?
The clock on the stairs has struck five:
The tape says that Stoddart is still at the stumps,
And has made a magnificent drive.
   Father, dear father, 'tis really too bad,
   The clock on the stairs has struck six:
   The eager spectators are mad with delight,
   For Stoddart is still at the sticks.
Father, dear father, you need not go now,
The clock stands at six fifty-four;
And Stoddart the smiter has carried his bat
For a grandly made three-figure score.

(Douglas Moffat)

Those showpiece occasions, the Gentlemen v Players matches, came early in July. In the first, at The Oval, Stoddart and WG walked out to face the best paid bowlers in the land. The younger man found more profit in the bowling than The Champion, and at 81, made in little more than an hour, he was caught for an excellent 59. O'Brien's hurricane 90 carried them to 347.

But Billy Barnes made 90, and with the long-established firm of Shrewsbury and Gunn doing steady business, the Players made 396. There was small resistance the following day, and the Players needed only 177 and got them easily.

Stoddart returned some very useful performances for the Gentlemen over the years, and in the next contest he took 3 for 41. Rain then ruined the Lord's pitch and the amateurs collapsed before Briggs and Lohmann. The showpiece fixture was over within two days.

Now, on each of three Saturdays, A.E.Stoddart made a century at Hampstead, as a reminder of his supremacy at this level. And in midsummer he recorded a duck for the Gentlemen of MCC against the touring Gentlemen of Philadelphia.

The heartening progress of Middlesex was checked by innings defeats to Lancashire and Kent, then the Oval crowd saw one of their idols, Walter Read, make a century, supported by sizable innings from the cast-eyed little Bobby Abel, portly Kingsmill Key, and George Lohmann, who looked even more god-like beside those other two.

"Stoddy" rolled his way through 30 overs as Surrey amassed 517, then he drove his way to a chanceless 72, an attractive innings, much overdue perhaps. But his side fell many runs short, and in the follow-on he was smartly stumped for 35 and might thankfully have adjourned that evening to one of his favourite pubs – the Winchester in South Hampstead – for a quiet drink with Jack Trotman or George Jeffery, or to the Constitutional Club (artist Romney's old house) on Holly Hill, or perhaps up to the Hampstead CC ground where his presence was always a stimulus. He and Gregor MacGregor often relaxed at the Conservative Club.

He enjoyed quietly coaching the youngsters, and they usually doted on every word, just as lads have done at the knee of Billy Beldham, through to gazing up into Kevin Pietersen's animated features.

The rest of the 1889 county programme was plainly woeful for Stoddart the batsman. Rollicking Bobby Peel's inexhaustible left arm cut him down for 2 and 1 at Halifax. Then at Cheltenham, "Father" Roberts, another left-armer, his physique slightly pear-shaped, had him caught for 0. Francis Ford led a fightback, and in the second innings Stoddart hit 45, the pair representing one of the most thrilling spectacles in late-Victorian cricket. In the closing stages Gloucestershire were forced to defend for their lives.

Stoddart was at least taking wickets, opening the bowling against WG's men and claiming 5 for 97, and taking his form to Scarborough, with five I Zingari wickets. But the dreaded Peel again had him twice in a 12-a-side match, and a man less gentle than "Stoddy" might have gazed at the North Sea and pictured the Yorkshireman's head bobbing down for the third time.

He went about things more constructively. In the South v North fixture he bowled Peel for a duck and punched his, Attewell's, Shacklock's and Flowers' bowling all over the place in a stirring knock of 77. The sweetest blow of all was a hit out of the ground off Attewell. The performane overall was described as "perfect".

In the follow-on Stoddart's wait was a long one as WG and Abel saved the match with a hundred apiece. Stoddart finally walked to the middle, got off the mark, then was given out lbw . . . to Peel. The Yorkshireman truly had a hold over him.

At Hastings the bowlers had it their own way as the North thrashed the South, and in the Gentlemen v Players match Stoddart took 4 for 51 with Abel's prized wicket and those of bowlers Peel, Ulyett and Lohmann, retaliation that must have been delicious. The amateurs finally had only 73 to get, yet Stoddart and four others were finished with cricket for the season by the luncheon interval.

CHAPTER 7

◆◆◆

County Before Country

DREWY Stoddart captained England at Dewsbury early in 1890 when Wales established a landmark, recording their first-ever rugby victory over England at the seventh attempt. The match was played in a sleeting snowstorm and the ground was a quagmire, which did much to immobilise England's tall, heavy men up front, Australian emigre Sammy Woods determined and boisterous as any of them. "Stoddy" tried hard to kick his team into a scoring position but the nimble play of the Welsh three-quarters, with the young genius Billy Bancroft at full back, defied all his efforts and reversed the pressure.

The English forwards scrimmaged well but the conditions at Crown Flatt were beginning to tell as half-time approached. As they sucked their oranges in the swirling white storm and trotted back into position hoping for better luck, surely the young England captain, his voluminous pants clinging damply to his thighs, must have glimpsed in his mind's eye the lazy sunlit terraces of the cricket grounds last summer.

He placed the soggy oval ball and booted it towards the fifteen hostile Welshmen awaiting his challenge. The ball came spinning back, punted by Welsh three-quarters sensing the chance of making history. There were tight scrimmages and much heaving and hooking and gasping.

Stadden, the Cardiff half-back, dodged his way through, fooling Fox by bouncing the ball out of touch and gathering it swiftly to go over for a try, not converted.

Now England stormed their opponents' line until a score seemed inevitable. Frenzied tackling kept them at bay, but back came Stoddart in what was amounting almost to a personal duel, loudly and generously appreciated by the crowd.

Those dying minutes saw England's forwards battling blindly to push the heroic Welshmen back, but the "no-side" whistle was blown and many a leek was waved delightedly in the chill air.

*The England team which lost to Wales for the first
time, captain Stoddart with ball, Sammy Woods front left*

That evening, at the dinner for the teams, Stoddart was outspoken: the ground had been "unfit for any ordinary player to play in and was an insult both to the English and Welsh teams to be asked to play on such a ground". This brought a rebuke from Dewsbury committeeman Mark Newsome, who said that he was "cut to the quick" by that remark, adding absurdly that the England captain was speaking "of something he knew nothing about".

Huw Richards has noted that Stoddart had had a poor game, the local paper having claimed that he had been out of form and showed a little "funk", and also seemingly a desire not to be "dirtied". It was not one of his shining sporting moments. A grim postscript to this match came seventeen years later when one of the outstanding Wales players, William "Buller" Stadden, a grocer who had scored the winning try, strangled his wife before cutting his own throat.

Four days after his 27th birthday in March 1890, with the injury which had kept him out of the Scotland match now cleared, Stoddart returned to the England side for the match against Ireland at the Rectory Field, Blackheath, where 12,000 people had gathered. Up north there were murmurs that Huddersfield's Delaney, a working man, had been dropped to accommodate Stoddart, a "toff".

"Stoddy" was to become notoriously poor at calling the toss in cricket Tests, and such was his form on March 15, 1890, when Ireland chose to take advantage of the wind. England's back line commanded play in the first half, with occasional spirited runs by the Irish pack, dribbling and pushing their way upfield against the stout wall of Englishmen, Woods, Evershed and Robinson prominent.

MR. STODDART PASSING THE BALL.

"Stoddy": much-admired rugby ace

The first try came when Stoddart made a short run and swung the ball across to Morrison, who penetrated well into the Irish twenty-five, when Evershed took over. He beat three men and crossed the line, only to drop the ball. Rogers pounced on it, and England had the try after all. Jowett failed with the wide place kick.

Soon Mason Scott took the ball from an Irish dribbling attack and got it to Aston. He ran for the line and threw the ball to Stoddart when his path was blocked. The captain grounded try number two, but Jowett was unsuccessful again with a difficult kick.

Early in the second half Morrison scored England's third try with a spectacular run down the right touchline, brushing aside tackle after tackle. Jowett now missed a kick from almost in front of the posts.

The Irishmen were unabashed, and pressed even harder. Johnstone was almost in when tackled by Stoddart, but the slate was kept clean and England's victory ensured a share of the title with Scotland.

> May nought on earth that union sever,
> May friends of football live for ever.
> May all who deserve it rise to fame,
> Keep pure and unsullied as Stoddart's name.

(Albert Craig, "The Surrey Poet", after the Ireland match)

As captain of Blackheath, Stoddart had scored seven tries, second on the list of scorers and something of a recovery from the previous year's poverty.

A contemporary pen picture helps convey his standing: "Very active and strong, he can well hold his own with heavier and more powerful men, and this he has frequently demonstrated. As for the speed with which he runs with the ball, and the quickness with which he can swerve and dodge without losing way when avoiding an opponent, his extraordinary starts and jumps, the certainty of his fielding, and his mastery of all the tactics of attack, are not these things matters of public notoriety?"

The writer recognised his British pluck and persistency by quoting another admirer: "He is a good-woolled one, and does not curl up after a pearler." Take note, squirming, fragile, mouthy soccer players of today – if you can comprehend this classic Victorianism.

A.E.Stoddart in Sporting Celebrities

Even at this early point A.E.Stoddart spoke of retiring from the winter game, but the alarmed interviewer hoped that he would "wait until the deterioration which he professes to find in his own powers is perceptible to others."

In February 1890 he was featured in the fashionable *Sporting Celebrities* journal, which paid him rich tribute and described his rugby play as "scientific" as well as "pretty"- an interesting word. Reference was made not only to his cricket and rugby skill but his ability as a tennis player and ice-skater.

His unselfishness remained forever in the memory of a club-mate who once watched him weave through the entire opposition, full back and all, then pass to a hitherto luckless three-quarter, who had the honour of making the try. "Stoddy" would, recalled this observer, often fling himself into the thick of his opponents and literally crash his way through. "He seemed not to know the meaning of the word 'fear'." But the injuries, some of which left him concussed, were taking their toll.

The year 1890 was the gateway for a glittering cricket decade notable for the gallery of fine cricketers who displayed their gifts daily throughout the summers in all the many cricket centres of the game. Their static portraits deceptively convey a sameness, but their characters were rich and truly Dickensian in variety in an age untouched by the great levelling movement in society. There were no television cameras to zoom in on them, no all-pervasive mobile phones to reduce cricketers and fans to gormlessly grinning robots, very few workaday journalists feeling for an angle or a loose quote, and no cardboard press conferences littered with cliché. A man could be himself. There was room for expression. With rare exceptions, cricketers made little money from the game they loved. Rare was the cricketer who took himself too seriously.

Archie MacLaren announced himself this year with a magnificent century at Hove, and F.S.Jackson made his debut for Yorkshire. Gregor MacGregor, one of "Stoddy's" special friends, kept wicket for England while still at Cambridge, where he stood up at the stumps for the wild slingers of Sammy Woods. And J.T.Hearne qualified both for Middlesex and for the title of the county's greatest bowler ever.

Timothy O'Brien, the Reads, Woods, the brothers Palairet, Lord Hawke and the fabulous Graces, pale-faced Shrewsbury and (automatically) Gunn, little Abel and big Billy Barnes, the formidable Lohmann, cunning Northern left-arm twiddlers Briggs and Peel, Wainwright, Mold, lisping Jack Brown, the awesome Lockwood and Richardson, and the much-loved, sad-eyed Drewy Stoddart. A truly rousing cavalcade to tempt people to the cricket grounds of England.

After endless hours in their company through photographs, sketches and text, it is with sadness that one has to accept that they have all been so long dead. The deaths of some were often as spectacular as their lives, a number of suicides robbing the game of many talents and much mature counsel.

But, for the moment, all was optimism, with Billy Murdoch's 1890 team about to arrive from Australia and the colourful signs of spring all round – so important to an Englishman.

It was a poor season for A.E.Stoddart. Having climbed two places in 1889, Middlesex slipped back again to seventh of the eight Championship counties. More of his thrilling bombardments on those depressingly damp pitches would have elevated his county.

It was the only year until 1898 that he failed to make a century for Hampstead, although he got as far as 97 not out. All the same, his 418 runs for the club in 10 completed innings must rate as failure on not only the Bradman scale but the Stoddart scale too.

Seven ducks quacked quite deafeningly at him in 45 first-class innings, his average a touch under 20. The season had started promisingly enough. In the nippy month of May the Australians opened their tour with a match at Sheffield Park, where Turner and Ferris had His Lordship's pride out for 27 (WG 20 of them). The Australians' total of 191 proved sufficient for an innings victory, although there was to be more defeat than victory for them in this summer of dreadful weather.

Soon "Stoddy" was playing one of the best innings of his life, for South against North at Lord's. After Shrewsbury had carried his canny bat through the North innings of only 90, Stoddart accompanied W.G.Grace to the middle to see what they could make of this awkward pitch and unrelenting bowlers a second time.

The Doctor concentrated on keeping the ball out and avoiding the kickers, but the younger man at the other end was soon banging the ball about, to the delight of the spectators and his companions on the balcony of the grand new pavilion. He cut almost brutally and pulled the short stuff with an elegant swivel. With model back defence to rising balls and a thumping drive against the over-pitched, he made 50 runs while that pillar of Victorian grandiosity, Dr W.G.Grace, made but three runs. The Champion was probably never so noticeably eclipsed in his half-a-century at the wicket.

In an hour and a half the opening stand mounted to 111. Then WG departed for 29. "Stoddy" continued on his chanceless way, until, with his score 115, he was stopped – by a Yorkshire left-armer, Peel by name.

Lohmann carried on the fight, hitting the metal-topped stumps seven times in taking 8 for 65, and the South had won by 135 runs.

Stoddart by the Lord's pavilion, which over the years became a second home to him

It was the first of eight consecutive games at Lord's that season for Stoddart. His 59 was the highest of the match against Kent, but it was followed by the mortification of being run out for 0. Then came the ignominy of defeat by Somerset, not then a first-class county. He took five wickets but made only 0 and 5.

Against Notts he had the cheeky satisfaction of bowling Shrewsbury for 11 (as detailed at the start of this book), a deed probably worth as much to "Stoddy" as his opening stand of 96 with A.J.Webbe.

Now, in a match at Lord's for which the admission price rose to the unprecedented level of one shilling (5p), Stoddart top-scored with 46 in another victory over Murdoch's Australians, this time for MCC, significant opponents for the tourists ever since the sensational affair in 1878, when the "colonials" unexpectedly humiliated the Lord's elite team.

His revival took a buffeting throughout June. Ferris, Peel and Mold all had his scalp for 0 in the course of seven innings, the match against the Australians being stiff with sensation: J.T.Hearne and E.A.Nepean had the touring team seven down for 13. A last-wicket stand of 80 by Jack Ferris and Hugh Trumble pulled the "colonials" up to 135. Middlesex batted, and soon the Australians were surprised to find themselves holding a lead of 22. Then Hearne bowled Murdoch for 0 for the second time (perhaps affording "Stoddy" some slight comfort), and the "Colonials" were soon 94 for eight. But the tiny Syd Gregory and John Barrett played out time, and the last day was mercifully washed out – which might have saved poor Murdoch, in his current runless plight, a third duck.

That disastrous June ended with a mauling for Middlesex by Surrey.

A fine 60 by Stoddart lifted Middlesex to 140 – 99 of them for the first wicket with Webbe. Lohmann and Sharpe tipped Middlesex out a second time for 57 on a tacky surface, Lohmann, who captured 220 wickets this season, taking 12 in this episode.

In late June "Stoddy" played for the Lyric Club against MCC at the St Ann's ground in Barnes, opening with the big hitter C.I.Thornton but failing. He did take six wickets in the match, and caught Harry Pickett, a future suicide.

No batsman was content with this wretchedly damp summer, least of all the Australians, notwithstanding the phenomenal success of Australia's Turner and Ferris, bowling into each other's damp, churned-up followthrough. Runs made off them were high-quality runs indeed.

Stoddart seldom succeeded in Gentlemen v Players fixtures, but at The Oval this year he stroked a superb 85 on a nasty wicket against Peel, Briggs, Attewell and Lohmann, a quartet of England's very best (John Shuter's 17 was next-best score). It was "Stoddy's" highest score in 21 such contests and one of the finest innings he ever played. A century was looming – and how he must have coveted it – when Lohmann threw himself across the pitch to scoop up the catch.

Today, Stoddart House, a large block of council flats, looks down on this historic piece of sporting England, Kennington Oval, where a Stoddart straight-drive once removed an umpire's hat, a green expanse which is to the cricket-lover what Hampton Court is to the romantic historian. The old Oval is surely replete with ghosts.

The Lord's Gentlemen v Players contest was spoiled by late rain, but "Stoddy" once more had the satisfaction of bowling the best professional batsman in the land with a break-back just when Arthur Shrewsbury must have been feeling he was set.

Now Andrew Ernest Stoddart was selected to make his home Test match debut in the first Test of the 1890 series against Australia, at Lord's. But, astonishingly to modern understanding, he was persuaded to withdraw his name and to assist Middlesex instead, against Kent at Tonbridge. Such was the unimaginable difference in attitudes between then and now.

The *Pall Mall Gazette* denounced this as a very bad precedent, saying that "the fact of the present Australian team having been found weaker than some of its predecessors does not, in our opinion, excuse the

Middlesex executive for departing from a proper and well-established plan."

Just how much pressure the county club exerted on Stoddart (an amateur and not a professional) is left to the imagination, but in assessing what his own attitude might have been it needs to be remembered that Test matches in those days were not subject to the massive hype (when major countries are involved) that we observe today. The sacrifice of his services to county in preference to country was considered praiseworthy by some, and not only Middlesex supporters.

WG led England to a seven-wicket victory in the Test match while Stoddart was making 42 for Middlesex at Tonbridge on a hard, true surface, following up with the bowling figures (4 for 35) as Kent went on to win.

He was chosen for the second Test match, but again withdrew, this time preferring to face Yorkshire at Bradford. When Lord Hawke received word of "Stoddy's" withdrawal from the Oval Test, he forbade George Ulyett and Bobby Peel to play against Australia too. But the county match was ruined by rain and Stoddart, who almost predictably was dismissed by Peel in both innings, must have wished that they had both been on the same side down in London, facing the common enemy.

Within the fortnight the England team was named for the final Test, with A.E.Stoddart's name immediately under W.G.Grace's on the list. This time there was no withdrawal – and, alas, no Test match as Manchester suffered a ceaseless downpour. The 1890 cricket season therefore had passed without any addition to "Stoddy's" international honours.

In the second half of the summer there had been a fine knock of 42 on a fiery wicket for the Lyric Club, who beat the Australians at Barnes in an intriguing match which, like so many others, was doomed to slip into glass bookcases and remain locked away, forgotten for decades to come.

Middlesex suffered further indignities against Surrey and Gloucestershire, and Stoddart's 15 was the only double-figure score in his county's second innings of 59 at Cheltenham. Somerset, moving nearer first-class status, and top of the Second-Class Counties table in this 1890 season, provided a happy talking point with a rare tie to conclude the match against Middlesex at Taunton, when a frantic run-out terminated the match. "Stoddy" fell in both innings to rugby team-mate Sammy Woods.

September, so often a felicitous month for batsmen, could hardly have been more ghastly for Stoddart. On imperfect pitches he scrambled nine runs in five innings. C.T.B. "Terror" Turner (13 wickets for 57) extra slaughtered a Test-strength Lord Londesborough's XI at Scarborough on a wet pitch, and would have been the only candidate for a Man of the Match award, had they had such an invidious system then, by top-scoring in both the Australians' innings. Johnny Briggs's 15 wickets kept His Lordship's men in the fight, but Murdoch's men gratefully scraped in by eight runs. (The tourists nursed a final tour record of 13 victories and 16 losses on this 1890 tour.) In what could readily have been seen here at Scarborough as a Test match, such was the strength of the two sides, Stoddart had to settle for one and five, and because of the strength of the Londesborough attack, he was deprived of a chance to bowl on a pitch made to order. So be it.

He went to Hastings, where the castle ruins surmounted a quaint setting, for his last first-class match of 1890. And before a large audience, perhaps appropriately for this year of struggle, he recorded a duck. C.T.B.Turner – who else? - had him caught at slip; and there was no prospect of a second innings.

His penultimate fixture had been the South v North match at Hastings, where Johnny Briggs, the popular little Lancashire left-arm spinner, got him for 0 and 8, rendering his future Test skipper's bat an inoffensive, ineffectual weapon. But "Stoddy" was in at the climax. Mordecai Sherwin, last man in for the North, might well have hit off the 10 runs required had not a smart pick-up and return from Stoddart done for him.

Wisden was to bemoan his average this season as "decidedly poor" for a player of such class, and conceivably he might have allowed his thoughts to wander to Colorado and brother Harry or somewhere equally distant. There is no telling either to what extent Seddon's death on the rugby tour continued to torment him.

But the advantage of being a dual sportman is that there is no need just to sit by the fire all winter contemplating past miseries.

And in 1890-91 he was busy. He returned to his position at the head of Blackheath's try-scoring list, and also had the distinction not only of playing in the first-ever Barbarians match (against Hartlepool Rovers), wearing the black skull-and-crossbones badge over his heart, but captaining them to victory.

Later on the Barbarians' tour Stoddart was running in to score against Bradford when a whistle blew. He stopped in his tracks. But the whistle had been blown by a spectator. Stoddart scored a try in the 6-6 draw.

A.E.Stoddart had the distinction of captaining the first-ever Barbarians team, in December 1890, at Hartlepool, with his pals MacGregor and Woods in the line-up. Here he leads the "Baa-baas" in their fourth match, against Devon at Exeter

As for extending his international record, although for some years his name was erroneously listed in one or two reference books as having played against Wales at Newport in January 1891, England did not select him for the rugby internationals that winter.

There was, though, a famous Middlesex v Yorkshire contest at Richmond, where the home side's superlative three-quarter line of Gould, Stoddart, MacGregor and Campbell failed to click because, it was said, they were all individualists. Yorkshire, so strong up front, simply crushed the home side, although the one Middlesex touchdown was a classic. From a scrum near their own line Middlesex broke away. Half-back Orr passed to Gould, who drew several opponents before slipping the ball to MacGregor at top speed. The Scot (Middlesex's wicketkeeper and "Stoddy's" flat-mate) swerved outwards as if dashing home for a short single and at precisely the right moment flung the ball to Stoddart, who set off at breakneck speed for the Yorkshire line. The crowning movement came at the end of this masterly run: he returned the ball to MacGregor, who had raced through in thrilling support, and the ball was finally flicked to Gould, who ran through a shattered defence quite easily to score a try.

"Stoddy" captained the Barbarians again at Exeter on April Fools' Day, 1891, against Devonshire, and went in for a try and converted three others.

Then came the 1891 cricket season, and a better year by far.

CHAPTER 8

Carrying the Bat

IN the late 1960s, I handed over a ten shilling note for some pipe tobacco, and among the meagre change was an 1891 penny. It was worn so smooth by the years of handling and contact with various bed-mates in sundry pockets that I saw this devalued disc as a symbol, a chronological yardstick. It may even have crossed the palm of Andrew Ernest Stoddart. He was fond of his pipe.

The sun did not always shine in those lustrous days, and 1891 was yet another shameful summer, with much cricket lost. Against Yorkshire in June he made the only "pair" of his career, Ted Wainwright catching him off Bobby Peel, who bowled him in the last innings of a match played on a treacherously damp pitch. There would most likely have been a shrug and a resigned smile before the dismal trek back to the relative warmth of the Lord's dressing-room. In his own signed *Wisden* there is no annotation, sorely as he might have been tempted.

Fast-medium maestro J.T.Hearne was the player principally responsible for raising Middlesex to third place this season, taking 118 wickets at 10 apiece. Timothy O'Brien, confusingly playing at times under an assumed name but apparently fooling no-one, headed the batting with 755 runs at 35.20, five per innings ahead of "Stoddy". The following match, against Nottinghamshire at Lord's, contained a typical display by the robust Irishman: 85 off an attack still rated among the best in the country.

"Stoddy's" gloomy contribution was 8 and 0 as he threatened to outdo any previous disastrous start to a season. Surely he wasn't "losing it" at the age of twenty-eight?

But then came the match against Lancashire, still at Lord's, and the sun shone gloriously. He made 37 out of Middlesex's first-innings 96 and furthered his restoration by getting within 13 of a hundred in the second innings before Arthur Mold, of the dubious action, broke through his defences. Middlesex won by the second evening, "Stoddy" having become one of the select few who ever collared Mold.

There were three matches now riddled with failure, with only the Gloucestershire contest providing the consolation of victory, O'Brien making a hundred. WG got Stoddart in both innings. Inexplicably, in the scorecard for Middlesex's match against Kent at Beckenham in late June, in *Cricket* magazine (but not in *Wisden*) "Stoddy" is bafflingly listed as "J.J.Evans" (no such name is listed in the *Who's Who of Cricketers*). Since he failed again (4 and 8), who is to say that he didn't bribe the scorer or reporter to bill him as someone else? Stranger things have happened in sport.

He continued to love playing cricket, taking every opportunity. Again he played at Barnes for the Lyric club, this time against Old Harrovians and sharing four wickets with "Demon" Spofforth, surely a strange experience, though they bowled together sometimes for Hampstead.

The great and thoughtful Spofforth gave his opinion on Stoddart's technique in an interview with *The New Review* in 1894: he considered him "unapproached" in the matter of science. It was wonderful to watch his pull, and to see the effect on bowlers, who lost both their lengths and their heads. He believed that he had achieved perfection in the stroke.

The Oval showpiece contest between Gentlemen and Players went conclusively to the amateurs, Stoddart opening with W.G.Grace and falling to a very fine catch by William Gunn in the deep. The Lord's fixture was ruined by rain – to nobody's surprise by now in this most wretched of summers – with the Gentlemen 89 for five in reply, WG (10) and "Stoddy" (8) both falling to Peel. Rain descended in torrents and the vivid flashes and deafening thunder-claps seemed to signal the end of cricket for the year, at the very least. By the time the splashing had subsided to a forlorn dripping, Lord's had become a lake. The cricketers had long since gone to their tea and toast.

Now it was mid-July, and the metropolitan county team made their way north, hoping for another win over Lancashire. A confident and substantial innings came from Stoddart's bat at last. The weather had brightened, the pitch was good, and he made the top score of the season. The *Wisden* report perpetuating the facts must have brought him much quiet pleasure:

"An exceptionally brilliant display of batting on the part of Mr A.E.Stoddart, who, going in first for Middlesex, carried his bat right through the innings, rendered this return engagement particularly noteworthy in the great county matches of the season. The Middlesex amateur may fairly be said to have on this occasion surpassed all his previous efforts, for not only was his score of 215 not out the highest innings played in first-class cricket last summer, but it was, by a considerable number of runs, the biggest score ever obtained in a good match by Mr Stoddart, his previous best having been 151 for England against the Marylebone Club at Lord's in 1887. His innings of 215 lasted five hours, and except for two chances, one at slip when he had made 86 and another at the wicket when his total had reached 109, it was quite free from fault. His hitting at times was remarkably fine, whilst the accuracy with which he got Mold's bowling onto the middle of his bat all the time gave the performance additional value."

The last three batsmen helped him add 214 runs, and it was in these latter stages that Mold suffered such untypical punishment. Hearne and Rawlin, establishing themselves as a pair of bowlers to be feared for most of the 1890s, twice got rid of Lancashire to seal a most welcome innings victory for Middlesex.

Now, at Hove, the page of Manchester glory gave way to the following blank sheet, and this time Middlesex were in for a reversal. Stoddart, alive with confidence, made 41, but a second-innings breakdown let Sussex in.

In August they went to Sheffield, where according to Australian Hugh Trumble's loving description, "the smoke from the factories is horrible, and they say the big factories always bank their fires when the visiting side goes in to bat." After lying on the grass he noticed black smut on his flannels when he got up.

The factories could not have banked their fires sufficiently this time, for Middlesex ran out winners. Stoddart made only 3 and 9 on this Bramall Lane pitch which was to be blown apart by the Luftwaffe during the Second World War.

It would have been pleasant to be home again and scoring runs. He made 90 at Lord's off the Sussex attack before Fred Tate bowled him – the same Tate with the pinned-back ears who was to be excruciatingly centre-stage as England lost to Australia by three runs at Old Trafford in 1902, and who was to see his son Maurice become a record-breaking bowler for England in Australia.

This 1891 season was an extraordinary one for Stoddart the bowler. For Hampstead he took his all-time best: 105 wickets at less than 9 each. Yet for the county, with Jack Hearne, "Turkey" Rawlin, Australian Jim Phillips, and Evan Nepean, an amateur, providing adequate artillery, Stoddart had but five overs all season, and they were against Somerset, the new boys in the Championship. He did at least take the wicket of W.N.Roe, who was a fellow quadruple-centurymaker with 415 not out at Cambridge in 1881.

The final county fixture was at Trent Bridge, and again the skies wept. Something must have upset them greatly this particular year.

Stoddart had been invited to tour Australia again during the forthcoming English winter of 1891-92, this time with Lord Sheffield's side, with W.G.Grace as leader. The thoughts of all invited members of the party during the festival games of September would not unnaturally have been directed to the delights and explorations that lay ahead. As another summer faded Stoddart managed only two innings of note: a 38 and an attractive 71 following a duck and followed by a duck for the Gentlemen when he was caught first ball of the match at Hastings.

Now, for the second time, it was goodbye to old England as the P&O steamship *Arcadia* pulled out of the Albert Docks, explorer H.M.Stanley among her company.

The forward thoughts of the 28-year-old Andrew Ernest Stoddart seem likely to have embraced a certain young lady he had met on his first Australian venture four years earlier.

CHAPTER 9

◆◆◆

Australia Again

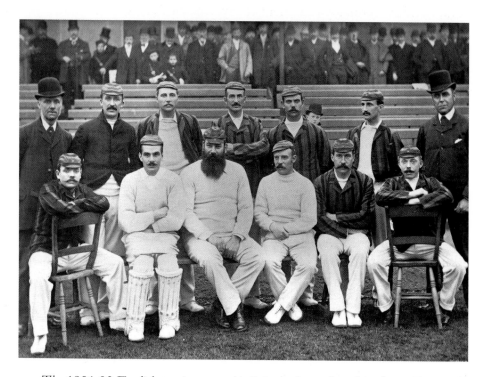

The 1891-92 English touring team, back from Australia. Standing: "Dick"
Attewell, George Lohmann, Maurice Read, George Bean, Jack Sharpe;
Seated: Johnny Briggs, Gregor MacGregor, W.G.Grace, Bobby Peel, A.E.Stoddart,
Bobby Abel. Absent are Philipson and Radcliffe (and, typically, Lord Sheffield)

LORD Sheffield's men played cricket on the island of Malta, in the
Mediterranean, and in Colombo, where WG soon tired of the fierce sun
and gave himself out "hit wicket". The match, played between a Ceylon
XIX and an England XII at the Galle Face ground, drew a crowd of 8000.
Stoddart batted on patriotically for 70 (next-highest score was 16) and

with blistered arms and florid face. Back on board, they continued to enjoy themselves at every opportunity. There had been a musical programme in which WG was the interlocutor for a Darkest African Minstrels show, with numbers featuring "Stoddy", George Bean, Maurice Read, Bobby Peel and Johnny Briggs to amuse the passengers. Everyone would have been very relaxed when they finally stepped ashore at Adelaide. "In spite of the seductive *dolce far niente* of a sea voyage", as one magazine put it, Stoddart ended landed seemingly fitter than at any stage of his life.

It had been 18 years since WG last toured Australia, and there was some apprehension as to the Old Man's endurance at the age of 43 through a tour which, although markedly more comfortable than the previous venture now that rail was taking over from coach and horse, was nevertheless a taxing expedition, even if he was being paid the fabulous fee of £3000 and had his family with him.

WG and Alfred Shaw, the tour manager, together with all these players who had been but lads when WG was first establishing himself as cricket champion of the world, were popular almost everywhere they travelled, retrieving the game from the doldrums where it had languished during the years of Australia's ill-success. Although receipts were to fall £2000 short of expenditure, Lord Sheffield was still moved in his appreciation to donate 150 guineas towards the advancement of cricket in Australia, and the following season saw Victoria win the first Sheffield Shield competition, the shield competed for ever since.

Australian pitches were much improved now, although WG's own shape and form were soon under less flattering scrutiny: "Great Scott — such feet! He could get £2 a week and his tucker [food] merely to walk about in the grasshopper districts to kill off the pest."

His fun had started on the voyage out, with a Christy minstrel act which featured Johnny Briggs, naturally, and which had WG's face blackened and the famous beard sacrilegiously powdered.

The team were photographed in Adelaide Botanical Gardens, where the flora provided an uncustomary setting for the Englishmen, bedecked in their light suits and straw hats. There sat WG in his Derby hat, black beard washed and restored; there he sat with his staff and crew, fit to take his place alongside the other pioneers of the awakening southern continent.

After a leisurely ten days they opened with an easy win over South Australia, Stoddart making a graceful 78. Then on to Melbourne, where all was gaiety: the drags and horses were all draped in Lord Sheffield's colours (navy blue, red and yellow, so like the touring MCC colours in years to follow), and the cricket match found W.G.Grace in all his commanding glory as he carried his bat for 159, which was to be his only first-class century in Australia.

The big opposition lay ahead, and at Sydney came the first great tussle, against a star-studded New South Wales side. The Englishmen made only 20 more than the home side's 74, and a second-innings recovery led by Harry Moses left the tourists 153 to win. When six were back in the pavilion for 88 it looked odds-on NSW. But Peel and Lohmann steered safely to victory. Stoddart, falling to Charlie Turner twice, made 4 and 28.

The touring cricketers stayed at the luxurious Hotel Australia, and it was here that the New South Wales Cricket Association staged a banquet in honour of Grace and his men, and of the Earl of Sheffield, of course. His Lordship responded elegantly to the speech of welcome, asserting that cricket was a binding force between the two countries and a factor in showing England how fine a place was the colony.

Briggs took 12 for 38 against Cumberland, but Lohmann outdid him next match, against Twenty-two of Camden, with 12 for 17, Bobby Peel bagging the other nine for 36. All but the politest of the English fieldsmen must have stifled yawns at the monotonous clatter of wickets, but the farmers and settlers were all going through an experience to be told and retold in the months and years ahead.

Next stop was Bowral, where Don Bradman's ancestor Richard Whatman played. Here the visitors beat "a poor lot". Briggs took 24 wickets in the match for 87.

Stoddart, still searching unsuccessfully for big runs, had some solace on Boxing Day back in Victoria with a 45 at Ballarat against shoddy fielding Then, on New Year's Day 1892, the first of the three Test matches began.

W.G.Grace lumbered onto the Melbourne Cricket Ground to toss with Jack Blackham, bearded and historic characters both. WG uttered a rueful remark as the coin fell Australia's way.

Alec Bannerman and Jack Lyons opened for "Combined Australia" and took their task so seriously that the crowd of 20,000 became restless. Tight bowling, careful fielding, and the diminutive Bannerman's innate caution restricted the score to 52 for 2 at lunch, and even the mighty Lyons had been barracked as Lohmann teased him with exaggerated off theory. "Hit 'im over the chains, Jack!" rasped one patriot in the outer. But Lyons was caught by WG for 19 and George Giffen failed. It took the tall and slim Victorian left-hander Billy Bruce to brighten play after lunch. He hit his way to a top-score 57, and all the while Bannerman, small, poker-faced, hair parted dead centre, chipped and steered his way to 45 in three hours and a quarter.

On Saturday, Australia reached 240, England bowling honours going to Jack Sharpe, Nottinghamshire medium-pacer who lacked a right eye and always offered a restrained profile to the camera.

The day was fine as WG took little Bobby Abel with him to answer for England, and runs were soon coming fast. Bob McLeod shaved WG's stumps once and The Champion enjoyed fooling the crowd by throwing back his head in horror and taking a step towards the pavilion.

Yet it was an omen. McLeod bowled him for 50, having already accounted for Abel. Stoddart avoided the hat-trick. But he was caught third ball by Giffen, and McLeod had three of the most valuable wickets imaginable in just five deliveries.

George Bean made 50, and a riotous 41 from Briggs put England ahead, although the eventual lead of 24 was only a morale flatterer.

It was extremely hot as Bannerman and Lyons began Australia's second innings. In faraway Paris, short-story writer Guy de Maupassant was taken into shelter that day after putting a razor across his throat, but the Australians shunned suicidal tendencies and proceeded steadily to 33 at lunch. Lyons went on lustily to 51, but Bannerman stayed for four hours fashioning his 41. Bruce again played a valuable hand, and that afternoon England knew their target: 213.

Stating that they would win by about four wickets, W.G.Grace this time took Stoddart with him, and they made a competent 60 before WG gave Bannerman an easy catch at mid-off. Then, at the same total, "Stoddy" tried to drag a long-hop from Callaway and was bowled for 35.

The gate was now open, and the Australians drove in. At close of play there were clouds of dust rising from the square, and soon England were swaying at 104 for seven, Abel and MacGregor together. Soon on the following day Abel was caught behind off a lifter from Turner, and the innings folded up.

Australia rejoiced in a 54-run victory that had been, above all, a reward for determined batting. Australia's batsmen had permitted 159 of the 343 six-ball overs to go unpunished. English batsmen had allowed only 47 maiden overs from the 174 bowled by Australia. The modern game of Test cricket was taking shape.

Stoddart must have been taking mental notes, for it was a feature of the batting that he took to Australia three years later that any flamboyance was quickly anaesthetised. The 1894-95 series, surrounded by unprecedented publicity and played with almost unnerving sincerity, would mark the beginning of Test competition as we know it. "Stoddy's" own attitude to batting was transformed in Australia from the free and dashing to the urgent and watchful. A sterner sense of responsibility was established.

Six fixtures against odds in Victoria preceded the second Test match at Sydney. Stoddart recorded some modest scores and a fifty against South Melbourne, who had in their line-up a certain A.E.Trott, whose life was to cross with his for years to come. There was another excellent 50 against Twenty Melbourne Juniors, and all this time the bowlers had been turning in such outrageous analyses as 9 for 73 (Briggs), 8 for 80 (Lohmann), 11 for 53 (Grace!), 7 for 7 (Peel), 13 for 29 (Briggs), 17 for 64 (Hylton Philipson, the wicketkeeper), 12 for 40, 13 for 57 and 7 for 67 (Lohmann), 9 for 30 (Attewell) – all single-innings figures. It took a bat full of Australian courage, know-how and impertinence to overcome this sort of bowling lust, and small was the number of local men and youths who managed to register a decent score.

This was hardly the sort of serious preparation for a Test match. Neither were the bushland capers in Gippsland, when Lord Sheffield's team almost went to bed one light after Bobby Abel's horse bolted through bushland criss-crossed with wire fencing. The party managed to get some kangaroos and emus without Abel's assistance, but the dead snake he found curled up in his cricket bag was a reassuring token of his team-mates' affection.

The dwarfish cricketer celebrated his return to the relative safety of the Test match arena by catching Alec Bannerman off Lohmann to start the rot in Australia's first innings, then carried his bat through England's 5½-hour reply.

The first Test had naturally fired optimism in the Australian camp, and George Giffen recalled that even the Englishmen seemed to feel that

Australia would win. That they did so was due to a sterling fightback in the second half of the match after England had seemed as certain of victory as a cricket team could be.

A tremor of controversy rocked this contest. Harry Moses was selected in spite of a leg injury sustained in the first Test, and WG made it clear that Blackham should not expect a substitute if Moses broke down. When, to add to this, a Sydney newspaper printed alleged criticism made by WG on his previous tour eighteen years earlier, sections of the crowd imagined themselves offended.

It was warm and sultry in Sydney that morning, and recent rain had left the pitch soaked. The sun was drying it slowly as George Lohmann flowed in to start the action. Alec Bannerman was his usual unsmiling self, but Jack Lyons thrashed about in thrilling manner, hitting consecutive balls over the chains for fives and quickly running to 41.

That was the only challenge as Lohmann proceeded to harvest eight wickets for the second time in a Sydney Test match.

The expected contretemps occurred while Moses was batting. As the batsmen took a sharp single his leg gave way, and he had to limp agonisingly thereafter without a runner, with the crowd raucously airing its disapproval until WG caught him for 29. Australia totalled 144 (*Wisden* incorrectly shows 145: an extra – or sundry – too many), and that evening the English team made 38 without loss.

Nor was Abel to be shifted. Before an enormous crowd of just over 20,000 (most on their feet, for there were few stands to accommodate them) he batted for most of that Saturday for 132 not out, carrying his bat through the England innings of 307. Stoddart had made 27 in good style, including a huge and very satisfying blow high into the reserve off Turner. Abel, batting beautifully and without risk, had good support from the lower order, and with Australia now well in arrears (163 behind), Blackham sent in Bannerman and Harry Trott.

It was quickly one for one; but Bannerman's renowned dourness and Lyons's hurricane hitting put Australia's nose in front and set the scene for a real game of cricket. They put on 174, of which Lyons pounded 134 in less than three hours: one of the finest of all Ashes centuries. The tempo dropped as Giffen stood by Bannerman as 79 more runs came. Giffen (49) was then trapped in front by Attewell.

Bannerman's marathon was accepted appreciatively, and even

provoked sympathy and good humour. An onlooker cried, "Look out, Alec! WG'll have his hand in your pocket!" England's captain was lurking very close indeed at point. Bannerman smiled faintly, that gesture alone rendering the match historic. Another likened the scene to the painting *Anguish*, Auguste Schenck's powerfully poignant oil of dozens of crows swarming around a dead lamb while the grief-stricken mother ewe stands helplessly by it. There was the impeccable slips fieldsman Lohmann, WG shuffling at point, Peel at silly mid-off, Stoddart at short mid-off, Briggs silly mid-on.

The crowd screamed with delight when Bannerman surfaced for an instant to crack a four past WG's ear. By Monday evening Australia were 263 for three, 100 ahead.

News then came through of the death of Bob McLeod's brother Norman, and the Australians wore black crepe as a mark of respect. Bob, greeted in sympathetic silence, did his duty with 18 runs, then set off for Melbourne on the night express, leaving poor Blackham to ask for a substitute for a second time.

The weather was unsettled on this fourth day, and heavy rain fell. Billy Bruce, with 72, was in fine fettle, and Bannerman, facing Briggs's tantalising slows, was at last caught by WG nine short of a century after an occupation of 448 minutes, with three lonely boundary hits, and an incredible 199 of Attewell's 204 balls to him unproductive. It was like the removal of a sliver of meat from between England's teeth.

An event of note at the end of the innings drew hardly any comment in contemporary reports: Johnny Briggs had bobbed in and taken a hat-trick. Moses, undergoing a course of electric baths, was unable to bat, and Briggs was thus denied the chance of taking four in four, which might have made the headlines.

Australia had amassed 391, leaving England 229 to win on a pitch which was giving encouragement to the bowlers. WG now made a decision which glimmers sinisterly from the annals, seemingly so wrong in retrospect: expecting the pitch to worsen, he retained the normal batting order. But, to deafening cheers, three important wickets toppled that evening for 11 runs before more rain sent the players off.

On the Wednesday the pitch rolled out well, and Stoddart and Maurice Read played the bowling comfortably enough. Stoddart swept and cut several boundaries, and hit Turner over the top for another five. The crowd squeezed their way forward in the sunshine, relishing the balance of the match. "Stoddy's" strokes were greeted generously, probably by some who had watched him play rugby three years before. But at 64 he lost Read to the ever-present Giffen. Shortly Peel was stumped, and when Stoddart, trying to pull a ball from the haunting Turner, finally had his stumps spreadeagled after a valiant 69, all hope seemed lost.

The tireless Giffen took care of the rest: he caught-and-bowled Gregor MacGregor and Dick Attewell, and Australia had won the rubber. There was tumultuous celebration at the conclusion, for Australia's *cricket* troubles at least were now unquestionably over for the time being.

During the seven weeks between Test matches, Drewy Stoddart had no cricket to write home about, apart from a couple of characteristic innings in cool Tasmania, where he spent his 29th birthday.

His contribution against New South Wales was trifling. Not for the first time he was bowled trying to flay a long-hop which kept low. The game brought further uproar when Percie Charlton was given not out to an apparent catch behind the stumps by MacGregor. W.G.Grace said something to umpire Briscoe, who left the field, and Charlie Bannerman had to take his place – Bannerman, scorer of the first-ever Test century and brother of the "dead lamb" at Sydney.

And so they travelled across to Adelaide for the third and final Test. Drewy Stoddart's hour had come.

The pitch looked plumb, and WG, in persuading Blackham to call, and wrongly at that, pretty well won the match and forgot his anger at hearing that the pitch had been covered the day before. A half-holiday had been declared, and 10,000 of Adelaide's 120,000 people were there to see the caricaturist's dream: W.G.Grace and Robert Abel opening for England. Abel soon misjudged a high, tempting ball from dreamy-eyed Harry Trott and wicketkeeper Blackham did the rest: 47 for one.

Stoddart began streakily. Blackham, standing at the stumps to Charlie Turner, missed a difficult chance when the batsman had made only one run: first a difficult catch followed a milli-second later by a stumping opportunity. But by the luncheon interval England's score stood securely at 65, W.G.Grace 32, A.E.Stoddart 9.

It was a testing time for Stoddart upon resumption, with Trott's parabolic slow spin at one end and Turner pounding away with offcutters and variations from the other. But "Stoddy" now faced his notorious adversary on level terms. The pitch was innocent and the English batsmen hit Turner and Trott from the firing line. Off George Giffen's first over Stoddart gathered two fours, and WG did the same next over to raise 100. Runs were coming fast and WG was looking dangerous when McLeod yorked him.

Maurice Read, pride of Thames Ditton village in Surrey, started shakily, but Stoddart was now in full flight, hitting grandly to leg. And Read, encouraged by the general outlook, square-cut McLeod with some elegance. At 138 Trott was brought back, and Stoddart got into a mess with one ball, moving out when back-play (to the eye of the observer in the cool sanctity of the shade) would have dealt with it comfortably enough.

*A.E.Stoddart (here with his pal MacGregor behind the stumps)
became a Test century-maker at Adelaide*

Runs came easily. Then soon after a short tea interval, Read was caught for 57: 218 for three. George Bean found things beyond him at first, but Stoddart continued to pile on the runs. The sweetest blows of all were a drive off Turner clean into the members' reserve (caught by

Lohmann close to the State Governor) and a similar space blast for another five off Giffen. These two fives off three balls took him to 94 and were followed by two glorious square-leg hits off Giffen. There had been no messing about. Andrew Ernest Stoddart had his first Test match hundred.

The ovation was loud and spontaneous, and as his score continued to mount it was suggested to WG that his own record 170 might be in danger, a possibility that seemed to appeal to the Old Man.

Bean made 16, and Peel stayed with "Stoddy" until the close of this first day, England comfortable at 313 for four, Stoddart 129 not out, the Australians having missed their chance towards the end when Trott erred. A substantial England score now seemed certain.

But any hopes of a long continuation were soon dashed on the second day. After adding four runs and being seen as fretting at Giffen's slows, Stoddart skipped down the pitch and was struck on the pad. Up went the umpire's forefinger, and his graceful tenancy of 230 minutes was over. There had been 15 fours and two fives in his 134, and if ever in middle age he sat and relived old battles, this careful but attractive knock must have been sharply in focus.

Yorkshire left-hander Peel registered what would be his highest Test innings, 83, and when Philipson fell it seemed all over: 425 for nine. MacGregor and Attewell, however, would not be moved and the score crept up to 490 when a heavy downpour put an end to Friday's play. Next day MacGregor, rather like Hanif Mohammad many years later, was run out going for a 500th run – his side's, not his of course. England's 499 was their highest to date in any Test, and remained the highest Test total not to include a century stand until Australia's 533 against West Indies at this same Adelaide Oval in 1968-69.

Australia, so cruelly slapped by the elements as the rain poured down, set about the uphill climb against the legendary pair Briggs and Lohmann. They bowled unchanged on that wet surface until Australia had fallen for exactly 100, tempers rising as WG insisted on quarter-hourly pitch inspections during the rain interruptions.

The Australians followed on, and apart from a good stand by Giffen and Bruce, they had no real answer to Briggs and, this time, Attewell, on the muddy strip. A feature of this last innings was Stoddart's stretching right-hand catch 100 yards from the bat, on the drive, to dismiss the thunderous South Australian batsman Jack Lyons. (Lyons and Stoddart each received a Zodiac Shield for their top-score centuries in this short Test series, items which reappeared in the auction rooms over a century later.)

Johnny Briggs's deadly slow left-arm efforts at Adelaide had carried him to his 50th Test wicket, with many more to come, but Australia had now seen the last of W.G.Grace.

Not that this spelt the end of the chatter that always seemed to attach to his name. Even a century later somebody wrote to a newspaper claiming that Lord Sheffield put a clause in WG's contract to the effect that if he didn't behave himself he would be paid off and sent home. An outburst to an umpire in Melbourne ("I don't believe you!") put the great man on final warning. The correspondent seems to have had inside information from this tour in that he further claimed that Dr Grace got into fights with team members, notably George Lohmann and twice with Stoddart, once on the morning of departure on the steamship *Valetta*.

So back home they journeyed, via the Suez Canal. Had he but known it, the man about to take the helm for the next couple of Australian expeditions was Mr A.E.Stoddart.

CHAPTER 10

◆◆◆

A Welsh Thriller

THE summer of 1892 was dry and filled with sunshine. Surrey carried off their sixth consecutive County Championship title. Arthur Shrewsbury headed the All England averages, and Stoddart made more runs than anyone else apart from Somerset's H.T.Hewett, whose 1407 pipped him by four.

Stoddart had now established his position among the aristocracy of English batsmen, no longer simply in style but in reliability. For the remainder of his career as a regular player not once was his season's average below 30, and twice it was over 40: against the standards of the time, proof enough of his high achievement. His legions of admirers would have noted the steeling process which had taken place. It gave them more of him, even if the risks were eschewed.

His caricature ("A Big Hitter") by "Stuff" (magistrate Harold Wright) appeared in *Vanity Fair* this year, a certain pointer to national pre-eminence.

A day after *Valetta* berthed, "Stoddy" was taking the cool English air on the Wormwood Scrubs ground, scoring 132 against Kensington Park and finding his land legs with almost rude impatience.

The Nottingham crowd were soon watching Lord Sheffield's side in a match played for Alfred Shaw's benefit: the touring team bowled out for 89, Stoddart 0.

Showers played an irritating accompaniment to the event, Shaw more than anyone wishing for a prolonged sample of that Adelaide weather. The team were photographed at Trent Bridge, and Stoddart faced the camera and posterity with conventionally solemn features. The thoughts of most of them might have been many miles away.

The dubious practice of staging benefit matches in May continued at Lord's where a Married v Single match took place, "Stoddy", still unattached, did his best for Robert Clayton with innings of 42 and 53 against strong bowling, and George Lohmann, every woman's dream, made sure of the match for the bachelors with 12 wickets and a handsome 58.

Now, for MCC against Kent, Stoddart stroked a brilliant 52 on a damp surface, with the exciting O'Brien belting 47.

Stoddart and Webbe opened the Middlesex season against Sussex, and 38-year-old Stanley Scott led them to a substantial first-innings lead.

In 1892 the society magazine Vanity Fair honoured Stoddart with inclusion

This was to be Scott's season: top of the Middlesex averages, a careful, unathletic batsman who at times could hit with the best. He made the cricket world sit up with an innings of 224 against Gloucestershire, when Middlesex extended a winning streak that put them in the right frame of mind for the derby over the river at The Oval. (Scott, in an article in *The Cricketer* in 1930, expressed a high opinion of Stoddart's bowling, and also reflected that Stoddart had condemned as a throw a ball from Arthur Mold that had dismissed Scott.)

Middlesex suffered a setback against Lockwood and Lohmann, who dispensed with them abruptly for 75 as a wintry wind swept under the awnings. Bobby Abel led Surrey to a sizable first-innings lead, and it was against these odds that Stoddart gave what the restrained *Wisden* considered "one of the finest displays of batting seen in London during the season". His 91 helped set Surrey 172 for victory, seldom in doubt as Walter Read and Abel, the darlings of South London, posted 117 for the first wicket.

The Yorkshire match at Lord's turned into a wonderful contest. Stoddart and Webbe posted 79 at the start, but Yorkshire, inspired by

George Ulyett, finally engineered a four-wicket victory, though things might have been different had a catch off "Stoddy's" bowling been held.

Nottinghamshire were the next visitors to Lord's – for a famous match. Shrewsbury carved out 212 in a Notts innings which stretched to nine hours. On an immaculate pitch it was going to need some exceptional bowling or irresponsible batting to see Middlesex out twice in the time remaining. But Shacklock, Attewell and Barnes broke into the first innings and Middlesex soon had lost four men in the second. With over three hours remaining and runs of no consideration, Notts seemed to have the contest sewn up.

As Stoddart and O'Brien set about mounting a counter-attack, "An Old Cricketer" (E.V.Lucas) was walking along St John's Wood Road in the warm afternoon air: "Mr T.C.O'Brien – as he was then, he became Sir Timothy later – was bringing off some of his own special late cuts and Mr Stoddart was putting the thick of his bat behind the straight ones and driving them to long-on and long-off as only he could do. His back play could be wonderful! I remember one ball he had to play back to, hitting the Pavilion railings and rebounding forty yards. There's strength for you!"

They put on 97, then Webbe dug in and a draw seemed even more certain as he and Stoddart put on 95 more. Stoddart reached 100 (only two were registered all season for Middlesex) and with only half an hour remaining and five wickets to fall, J.S.Robinson (who was to be killed in a fall from his horse six years later) took over as wicketkeeper while the big man, Sherwin, had a bowl. It worked: Webbe, so safe, so dependable, was bowled. It was, he said as he unbuckled his pads, like being run over by a donkey-cart. His downfall had been followed by stunned silence apart from "a few stray Nottingham yells".

"Turkey" Rawlin came in, and next over Stoddart was given out leg-before to Attewell for 130, spreading alarm in the home dressing-room.

"You could see in the hush every hand going to the waistcoat pocket. Those were the days before wars and wristwatches, you must remember."

Ten minutes remained and three wickets separated Notts from unlikely victory. Thesiger took Stoddart's place, made a single, then faced Mordecai Sherwin, the "donkey cart". Two runs, then he also was bowled by an innocent-looking ball.

Attewell struck a vital blow by bowling Rawlin several minutes later, and with R.S.Lucas looking on helplessly, Jack Hearne slashed away and was caught. Notts had won by an innings and 14 runs a mere four minutes from time.

"An Old Cricketer's" thoughts lingered nostalgically: "But when I think of that great match it is not only Mr Webbe's joke that I remember, but the tragic end of the two greatest batsmen: Mr Stoddart and Arthur Shrewsbury. It's odd how cricketers are often not very happy men. I suppose it's got something to do with the disappointments of the game – its glorious uncertainty, as they call it. Uncertainty can be very depressing as well as glorious, and it makes men moody."

For MCC, Stoddart made a very powerful 52 and 60 against Oxford University, caught each time by Douglas Jardine's father, Malcolm. One leg-side full-toss ended up in the scorer's box and another was lofted into the outside world. Young C.B.Fry, who became a celebrated all-round sportsman himself, initiated a hat-trick in this match with "Stoddy's" wicket. Some years later, in what remains probably the best surviving technical analysis of A.E.Stoddart the batsman, Fry recalled his style: "All Stoddart's batting is distinguished by a most fascinating elasticity of action; indeed, this quality is what makes his style when at his best so charming."

"Stoddy" in similar style to Victor Trumper

He considered the drives the choicest of his wares. Sometimes, he said, they were firm-footed, other times he ran to the ball. The right shoulder never dropped, and the left elbow was always well up. When he drove in the air it was never in ballooning fashion, but on a skimming low course. "He has," wrote Fry, "a hook stroke that is the despair of all imitators." The cut was played grandly – as pleasing as anyone's – yet often, even in a long innings, he had seen him refrain from using it at all. To off-break bowling he used to turn the ball away towards forward short leg with the turn (probably in the manner of Tom Graveney). The wrap-up would have left anybody who ever saw him bat simply yearning to see him again just one more time: "He makes everything he does look nice, and yet no-one was ever freer from any attempt at effect."

From an Australian viewpoint, George Giffen, who played in Tests against Stoddart, wrote of his "gracefully easy" stance, his "jump or bound" out to the drive, and a splendid forward cut. And when A.O.Jones of Nottinghamshire toured Australia in 1901-02 with the English team, he was compared to the Stoddart of 1888, who "used to jump in and smack the ball in brilliant style".

The Gentlemen v Players match at Lord's in July 1892 had been shaping into a fascinating fight for first-innings honours as WG and "Stoddy" made a bright 88 before the rain fell, but Stoddart was bowled first ball next morning by Wainwright for 49, and in the follow-on Attewell trimmed his bails with a devilish ball before he was even into double figures.

At The Oval, where WG's absence through injury deprived the Gentlemen of their powerful figurehead, Stoddart opened with the elegant Somerset batsman Lionel Palairet and posted good figures for the first wicket both times with enchanting strokeplay. Bill Lockwood was unnervingly lively and had Stoddart ducking to avoid trouble. He and S.W.Scott actually had words with the bowler as the ball continually reared back towards their faces. Stoddart fell to him both times.

Later in that 1892 season Palairet was party to sensation in posting 346 with Hewett for the first wicket against Yorkshire, a Somerset record still standing over a century later. It sparked off a spate of marathon openings, and before the 19th Century was out the record had been passed by Abel and Brockwell (Surrey), Shrewsbury and A.O.Jones (Notts), and then, after a dress rehearsal of 378 in 1897, J.T.Brown and "Long John" Tunnicliffe dwarfed them all with 554 against Derbyshire at Chesterfield in 1898.

These records were symptomatic of the changes sweeping through the game as pitches were given better preparation and competition intensified. Oxford and Cambridge Universities were now scattering their riches among the county clubs: carefree young men who injected splashes of colour into the county cricket fabric.

The men who alternately provided their fodder or cut them down were the army of ripe characters, nearly all professionals with little formal education, who bowled a cricket ball for a poorly-paid living. Stoddart's next encounter, against Lancashire at Old Trafford, was played out by four of the best of them: J.T.Hearne and J.T.Rawlin, who took 18 wickets between them; and Arthur Mold and "Stoddy's" team-mate in Australia, Johnny Briggs, who also took 18 wickets, all serving up satisfactory production figures to their respective county club employers and finding the pitch a handy selling aid.

During this match Gregor MacGregor, "Stoddy's" pending Hampstead flat-mate and team-mate, making his debut for Middlesex, suggested to him that a catch at the wicket might result if the bowlers pounded the ball down short outside off stump. But Briggs's blazing cuts caused fielder O'Brien to remonstrate with skipper Stoddart, who quickly abandoned the tactic. Briggs slashed his way to 98 and helped set Middlesex a stiff target. In the end the last Middlesex pair held out for a nail-biting draw.

The Yorkshire fixture at Headingley was another bowlers' feast on a soft surface, but Stoddart kept Peel at bay and made 46, top score of the match. The chroniclers again looked for suitable descriptions and came up with the repetitious (but gratifying) "brilliant". Yorkshire slipped away for 46 in their second innings.

Drewy Stoddart now returned to London and took part in a spectacular sequence of club matches with Hampstead, making hundreds against Crystal Palace and Hendon, and captaining the club on tour, making centuries off Bournemouth and Hampshire Hogs. He collected 500 runs at an average of 100 during this club cricket sojourn, and during the periods on tour when his open-ribbed pads were removed, this club colossus grabbed 31 wickets in the three matches, including a hat-trick against Bournemouth, who were 0 for five wickets at one amusing point.

Back with Middlesex, it was all Hearne and Rawlin in low-scoring August. In seven matches Middlesex achieved victories only over Lancashire and Sussex. Stoddart's best innings of the month was an 88 against Kent, and later there was a 41 against WG and his Gloucestershire yeomen, pursued by a fast 43 pulled and swept off Sussex at Hove.

And so the 1892 county programme was completed, with Middlesex disappointingly in fifth place. The festival matches were enacted like a wake over yet another dead cricket season. At Scarborough, "Stoddy" dished out to Lohmann one monumental blow, and had an enjoyable stand with

W.L.Murdoch against county champions Surrey before rain again drifted across.

For South v North at happy Hastings he made 32 runs in even time off Spofforth, Attewell, Wainwright and Peel on a bad surface, and the Saturday was devoted to a match played with broomsticks. On the same ground, against the Players, the Gentlemen curiously had only one regular bowler, the doughty Aussie Sammy Woods, who worked a small miracle in the first innings, taking 8 for 46, sending the professionals back for 109. One man was run out and the other wicket went to Stoddart, who drank his pal Woods's health that evening over dinner, remarking, "Well bowled, we two!"

In the follow-on the almost inevitable happened: Abel and Lohmann got runs, Peel, Attewell and Bean lent support, and poor S.M.J.Woods wheeled down 65 overs, taking 3 for 201. WG strained his knee, and the only other bowler in sight was one A.E.Stoddart, who manfully bowled 40 overs and took 1 for 96. The Gentlemen salvaged a draw in the end, and Stoddart, off what was probably a tired stroke off Lohmann, packed his sweat-soaked gear and prepared for some rugby football.

He had captained Blackheath for two seasons and missed the last owing to the tour of Australia. Now W.P. "Tottie" Carpmael led the club, and Stoddart was sitting by his side in the team photograph, moustache luxuriant as ever, eyes fixed distantly beyond the camera. This was to be the season of his final appearance in an England rugby shirt. It was also the year that "A Country Vicar" (R.L.Llewellyn) first saw him play:

"He was drawing near the end of his football career, and wore the badges of long service and many injuries – elastic knee-caps on both knees, anklets on both ankles, and a rubber bandage on one elbow! But he played beautifully – tackled, passed, kicked, and ran in the grand manner of the finished master. We undergraduates had gathered in force on the Corpus ground, where the University matches were then played, and we had all gone with the idea of 'seeing Stoddart'. He showed us a perfect performance by a wing three-quarter – how and when to part with the ball, and what to do when he kept it. I still see two runs of his – one, from halfway, when he was pushed into touch just the right side (from our point of view) of the Cambridge goal-line – one of about 30 yards, when he flashed down the field and scored in the extreme corner. That game was played in a tornado of cheers, but it was Stoddart's try that brought the longest and loudest applause — Stoddart himself, limping a little, who received the great ovation at the end."

Blackheath 1892-93, with W.P.Carpmael as captain, Stoddart on his right

He played for Barbarians against Cardiff on Boxing Day, but throughout the first week of 1893 Britain endured blizzards, and it was only late on the Friday afternoon, January 6, that the English rugby men decided to set off for Cardiff for the international match. They arrived in a raging snow-storm and went straight to the shelter of the hotel.

In polar conditions they went down to the Arms Park after dinner and beheld one of the strangest sights conceivable on a sporting surface: 500 perforated buckets full of hot coals glowed across the frozen expanse of the ground. Local children darted gleefully about like junior citizens of Hell. It was estimated that 18 tons of good Welsh coal were used to save this rugby international.

The Englishmen returned to their rooms holding out meagre expectation of play. There was no relief next morning. It was still extremely cold. Surely the match had to be called off? But the braziers had done their work, and the ground was declared playable.

The players changed into their gear at the hotel and walked to the ground through hordes of admiring boys, each trying to place a cold hand on the great men for a fleeting moment of magic.

England were fielding three three-quarters and nine forwards; Wales, with eight Newport players, four three-quarters and eight in the pack.

Stoddart and Gould tossed and England's captain chose to have the wind advantage. His back line soon started a movement which ended with Lohden, his Blackheath club-mate, falling on the ball for a try within minutes of his international debut. Sammy Woods missed the conversion, but England kept up the pressure. Stoddart missed an easy penalty which may not have seemed important when Marshall followed through a forward rush and touched down for England's second try, Lockwood converting. But the extra points would have been invaluable later on.

At the interval England were comfortably placed after some superb work by a great pack, with Woods, "the father of modern wing forwards", formidable among them. His tackling was crushingly effective, and he was famous for quick breaking and relentless dribbling: as fast bowler or rugby opponent, an awesome competitor.

The Welsh backs had been starved of the ball, but now, with the wind helping, they and their forwards stormed into the English half and pressed hard until Field gathered a high punt near his own line and raced out through the Welsh ranks. He was brought down after a stupendous run, and Marshall scooped up the ball to plant another try for England, unconverted.

Now Wales fought back, and the 17,000 onlookers welcomed the chance to clap their numb hands together as Gould raced in for Wales's first try and Billy Bancroft kicked a superb conversion. Wales took heart. The back line responded, and Phillips and Biggs set up another try for Gould which Bancroft only narrowly failed to convert. Soon one of the English forwards got the ball out to Stoddart, who made some ground and fed Marshall. Playing his only international, Marshall slid over for his third try. But Woods missed with the kick

This had still seemed to have sealed the match for England, but a sudden move down the flank let in Gould for *his* third try. Bancroft, from the touchline, was unsuccessful.

The contest moved on towards its hysterical finish, when confusion after the final whistle was so great that the result of the match wasn't known for some time. It began when England conceded a penalty and young Bancroft, unaware of the score, was called up by Gould to take the kick. As no further instruction seemed to be forthcoming and with the crowd bellowing for some action, Bancroft picked up the ball, took three strides, and drop-kicked. "It's there, Arthur!" he cried to his captain as the ball sailed between the uprights.

The English rugby players shiver in Cardiff. Skipper Stoddart seems to be feeling the freezing conditions even more than the others

The difficulty was that only two days previously the system of points-scoring had been rearranged by the International Board. A try was now worth two points, not three; a conversion was worth three, not two; and a penalty was three points as before. This must have caused widespread arithmetical distraction as the final furious minutes were played out in the biting wind which made this classic match such an endurance test for players and onlookers alike.

So Wales held on and went on to win their first Triple Crown. The English boys, if the match had been played a week earlier under that points system, would have earned a draw – and without the blizzard's nasty chorus.

A month later Rowland Hill was informed that Mr A.E.Stoddart would be unable to play for England in Dublin. A further month on and England now assembled at Headingley, Leeds to tackle Scotland. In fine weather and before a crowd of 20,000, Stoddart led out the national team for the last time. For him it was to be a somewhat dismal event.

Boswell won the toss and took the wind at Scotland's back. Among Stoddart's opposing three-quarters was his dark-haired friend Gregor MacGregor, and it was he who relieved the initial pressure on the Scotland line with a good run that put them on the attack. The Englishmen, without Woods up front, tried desperately to push the Scots upfield. Scotland's scrimmaging was powerful, however, with McMillan and Boswell outstanding. It was the unlikely defence of England's halves, Duckett and the cricketer C.M.Wells, that kept them at bay, tackling bravely and making short runs to relieve the danger.

England made some progress. Dyson claimed a lot of territory with a penalty, Simpson returned the ball, then Mitchell sent a penetrative kick into Scotland's half. Wells had the ball and ran for the line. He passed to Stoddart, who had a fairly clear run. But he dropped the ball. And the Scottish forwards seized the chance to surge forward again. Within seconds England were desperately defending.

Middlesex rugby XV 1893, with Stoddart, in his final season, on the extreme left. MacGregor at the rear, centre

Play was balanced for a time, then Scotland rushed, and rushed ferociously. Stoddart again failed at a critical moment and Boswell had the ball just within kicking range. He dropped a lovely goal, the ball bouncing over via the crossbar.

The same pattern fell across the second half as the Scottish forwards marauded and harassed. Before long Campbell was gathering a loose ball and dropping another goal. The monotonous tidal attacks continued, with England's forwards being outgunned and the backs playing themselves into the ground. Only a long kick by Stoddart created some breathing space, though only briefly.

A Boswell penalty sparked off another sharp attack, and as the curtain was poised to fall, Stoddart, choked with remorse, made several desperate long drop-kicks, causing Scotland to fall back.

Two dropped goals (eight points) to nil gave little idea of the disparity between the sides, and with Scottish match reports justifiably rapturous, one English journal summed up by stating that "generally the English game was disappointing and the three-quarters were weak". Looking back many years later Sammy Woods remarked with cryptic brevity that Stoddart was "alas, a little too gentle when playing against Scotland". Might it have been fear of causing injury to his pal Gregor MacGregor?

Thus exit A.E.Stoddart, one week away from his 30th birthday, greatest of three-quarter backs, most agile and sophisticated rugby footballer of his generation.

Within days word came through that the *Orizaba*, carrying the Australian cricket team to England, had sailed from Melbourne. This kind of report – every touring year – sends a tremor of excitement and anticipation through cricketers everywhere.

CHAPTER 11

England Captain at Lord's

WISDEN for 1893 honoured him with inclusion in its Five Batsmen of the Year. Concise words of praise were now indelibly inscribed in the "gospel": "He continually gets runs under conditions that find most batsmen at fault, his play both on slow and fiery wickets being quite exceptional." The panegyric entered the shade with passing comment on his football career, lamenting that "he is now rather past his best". But for lovers of the summer game "Stoddy" was still very much in vogue.

It was again generally warm and sunny this year, and after the customary early practice at Mitcham the Australians went to the salubrious Sheffield Park for the opening match of their tour, which they lost by eight wickets. One scribe, searching for signs of sophistication in this eighth Australian touring team, wrote cheerlessly that the visitors had, as before, failed to please the critics with their batting style, although he granted that they amply demonstrated its effectiveness. The erratic performances of some of the Australians this season was put down to the periodic bulletins from Melbourne, where the land boom, in which many of the players had speculated heavily, was collapsing.

Stoddart was welcomed back at the Hampstead ground and initiated a dazzling club season with 75. In his seven matches for the club he was to average 111 this summer, with a century and a double-century and not a match lost. Gregor MacGregor joined Hampstead this year and shared comfortable bachelor accommodation with "Stoddy" at 30 Lithos Road, on the breezy slopes of South Hampstead, where from the

Lord's in the 1890s

rear window they could see across to the cricket ground in Lymington Road.

Stoddart stroked 62 runs in less than an hour for MCC against Sussex, having bowled leg-breaks to Fred Tate, who "hit at them with immense energy" but could not connect. Then when MCC played the Australians, WG clocked up 41 with him for the opening stand. The pitch was at its worst during this early period, and again a promising start had been made before Stoddart was caught after a determined 58.

Hampstead CC dinner menu:
AES in the chair

MCC amassed 424, and soon had the Australians following on, with Jack Lyons now playing a phenomenal innings, battering the bowling into the crowd and onto the awnings of the covered enclosures. His hitting had spectators and fielders silent with awe. Only the clang of the ball's landing disturbed the spell. He thrashed J.T.Hearne for four gigantic blows in an over, and then shouldered his way greedily into Attewell's and Nepean's servings.

Lyons's century came in 55 minutes, the score 125 without loss, and the pace seemed to sag momentarily as the giant seemed to step back and savour his destruction. ("When I taps 'em they hit the fence!") Then it was on again, and the figures on the scoreboard (crawler Bannerman's excepted) were no sooner up than they were making way for higher numerals. Lyons steamrollered his way to 149, when the arrears were exactly accounted for, then with fine dramatic sense, without further ado he was caught in the deep.

MCC needed 167 to win, and WG and "Stoddy" set about the task. There were hopes that the younger man might do something similar to Lyons, and he did hit one ball over the stand near the new score-box at square leg, and 72 runs were quickly posted before the rain returned.

Upon resumption both men were caught, and a collapse had to be checked. Although drawn, it was one of those matches which, if ever played out again in the fields of asphodel, simply must be televised. Stoddart was in spanking form in the Whitsun match against Somerset, and Surrey were beaten comfortably at The Oval, always a worthy performance. At Lord's, Middlesex seemed well placed against Gloucestershire, too, until Stoddart was hit by fast left-armer Fred Roberts in the last innings. Unsettled, he was caught by WG, and Middlesex crumbled to defeat. At least his first innings of 74 in 65 minutes had been a display of all his well-known artistry.

Again at Lord's, on the first day of June 1893, George Hirst burst a fast swinger through him for 2, but a second effort of 88 plus a solid Stanley Scott innings left Yorkshire a few to get after all. The Northerners scraped home, and ultimately took the Championship title this season.

A couple of days later, still at Lord's, Middlesex faced Notts, and A.E.Stoddart accomplished the then very rare distinction of a century in each innings, a deifying performance in Victorian times. Not since William Lambert in 1817 had a batsman made two centuries in a match at Lord's.

The contest began with a stand of 50 in only 20 minutes with A.J.Webbe, but no more real support came until F.G.J.Ford (45) batted, followed by MacGregor's useful 31. All the while "Stoddy" was absorbing the experienced Notts attack and placing it expertly through the field. A further record came this remarkable sportsman's way when he became the first batsman ever to score a hundred before lunch on the first day of a County Championsip match.

Last man Jack Hearne came in, hoping desperately to see him to his double-century, but he was bowled by Dixon, leaving Stoddart to carry his bat through the innings for 195 (215 minutes, one five, 28 fours, eight threes, 14 twos, 26 singles). This was to be the highest score registered by anyone in that 1893 summer of first-class cricket.

Billy Gunn, tall and commanding as any military leader,

AES: records aplenty in 1893

led the Notts reply with 120, and Middlesex had to make another big score to prevent defeat. At the end of the second day they were 184 for two wickets, Stoddart 94 not out, a careful innings so far, with no loose ball wasted.

With overnight rain sprinkling the pitch, the people came early to Lord's to be sure of seeing the hero of St John's Wood get his second century. It soon came, to storms of cheering and the waving of straw boaters as he cut a three off Bob Mee after 2½ hours in the middle. A boy ran out to him with a telegram, surely of congratulations, which Stoddart stuffed into his pocket unread.

There was conjecture as to his limits this day, with 300 runs already under his belt off this highly professional bowling line-up, and much of the day to bat. His manner was increasingly radiant with confidence, but eventually, at 124, after 195 minutes at the crease, he skyed a catch to Flowers at cover off Mee, the tall fast bowler who had taken a career-best 9 for 54 against Sussex in the previous month and had done most of the work here with "Dick" Attewell. "Stoddy's" second masterpiece of the match had included 13 fours, seven threes, nine twos and 33 singles.

Notts wickets tumbled all afternoon, and Middlesex pulled off a 57-run victory ten minutes from the scheduled close. Hundreds of spectators rushed to the pavilion at the end and shouted "Stoddart! Stoddart!" for five minutes before a man in a tall hat ran into the pavilion, "and soon afterwards the hero of the great match appeared at the entrance-door, cap in hand, while his admirers shouted themselves into a perfect frenzy of delight". The undoubtedly weary batsman acknowledged this remarkable demonstration with "a profound bow".

For a long time afterwards his great double was a talking point of widespread delight. "Verily," stated *The Cricket Field*, "we are lucky who are living to see such things."

As for a memento of this epic performance, he had secured the two balls off which he had made his twin centuries with the object of having them mounted as a "striking memento". There seems to have been no sight of them on the collectors' market during the past half-century or more.

STODDART FIN-DE-SIECLE

O Stoddart, dear Stoddart, explain by what odd art
You manage to knock up three centuries;
For beyond all denying it's all through your skying
Your county safe out of its venture is!
   With rigorous vigor you make your big figurehead
   Still bigger, till everyone wondered
   At your "190s"; and surely a sign 'tis
   You could have run up to 200.
O Stoddart, dear Stoddart, thou some demi-god art!
Such scores in one fixture! Why, that's, man,
A triumph so great as to give thee the status
Of an end-of-the-century batsman.
   But though it's delightful to yield thee thy rightful
   Applause, while admiringly patting
   Thy back with great glee, yet we won't want to see yet
   The end of thy "century" batting.

(Albert Craig, "The Surrey Poet")

The Australians faced MCC again, and this time Lyons made a competent 83 which would have been regarded as exceptional from the bat of any other player. He had to face Charles Kortright's lightning deliveries, and as with Harold Larwood forty years later and Frank Tyson twenty-two years after that, the near-invisible bowling onslaught cast a paleness across Australian faces.

Stoddart, the man of the hour, played on to nemesis Turner early, but late on the second day he reminded the tourists of his powers. With MCC needing 175 to win, he made the majority of 83 with W.G.Grace in a mere 45 minutes, taking the stand to 120 next morning before "Stoddy" played on to a ball from the tall off-spinner Hugh Trumble for 74. MCC's seven-wicket victory seemed a promising augury for the first Test match.

The Cricket Field paid him a prim compliment around this time: "His is the best sort of cricket to watch. All he does is done without effort; he rarely seems to have a difficult ball to play, because he plays it so easily; he is a comfortable bat to watch."

E.V.Lucas, recalling the way Stoddart often moved down the pitch, branded him as the immortal "Silver Billy" Beldham's worthiest disciple.

On a sub-standard pitch his ripe form continued with 95 in Hove's salty air, MacGregor attracting attention with his splendid wicketkeeping as Hearne and Rawlin bundled Sussex out. At Gravesend, "Stoddy" made a fine half-century on a bumpy pitch. Then it was back to Lord's to meet Surrey.

He took the bowling honours with 3 for 45, causing amusement at one point by running in to bowl then stopping suddenly for something (probably imagined) in his eye. He topped a bad first innings with 31, falling to the strapping new fast bowler Tom Richardson. Soon Stoddart and Timothy O'Brien were walking out through the gateway, a pair to make the pulse throb even when their team were trailing by 179 runs.

In 140 minutes Stoddart hit 125 runs (11 fours, six threes, 18 twos) and the pair lashed 228 in partnership. O'Brien's 113 contained some rumbustious strokes, including some controversial drives past a worried wicketkeeper off Walter Read's provocative leg-side lobs. When the dust had settled after another of these absurdities a bail was on the ground. A sharp discussion ensued between the principal parties, but since neither umpire had seen things clearly O'Brien settled the matter with characteristic decisiveness: "Anyhow, I'm not going out!" And the game proceeded.

The faithful Hearne and Rawlin saw to it that Surrey fell well short of the required 199, and at the end the crowd swarmed around the mighty Lord's pavilion, calling for their adored Middlesex cricketers.

There was no stopping "Stoddy" now. Against the Australians he hit a magnificent 94 (match top score) on a perfect Trent Bridge pitch for "Shrewsbury's England XI" (a welcome benefit match for the loss-making 1888 football tour organiser), and posting another century opening stand with W.G.Grace.

Then came a sojourn into club cricket. Australian "Demon" Spofforth, now playing for Hampstead, arrived late for the Uxbridge match, so Stoddart and George Thornton bowled Uxbridge out cheaply. The Demon then amazed everyone with an innings of 155 that overshadowed Stoddart's 68.

Soon Spofforth was hitting the local headlines again by taking 10 for 20 and 7 for 20 against Marlow, a suspicion remaining that some of those wickets were surrendered to his overwhelming reputation, even though the fire-breathing monster was already mellowing into the businessman and well-respected gentleman who, in his sixties and seventies, was to be found exhibiting fine chrysanthemums in Surbiton.

Hampstead, one of the strongest sides ever known in English club cricket. MacGregor and Spofforth are on the bench, with Stoddart to the right in fashionable cape

Stoddart made one further score of note before the first Test match – a 68 against Sussex – but failed to make his mark in yet another Gentlemen v Players showpiece. On 13, he hit a ball straight to Johnny Briggs at cover and bolted. WG didn't even leave his crease. The incident was commemorated in jocular verse by someone calling himself "Misericorde": "stumps went down and Andrew E. went back to th'pavilion creeping". On a final day of thunderstorms he fell for 11.

A week before the opening Test match the cricket world was shocked at the news that Will Scotton had committed suicide. This acutely sensitive man with the heavy eyelids, dourest of left-handers, had lodgings in St John's Wood Terrace, and after umpiring at Clifton College he had returned to London deeply depressed. He stayed in bed all next day, rambling incoherently.

Scotton had been photographed only days before, and liked the portrait so much that he ordered copies for friends and relatives. Now those friends and relatives were invited to view his body instead when the coffin was unlidded on the railway station in Nottingham.

So the legendary Scotton was laid to rest as the rain cascaded down, and now two other tragic figures walked to the wicket at Lord's to open for England against Australia: Stoddart, the lad from South Shields, playing his first home Test match and captaining England (WG was out with a broken finger) for the first time, emulating A.N. "Monkey" Hornby's achievement of leading England at both cricket and rugby. And Arthur Shrewsbury, the batsman WG placed highest of all others, was about to compile his third and final Test hundred against Australia.

A hot sun smiled derisively on the damp pitch, posing Stoddart a dilemma when he won the toss. He felt obliged to take first innings: if the first few unpredictable overs could be negotiated England might perhaps make a solid score.

Fifteen thousand people were crammed into an under-developed Lord's ground as "Terror" Turner ran in, the bell-topper hats and frock-coats darkening the pavilion behind him, no sightscreen then being in position. He let the first ball go, and then the second, which Shrewsbury aimed to flick to leg only to see it fly towards slip. By the last ball of the over Stoddart was facing the most formidable of all his cricket adversaries. He played him square for three.

Soon he was making a stirring off-drive that panicked the crowd at the Nursery end. He hit Billy Bruce again next over, a thumping blow that again gave a handful of spectators at square leg a chance to inspect the bright red ball. "Stoddy's" score spun round to 20 out of 21 in twelve minutes. But trouble overtook England in Turner's next over.

Stoddart took an agonising crack on the elbow which hurt him beyond concealment. The joint stiffened up, slowing his freedom of movement He was nearly caught at point from a desperate parry, and minutes later he played forward to Turner and failed to cover a sharp cutter that hit the off stump. First blood at 29: Stoddart 24.

William Gunn made only two. Then F.S.Jackson, the elegant Yorkshire amateur, walked out for his first Test innings. Shrewsbury was hanging on without causing the Australians much concern, though they must have yearned for the sight of his sloping shoulders receding towards the pavilion. He reached double figures after an hour's grafting.

England's team at Lord's for the first Test against Australia in 1893.
Although injured, W.G.Grace sits centrally among them, alongside the new
skipper, Andrew Ernest Stoddart, who became the first captain to declare a
Test innings closed. His crew consisted of: standing – Ted Wainwright,
Arthur Mold, William Gunn, Maurice Read; seated – Bobby Peel, AES, WG,
Bill Lockwood, Arthur Shrewsbury; front – Gregor MacGregor, F.S.Jackson,
Wilfred Flowers

Jackson meanwhile was delighting the crowd with some leg hits and drives. Shrewsbury stirred himself occasionally, but the style and approach of "Jacker" proclaimed him a species apart. Harry Trott for once failed to drop his leg-breaks on a length and Jackson punished him with three fours to leg; so Blackham hurriedly withdrew him.

It was tense and engrossing cricket as the Englishmen took the score to 168 before Jackson was caught nine short of his hundred. The pitch had settled down apart from occasional antics at the Nursery end, and it was now up to England's middle order to consolidate.

Maurice Read failed, however, and as Peel tried to push things along the crowd became restive. It may have gained Australia a wicket, for Peel let fly at the lanky Hugh Trumble and skyed a catch to Bruce. Five were out for 213.

When Shrewsbury fell at last to Turner for 106 he had been in for over four hours, with late cuts and leg-side placements mixed with great care that endeared him to all patriots.

The England innings ended at a solid 334, leaving Australia an awkward evening session to see out. And it went all wrong. Lockwood removed Lyons's leg stump and Giffen suffered an identical fate without scoring. Two down for 7, little Alec Bannerman sphinx-like at the other end.

No-one envied MacGregor as he tried standing up at the stumps, eventually wisely to revert to standing back. Thirteen extras helped towards Australia's 33 for two as Bannerman and Trott strode off at the end. Stoddart was well content with the situation.

Tuesday, the second day, was bright and the pitch appeared to have eased, as expected. Yet Shrewsbury was soon dropping onto his left elbow to catch Bannerman for 17, and Bob McLeod was beaten by a sizzler from Lockwood. At 75 the fifth wicket fell, and Lockwood had all five – almost six as he dropped a return catch from Harry Graham which would have made a staggering difference to this Test match.

Stoddart had got all he could out of Lockwood, and the Surrey fast man gave way to Arthur Mold after a stretch of almost two hours of potential devastation. Yet the last few overs had been played with growing confidence by the youthful little Graham, in his first Test innings, and tiny Syd Gregory, still to show his true worth at this highest level.

Like so many subsequent captains of England, Drewy Stoddart had to face criticism from many angles: he had kept Lockwood on too long; Jackson should have bowled more; it was less a case of determined batting than a slight case of mismanagement. Opinion without responsibility. Perceptive romantics wondered what might have happened had Graham's catch been held. But it was past, and now the young Australian pair took runs easily.

Sturdy Lockwood, England's likely matchwinner, was granted only half-an-hour of rest before taking up the attack at the Nursery end, and Shrewsbury undid much of his own good work by missing a high chance at point off Graham, who was scoring much faster than Gregory. The hundred stand came in little over an hour, and Gregory was finally out to an excellent high catch by MacGregor off Lockwood. At 217 for six Australia were right back in the match.

"Grummy" Graham, his boyish face flushed, reached 98, and the whole of Lord's tensed. He played uppishly to point off Flowers, and Shrewsbury got his hand to the ball . . . and dropped it. Graham's century came, warmly applauded, and when MacGregor finally held him off Mold, his 107 had been made in only 140 minutes. Australia, who had clearly made a very special discovery in this little fellow, finished a mere 65 behind after all.

Stoddart shaped better in the second innings, and the early sensations concerned Shrewsbury, who, as Trott missed him at point, smiled innocently and took a couple of boundaries. From a Stoddart late cut they ran four smart runs, but with 27 on the board Turner yet again broke through the England captain, this time for 13.

Gunn strode in and the Nottingham men took it to 113 by the day's end – Shrewsbury 45, hitting Turner over the fieldsmen's heads and picking the gaps as fast as they were created, like the master he had long been. Gunn again fell into step behind his businesslike little mentor.

They wore the bowling down on the third and final day, and as grey clouds came across the run rate began to accelerate. Shrewsbury was heading determinedly towards his second century of the match when Gunn was caught near the rope.

The Honourable F.S. Jackson knew what was needed. He hoicked and was missed by Bruce, who compensated almost immediately. Read made only a single, and after rain Shrewsbury was bowled for 81. When Lockwood went, it was suddenly six down for 198.

Stoddart's thoughts were now on the weather and the clock as Wainwright, the bluff Yorkshireman, hit hard. Eight were down for 234 at lunch, which would have left Australia needing 300 to win. But not until 3.15pm, when the drizzle had ceased, did Stoddart declare the innings closed.

This was the first declaration ever made in a Test match.

Jack Blackham had the pitch rolled, but rain fell again, and the match was eventually given up. The people, cheated miserably by the weather, drifted away from the dreary roped-off space.

In the county match at Old Trafford, O'Brien and Stoddart repeatedly hit Briggs over the railings before being stumped off him one after the other. This was County Championship cricket 1890s style, not the Twenty/20 of the 21st Century. Johnny Briggs, the laughter-maker with the tell-tale "grimace of Grimaldi", as Cardus saw it, gathered seven wickets with his ingenuous and persistent slow left-armers. Arthur Mold took twelve as Lancashire, so often the bridesmaids in the Championships of the 1890s, chalked up a victory over the Middlesex "swells". Stoddart had taken the ball in this game too, and did something with it: 4 for 23 and 2 for 23 helped render the trip worthwhile.

Then for Hampstead he thrashed Hampstead Nondescripts for 129 runs, and within days was striking 40 boundaries in an innings of 210 which helped his club to a lead of 400 over Willesden. Well, he *was* just about the best batsman in the world.

The Middlesex men went to Taunton in August, and in the blazing sunshine there was a feast of run-making. "Stoddy" was reported as lame when Middlesex fielded (an obstinate football injury?) but he managed 34 before England rugby colleague Sammy Woods had him in the slips. One memorable hit had been a drive into the river off Hedley, the ball's flight path showing the way for Botham and Richards around a century later. It took an astonishing catch by Woods to end Stoddart's at 25 in his second innings in the scorching heat.

At Bristol, against the puzzling spin of Charlie Townsend, the teenage wonder, a typical 75 from Stoddart helped Middlesex to 385. Gloucestershire then crashed against "Turkey" Rawlin after misty rain and sunshine on the Saturday.

Big attendances on the first two golden days of the second Test match at The Oval helped swell Maurice Read's benefit fund. (How lucrative it would be for a modern cricketer to be awarded a Test match for his benefit.) There was the usual rumble before the Test got under way. Wainwright was retained by Yorkshire for their Middlesex match, but Stoddart and

MacGregor played for their country (allowing that MacGregor came from north of the border). Fortunately for the Oval crowd, F.S.Jackson preferred to play for England, but this thing was coming to a head. There was a feeling that priorities, particularly Lord Hawke's, ought to be reviewed.

WG was fit again and resumed his place on the mount, succeeding in his first obligation by winning the toss. A smile creased his face as he came down the pavilion steps, although to one observer Stoddart seemed tense with the responsibility of opening for England.

Turner measured out his run at the pavilion end, but the field setting arranged by him and skipper Blackham seemed as respectful as for a mere change bowler. Only two slips and a third man stood behind the bat; Trott crouched at point, as usual; then, challenging the driving power of Stoddart, whose right hand gripped the bat so unusually low, was an array of off-side fieldsmen.

It wasn't easy at the start. "Terror" Turner caused frowns as WG got things going with a lofty square-cut. Trumble, the commanding off-spinner, had almost the same field setting, and for six stringent overs this pair tied down England's openers. With only a single to his name Stoddart was dropped at slip before getting his off-drive away. Then he was reprieved again, an easy chance to Trott. He was mistiming Turner embarrassingly, and WG himself was surprised by a kicker from Trumble which hit the top of his bat-handle.

Stoddart edged through the slips. And then came the break from bonds that comes often to batsmen in the horrors: he saw a short ball early and swung it serenely to the chains. It heralded a string of thrilling strokes played without inhibition to all sections of the shirt-sleeved crowd. Forty came up fairly promptly after all, and WG pulled Turner masterly for four. Stoddart then drove McLeod beautifully through mid-off, reaching 30, and then was dropped again. His luck stretched credulity.

The crowd gasped again as WG edged George Giffen over the slips to the boundary to raise the fifty, and runs now came thick and fast, especially from a fatalistic Stoddart, who reached his own fifty in 70 minutes.

WG slammed Harry Trott's leg-break through the cover field then galloped a swift single. The century partnership came as Stoddart lifted Trott over long-off for another four, then hit him to leg for three – the three-figure stand in only 90 minutes.

Trumble bowled a maiden over or two, but WG made a fine stroke to leg to register his own fifty. Giffen ended a tidy spell of bowling which had time and again brought WG tentatively forward and forced the less rangy Stoddart often to drop down late on the ball. They went to lunch 134 for no wicket, the aggrieved Australians following thoughtfully.

The England pair were late coming out after the break, and stories circulated that WG's finger had let him down and that his partner had been stricken by sunstroke. But the rumours probably started in the Oval bars, for the batsmen finally appeared, and the battle was resumed.

W.G.Grace barges through the clamouring
Oval Test match crowd, Stoddart right behind him

There was a confident howl when WG's pads were rapped, but Stoddart restored confidence with an on-driven four, quickly supported by a cut and a pull to the rope. Things quietened as the 150 came up. Then Stoddart was put down at short leg and McLeod muffed an easy catch at second slip off Turner, and the crowd murmured. It was as if the proverbial cat with nine lives had donned flannels.

But the fortunes had now exhausted themselves, and Stoddart played the next ball from Turner into his stumps. The flukiest of all his innings, an innings he declared he was positively ashamed to go on with, was at an end. If anything the shame rested with the butterfingered Australians. *The Bulletin* years later, whether exaggerating or not, bemoaned its countrymen's dismal display in the field: "What a night the Australians must have had previous to the Test match at The Oval! Eleven catches were missed off Stoddart's batting."

There had been 11 boundaries in his 83, made out of 151 (WG and he had now reached three figures in each of their last three openings against the Australians) on a pitch which had interested the bowlers all the while. There had been frequent errors, but also some explosive hits, and although an artist considers firstly the quality of his work, this innings, "Stoddy's" highest ever in a home Test match, had gone into the scorebook with enough weight to ensure the likelihood of ultimate victory.

Now, at the other end, and without a further run added, the Champion was caught by Giffen off Trumble for 68. Shrewsbury and Gunn were now together, and the game changed colour. Shrewsbury was in commanding, almost flamboyant, mood. The 200 came up, and the tireless Giffen returned to his domain, the bowling crease. With his second ball he bowled Gunn for a worthy 50th Test wicket.

When Albert Ward, in his first Test match, snicked a four through slips, that other serious man, Giffen, pretended to examine his bat for holes. Shrewsbury reached 50, and celebrated with 12 off an over of Trott's leg-breaks, and Ward cut cleanly and hit to leg. In the sunshine the runs happily mounted.

A stand of 103 had been constructed before Shrewsbury was tempted to hit out once too often. Ward soon fell for 55, and Jackson strode in at number seven.

Calamitous fielding cost Australia heavily again as Gregory missed Jackson in the outfield, and by the end he and Read (W.W.) had added 67, England waxing fat at 378 for five.

In the high heat of the following day Jackson drove Trumble's third ball to reach 50 in only 45 minutes, and the eager crowd saw Read let go at last with a characteristic pull-drive. The 400 was rolled onto the scoreboard and everywhere English eyes were smiling.

The cricket sparkled until Read finally played back and was bowled, the stand worth 131. Someone moved behind the bowler's arm as Briggs faced Giffen. His off stump was hit. Lockwood prevented the hat-trick. But soon the eternal Giffen trapped him too. And now MacGregor ran "Jacker's" quick singles and watched him drive with Olympian power. At 98 Jackson lost his penultimate partner, and Mold, almost the world's worst batsman, played out the over with legs and bat. The ground then settled to watch Jackson hoist his century. The ball ran down to third man and Mold came stampeding down the pitch. Jackson unselfishly consummated the run, and it was left to Mold to see out another nerve-racking over.

He managed it, and F.S.Jackson faced off-spinner Giffen. He drove mightily at the third ball, and the clunk as it hit the pavilion (such a hit was worth only four runs at the time) was lost in the roar of jubilation rising from members and the throngs in the outer. Mold, who was not thinking all that clearly, ran him out shortly afterwards, and England wound up with 483, their highest total so far in England.

The cream figures in their assorted headwear played out the second act of this game of Test cricket under the gaze of the gas-holders in August of 1893, when Victoria was ruling with motherly supremacy, Gladstone was enjoying his fourth and final term as prime minister, and the occasional "four-wheeled petroleum gig" could be heard and seen along the Queen's highways.

Australia started well, but Briggs had Lyons playing across the line at 30, Trott and Bannerman were snapped up by Lockwood before lunch, and young Graham was caught behind second ball after the break. Thus Australia were soon in deep trouble.

MacGregor bravely moved up to the stumps to take Lockwood and was rewarded for his pluck with a full-toss which smashed him on the knee. But these things were forgotten (except perhaps by MacGregor) as Briggs dealt Gregory his fate, and Australia had lost five for 40.

Giffen and Bruce made a bright little stand that promised much until Giffen fell to England's bowler of the series, Bill Lockwood, and the collapse continued unchecked as Briggs chimed in with a series of tailend wickets. F.S.Jackson finally ran out Blackham after the last-wicket 32 had lifted Australia to 91, a tired performance. The compulsory follow-on with a deficit of 392 could hardly have been more dispiriting.

But Billy Bruce, spurning Australia's wobbly position, hit away when the second innings got going at half-past-four, boundaries flying in all directions. The fifty came up in half-an-hour. Then Mold's first ball flew from the edge of Bruce's lightweight bat into the slips, where Jackson held a sharp catch. Big Gunn nearly ran out little Bannerman as he scrambled a run to open Giffen's score, and when Lockwood dropped a few short Bannerman suffered some stinging blows. He walked rhetorically down the pitch and patted a spot.

Slowly it began to seem that the outcome might not be so straightforward. The pitch was holding up well and the other Australians were resting up in the dressing-room and on the balcony as WG and his army sweated it out. Fieldsmen's tiredness began to show. A misfield gave Australia their 100th run. Soon Giffen was missed, and disdainfully cut the next ball for four, perhaps hoping that Stoddart's lucky star now hung over him.

Then Bannerman, 55, was caught by Read running back at mid-on, and two were down for 126. The grim-faced little Sydneysider had become the first Australian to score a thousand Test match runs, although in an age when statistics were only of casual interest it is just possible that he and most others may not have known it.

Australia at the close were still 234 behind. It was going to take something special from Giffen and others next day. The public gave little for Australia's chances. Only 2000 turned up to see Briggs and Lohmann spearhead the attack. The only runs Giffen made today were gifted to him: he cut and MacGregor failed to take the return and four overthrows resulted. Lockwood then yorked him for 53.

Syd Gregory's dreadful run continued, Shrewsbury toppling over as he caught him for six. Harry Graham, on a "pair", was soon liberated, and runs came fast. He pulled Lockwood defiantly to post Australia's quick 200, four wickets down.

Graham, moving quickly out to Briggs, and clubbing a slowed-down Mold, had the crowd in ecstacy. Trott, who had been quietly beavering away from the drop of the second wicket, reached his fifty, and W.G.Grace's tactics, not for the first time, were questioned. Why not Walter Read with his strange lobs? Or Stoddart? Or some cunning from the Old Man himself?

Trott and Graham put on 106 in little more than an hour as the crowd grew ever more impatient. Then Johnny Briggs looked very pleased with himself as he turned away, hands in pockets, having deceived and bowled Harry Graham for 42.

Jack Lyons's first ball was popped comfortably up to Jackson at mid-off . . . and was dropped. The 300 came up, but soon Trott's gem-like 92 was terminated like so many innings in an age of robust driving – by a catch at mid-on.

With little to lose now, Lyons struck out at Briggs, then turned his attention to Bill Lockwood, hitting him for four, his third successive boundary. Read was sent to field in front of the members, but Lyons's next effortless stroke lifted the ball onto the pavilion roof. Lockwood bowled again, and the mighty Lyons got underneath the ball with a huge heave. Read rubbed his hands together, but the ball zoomed well over him as he leaned back against the railings. This was Lyons's fifth four in a row, but to the next delivery he drove to mid-off, where WG surprised everybody with a sharp catch low to his left. It nearly rocked him off his feet, but for Australia it really was the end.

F.S.Jackson aptly finished the contest by catching Bob McLeod, and England had won by an innings and 43 runs.

Next day, in a county match, "Stoddy" was bowled for a duck at Trent Bridge by the six-foot-four Mee of Notts. Middlesex won easily.

The *Windsor Magazine* once looked at cricketers' fingers, and A.E.Stoddart's were found to bear no trace of rough usage. Most bowlers had fingers of considerable length; Stoddart hadn't. His hands were on the small side, well-proportioned, characteristic of their owner: "thoroughly neat and workmanlike". They had done a goodly share of work in that match against Nottinghamshire, taking three wickets and holding five catches.

There was one further Championship match before the third and final Test. It was against Lancashire, who needed a win to stay in the race for the title, and Lord's was filled on a showery morning. Middlesex made 304 (Stoddart 12). Then Lancashire twice fell apart against Jack Hearne. With time fast running out after rain interruptions, Middlesex went out to get 29 in the slithery conditions. Stoddart, swinging a short one from Mold for what looked a certain four, stood nonplussed as Archie MacLaren made a catch of it, dismissing him for 0. Mold's figures were 3 for 3 as A.J.Webbe sealed Lancashire's fate for another season.

At Old Trafford, as August 1893 drew to a close, England had to resist any Australian attempt to level the Ashes series.

Manchester had been drenched, but a drying wind had left the pitch suitable for a prompt start Thursday morning. This time Lord Hawke kept F.S.Jackson and Peel in the Yorkshire ranks.

There were 8000 present to see W.G.Grace lead out an England team containing two new faces, Surrey's Billy Brockwell and his close chum Tom Richardson. The doubling of admission prices may have had something to do with the moderate attendance, yet those who saved their money missed a highly entertaining day's cricket, initiated by the incorrigible Jack Lyons.

It started with a boundary first ball of the match to stonewaller Bannerman, a freakish beginning. Then for a thrilling fifteen minutes it was Lyons unlimited. He made 27 of the 32 for the first wicket, thrashing Mold and Briggs, who were bowling before their own crowd, and with a defensive field. MacGregor eventually caught Lyons. Then at 59, the colossus from Mitcham, Tom Richardson, took his first Test wicket. The dour Giffen was a good one to start with. When Bannerman unhappily went to a touch off the glove against Briggs, Australia were three down for 69. Richardson thundered in again and had Trott edging to WG, who clung to the ball low down. Four down for 73. Harry Graham entered, and by the luncheon break the total had eased to 100.

Mold hurt Graham twice, then hit his boot and gained an lbw decision. Half the side out for 129, and Stoddart at mid-off feeling happy with life, exchanging pleasantries with skipper Grace as they crossed between overs.

Swarthy little Syd Gregory was bowled first ball by Briggs and drooped off, probably wondering at the perversity of international cricket and questioning why the English authorities could be so inhuman as to select this slow left-armer match after match.

Billy Bruce and Hugh Trumble set about restoring the situation. The left-hander clubbed Briggs for 16 off one over, and Trumble employed his distinctive cut. The 150 came up, Mold and Briggs making way for Richardson and Brockwell – who today lie in close proximity to each other in Richmond cemetery, Richardson beneath a broken wicket of marble and Brockwell anonymous beneath a grassy patch.

In 1893, with blood coursing urgently through their veins, they strove to improve England's advantage as Bruce and Trumble dug in. Bruce drove Brockwell through the field for four to bring up his well-earned fifty, then cut Richardson and hit him to leg. As the 200 loomed, Bruce was well caught by Read, and the tail went quickly when WG brought back Briggs. Richardson strode off with 5 for 49, Briggs with 4 for 81. Australia had made a paltry 204 that soon seemed far more comfortable as England squandered their position.

Giffen opened the bowling without a slip, and the other end was taken by Charles Thomas Biass Turner, also with men plotted out to deal with the lofted drive. Trumble, as usual, bestrode the slips area.

WG drove towards mid-off and started to run. Stoddart, still scoreless and perhaps not impatient to come to grips with Turner, was not backing up very well. He was a long way from home as Gregory broke the wicket with his punctual return. It was a nauseating way to go, and it seems that WG was upset too as he grafted his way into the thirties by close of play. Shrewsbury had made a fearfully slow dozen before Giffen had him caught.

On the Friday, William Gunn and William Gilbert Grace began confidently, cutting boundaries and off-driving. Then a ball from Bruce kept low, thumped WG's pad, and went on to disturb the leg stump: 73 for three wickets.

Gunn took matters most seriously. His first hour brought him 14 runs, and Bannerman at mid-off must have squinted across with mixed emotions. The resolute Albert Ward was caught behind, and Walter Read, after two spanking boundaries, was bowled by Giffen. Now, with an end to bowl at, the Australians still led by 90.

Brockwell stayed a while, then made way for Briggs. A fascinating partnership saw Gunn finding his strokes. Then Briggs, unable to stand by any longer, tried to hit Giffen and was bowled for 2. Eventually the Australian total was passed, and once more Mold, for all the satirical remarks, stayed long enough to see a batsman to his century. When he fell for a duck, Gunn had reached 102 and England, with 243, had a token lead of 39.

Bannerman and Lyons soon wiped off the arrears, but Mold got Lyons at 56, the muscleman from South Australian having hit 33 in even time. Giffen went to a nimble slip catch by Brockwell, and near the end Trott was bowled by a worrying shooter from Mold. Australia led by 54 with seven wickets in hand and a day to play. The balance was delicate.

It was, surprising to note, the first Saturday of the Test series, yet, probably owing to the threatening weather, only 5000 came to the ground to see Bannerman and McLeod resume for Australia. Following a shower of rain, McLeod was caught off Richardson, who was getting the ball to kick off the Old Trafford turf.

The mighty and tireless Tom Richardson
(one of a number of previously unpublished pictures in this volume)

Bruce raised some excitement with four fours and a two off a Briggs over, and after another break for the weather he edged one close to Stoddart at third man. Then he played to point, into Shrewsbury's reliable hands.

England had to get wickets quickly, but Bannerman seemed immovable. After 2½ hours he reached 50 – and was dropped by Read at slip. Johnny Briggs was called up again and had Graham stumped.

Three runs later Gregory went leg-before to Richardson, and Australia were 173 for seven. Trumble needed to stay with Bannerman now. Time was as significant as runs.

But only nine were added before Bannerman refused a call and the lofty Trumble slipped in turning. Australia, with two wickets left, led by 143. Soon after lunch Richardson smashed a ball into Turner's hand.He ran the run but went straight to Dr Grace, who pulled the finger back into place.

The 200 was posted. Then Richardson took his tenth wicket of the match, an impressive debut performance. Bannerman's 60 had taken 205 minutes, a grim defiance lightened by eight fours.

Turner and Australia's skipper Blackham now swung the mathematics of the contest around. This tenth wicket, so often the most crucial of an innings, realised a swift 36, so when WG came out with "Stoddy", England needed an awkward 198 in 130 minutes on a surface still playing truly.

Stoddart got off his "pair", and both openers hit early fours. Twice Stoddart pulled Trumble to the boundary almost off his face. Then he drove Turner deep. Hopes rose around the ground as WG lustily drove Turner high into the crowd, temporarily losing the ball. In 70 minutes they had 78 up, though it wasn't quite good enough. Stoddart, after eight stirring fours, tried to place Trumble to leg and was snapped up by "Tich" Gregory for 42.

Shrewsbury hit Trumble hard, but as the pointlessness of the situation became obvious he became quiet. At half-past-five WG was caught for a 45 which had taken the 45-year-old almost two hours. The match had long since been doomed to stalemate. Gunn, the first-innings hero, made only 11, and Trumble bowled Ward next ball.

Thus England, with their Oval victory, had won their fifth home rubber in succession. A year from now it would be time to look forward to the next compelling chapter of Anglo-Australian competition.

The first game of the Scarborough festival provided A.E.Stoddart with memories gloomier than he would have prescribed for himself. The Reverend R.S.Holmes had urged him to make a tall score, but the response was a doleful shaking of the head and a gentle protest that he was worn out. George Hirst, swinging his left-armers late, gave him a hectic time in both the MCC innings.

Then recovery: for the South against Yorkshire he and H.T.Hewett had a cracking century stand, and although Stoddart fell to Hirst both times, he put 77 runs in the book.

Next, as the summer neared its end, for C.I.Thornton's XI against the weary Australians, in beautiful weather and on a Scarborough ground filled to capacity, the Honourable Stanley Jackson, the local god, and A.E.Stoddart, the champion from the South, played through a stern opening spell from Turner, then began to play some strokes. Similar in appearance, the elegant pair accelerated the longer they were in. "Stoddy" relaxed into carefree cricket, and outscored "Jacker" almost two runs to one, chipping out for himself the honour of a century before lunch, when the total was 170. He finally fell for 127.

The Australians went on to pass the Thornton score on first innings (95 to the brilliant little Harry Graham). "Jacker" charmed another 60-odd, and there was eventually time only for another brief sample of Jack Lyons's heavyfooted homicide with the bat.

The 1893 season was wound up at Hastings, a major talking point being the possibility of Stoddart achieving the very rare tally of 2000 runs for the season: two fixtures left, only 35 runs required. After batting for the South against the Australians the odds lengthened. Turner reminded him of the personal jinx, having him caught for four, and the well-informed girls in their puffed-sleeved dresses felt sad at heart. "Stoddy" had seemed oppressed by the thought of completing his 2000, an achievement hitherto the boast of only W.G.Grace and, this very

Romantic image of Stoddart the gipsy

season, William Gunn. While he dithered over those four runs, WG had made 24, a rare instance of the elder outscoring the younger.

The Australians now collapsed for 64. But in the follow-on Lyons gave another Herculean display, and the South after all needed 111 to win.

There was a sense of urgency this time, and Stoddart and Hewett made runs fast. The 2000 edged teasingly within reach: one boundary shot would do it. After all the square-drives and hooks, the skimming off-drives and crisp cuts of this summer of 1893, "Stoddy" wanted just one more well-placed stroke and the momentous achievement was his.

Turner purred in and bowled. The ball deviated and slipped through Stoddart's defence. The stumps were rattled. Stoddart, bowled Turner, 27. Season aggregate: 1996.

For the cream of English cricket one more first-class match remained before the leaves began to fall from the trees. It was mid-September, and the gaiety of Hastings was tinged with the poignancy of farewell.

WG and Stoddart took up the South's reply to the North in mid-afternoon. Stoddart played the first ball away and they ran a three which might have been four if he'd had a younger, swifter running mate. Season's aggregate now 1999. WG played the remaining four balls, then it was Briggs to Stoddart, a half-volley floated outside leg stump. "Stoddy" opened his shoulders, the umpire flinched, long leg peered eagerly, but the ball was through to Sherwin as a murmur of disappointment went up.

The next ball was short, perhaps compassionately so, and Stoddart banged it away for four. The 2000 was his, a rare and grand accomplishment.

On top of all the other acknowledgements of his performances at the crease the accolade of starring on the rare Leibig menu

W.G.Grace, England's father figure, recorded a duck, and Stoddart soon followed for 13, but a lead of almost 100 accrued, and in the fourth innings the South had to get 261 runs. WG again went cheaply, but Stoddart, with the monkey off his back, made a pulsating 63, for which Nicolls, the batmakers, awarded him a new blade. That innings to close a memorable summer embraced 11 fours and five threes and came in only 55 minutes.

The 1893 season found A.E.Stoddart top of the run aggregates for the only time in his life. His total was 2072. His average of 42.29 was 0.56 behind William Gunn's. Arthur Shrewsbury's tally of 1686 was third-best.

Middlesex CCC presented

"Stoddy" with an elegant silver bowl at the end of this wonderful season, "in appreciation of his splendid cricket for the county". Over fifty years later it stood on his widow's sideboard, bright and pleasing as the man's batting.

This year also saw his retirement from rugby football, a gap that was sorely felt at club and national level. Henceforth it was to be cricket first, and dalliance with golf and racquets, lawn tennis and winter skating, betweentimes.

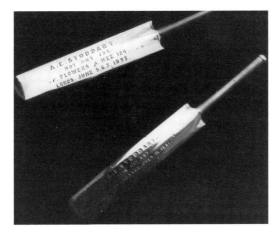

Commemorative miniature bats - souvenirs of his twin hundreds at Lord's and his double-century two years earlier

CHAPTER 12

♦♦♦

The County Grind

"WHO is the greatest cricketer, please?"
And Mr Simon of course replied, "Dr W.G.Grace."
"And the second-greatest?"
"Perhaps," the minister answered, "A.E.Stoddart."

A mighty club side: Hampstead 1894 – Spofforth, Stoddart, MacGregor, Thornton, Hayman et al

In 1894 Stoddart was elected as a vice-president of Hampstead Cricket Club. Once more every match in which he played resulted in victory for the club, his contribution with the ball surpassing much of his batting this summer.

In June, against Beckenham, considered a strong club at least until this particular match, he and Spofforth swept the opposing batting away for 13 and 21. "Spoff" took 8 for 7 and 4 for 4, "Stod" 2 for 5 and 6 for 7. Hampstead made 269, Stoddart 148.

He took a century off Emeriti and chopped Willesden about with 226 not out, having hit 210 against them the previous year and 238 in 1887.

Yet despite these pyrotechnics, his club batting average was restricted to a modest 64. His 37 wickets cost only 5.5 each.

His showing for Middlesex was less satisfying. *The Cricket Field* remarked in mid-season that "centuries in first-class matches have become quite common, and almost the only man who has not greatly profited is Stoddart, the best batsman of all".

Early in 1894, after Lord Sheffield had declined their invitation, the Melbourne and Sydney cricket authorities had asked Stoddart to gather together a team to tour Australia at the close of the English season. The job of seeking a balanced array of talent for a tour party may have caused him some distraction as the summer progressed from one damp week to the next.

The curtain-raiser at Lord's was a curious match between MCC and Sussex which got under way at five minutes past noon on May 2 and finished at 5.25pm that same day. Sussex crashed for 42; Stoddart hit 44 out of 103; and Sussex fell again for 59.

He gave customers value during the dawn of this cricket season: 32 in Sherwin's low-scoring benefit, a magnificent 81 for MCC against a high-class Kent attack, 41 in 40 minutes against Lockwood and Richardson's unpatronising stuff at The Oval (when "Stoddy" bowled he was hit for a seven to leg by Bobby Abel), a tortured 45 in the brief Gloucestershire match (WG 0 and 1) – all this before May was out.

Middlesex did well in June, the bowlers having things to their liking. Stoddart had a 70 at Hove, but the big innings came in Billy Barnes' benefit at Trent Bridge. For the Gentlemen of England he made 148 that was all style and charm, helping build a total of 340. Notts got to within one run, and by the time Stoddart and Hornby (England's only double cricket-rugby captains) had made forties in the second innings there was no time for a result. The attendance had been poor, but Barnes sought out Woods and Stoddart after the game and bought them a grateful drink out of his meagre takings.

Against Oxford University, Stoddart again found himself seeing the ball clearly. His 78 was easily the highest score of the match, which was made notable in a way by "Shrimp" Leveson Gower's "pair". Stoddart caught him second time round and comforted the victim as he passed by saying: "Congratulations! WG maintains that no-one is a first-class bat till he has made 'spectacles'!"

WG and Stoddart made a quick 56 for the Gentlemen's first wicket at Lord's, where the historic performance came from F.S.Jackson and S.M.J.Woods, who bowled through both the Players' innings unchanged as

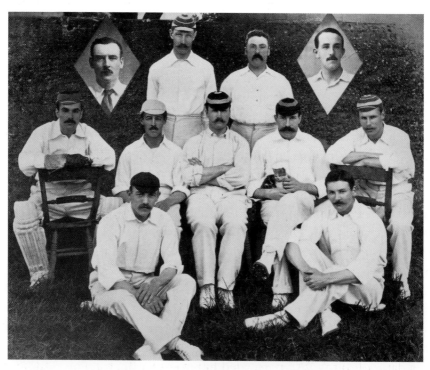

Cricketer with kitten. Middlesex 1894:
Standing: S.S.Pawling, J.T.Rawlin;
Seated: G.MacGregor, P.J.T.Henery, T.C.O'Brien, A.E.Stoddart, H.B.Hayman;
Front: J.T.Hearne, R.S.Lucas; Insets: A.J.Webbe, C.P.Foley

the professionals slid to an innings defeat.

The Somerset fixture brought Middlesex their last victory of the 1894 season, with T.C.O'Brien hitting and hooking 110 not out, the only century recorded for the county through the entire season. This was also P.F. "Plum" Warner's first county match, and some years later he was to describe his introduction to the team at the Castle Hotel in Taunton: "It was a very shy and strange boy who walked into the sitting-room. I can see [A.J.] Webbe getting up at once, coming forward and shaking hands with me, and welcoming me in the most affectionate manner. In the room were Stoddart, O'Brien, and MacGregor, and I was delighted when any of them spoke to me. I thought them all heroes. In later years when I became captain I always, when a new man came to play, had in mind the way Webbie first met me. To know Webbie is to love him."

Stoddart's reaction upon making the big time nine years previously had been almost identical.

August 1894 was a cheerless month, with only the Lancashire match touched by the Stoddart personality. Against Briggs and Mold he dominated both Middlesex innings with 68 and an 84 which took him past his thousand runs for the summer. The match was lost, however, and it might have been after this debacle that the team photograph was taken. They look glum, those nine men, with Webbe and Foley in insets. Rawlin, with his inverted-horseshoe moustache; Pawling, once "Stoddy's" school opponent, tall and solemn; MacGregor in his insubstantial gloves; the frail Henery; the muscular O'Brien, arms folded truculently, cap-peak vertical as a guardsman's; Hayman, who modelled himself on Stoddart, the Hampstead favourite; Drewy Stoddart himself, tenderly nursing a piebald kitten, thinking perhaps of the task ahead, the trip to faraway Australia, this time as chief of staff.

Lord's would soon be emptied for another winter, and the kitten would have to find affection from another source.

Stoddart's three matches in September were all rain-affected. Yet he came up with an amazing performance for the Gentlemen at Hastings. On a dampish pitch WG persuaded him to open the bowling, and he and Ferris, the Australian left-armer, sent the Players back for 85. In 25 overs "Stoddy" had Bobby Abel, Billy Brockwell, Albert Ward, Alec Hearne and Bobby Peel for 34.

Now WG made a hundred and the Gentlemen built up a lead,

Lord's Ground.

GENTLEMEN v. PLAYERS.

MONDAY and TUESDAY, JULY 9, 10, 1894.

GENTLEMEN.	First Innings.		Second Innings.
1 W. G. Grace, Esq.	c Storer, b Lockwood	56	
2 A. E. Stoddart, Esq.	st Storer, b Briggs	21	
3 H. T. Hewett, Esq.	c Ward, b Briggs	12	
4 F. S. Jackson, Esq.	b Flowers	63	
5 G. J. Mordaunt, Esq.	b Brockwell	28	
6 A. C. MacLaren, Esq.	b Brockwell	21	
7 J. Douglas, Esq.	b Flowers	2	
8 J. R. Mason, Esq.	l b w, b Briggs	7	
9 H. W. Bainbridge, Esq.	b Flowers	0	
10 S. M. J. Woods, Esq.	not out	27	
11 G. MacGregor, Esq.	c Lockwood, b Briggs	5	
	B 10, l-b 2, w , n-b ,	12	B , l-b , w , n-b ,
	Total	254	Total

1-56 2-70 3-119 4-167 5-195 6-197 7-213 8-216 9-240 10-254
1- 2- 3- 4- 5- 6- 7- 8- 9- 10-

PLAYERS.	First Innings.		Second Innings.	
1 A. Ward	b Woods	2	b Jackson	13
2 Chatterton	c Mason, b Jackson	0	run out	0
3 Brockwell	b Jackson	17	b Woods	12
4 Gunn	b Jackson	1	b Jackson	22
5 Briggs	c Hewett, b Jackson	12	c MacGregor b Jackson	13
6 Flowers	c and b Woods	16	c Mason b Jackson	2
7 Lockwood	c and b Jackson	0	b Jackson	3
8 Wainwright	run out	34	b Jackson	27
9 Storer	b Woods	5	c MacGregor b Jackson	0
10 J. T. Hearne	c MacGregor, b Woods	1	b Woods	
11 Martin	not out	0	not out	11
	B 10, l-b 1, w, n-b,	11	B 3, l-b , w , n-b ,	2
	Total	108	Total	107

1-2 2-2 3-31 4-49 5-53 6-53 7-84 8-107 9-107 10-108
1-3 2-7 3-23 4-35 5- 6- 7- 8- 9- 10-

Umpires—W. Hearn and Titchmarsh.   Scorers—T. Hearne and Clayton.

ONE PENNY.   Three-day Match.

*** The figures on the scoring board show the batsmen in.

Metropolitan Railway Tickets can be obtained at the Booking office on the Ground.

Scorecard for the Gentlemen v Players match at Lord's, 1894, a triumph for F.S.Jackson

though Stoddart fell to J.T.Hearne that evening, to the general regret of those who had booked seats for the following day.

This time the professionals did better, and Stoddart, bowling 26 overs, was cut down to size with 0 for 47. Gunn's declaration made a game of it, but WG couldn't resist altering the batting order, and at the close his side had slipped to 73 for 7, and Stoddart had still to unsheath his sword.

About this time he began to take a keener interest in golf, and the spectacle of the three beginners, "Stoddy", Murdoch and Grace, thrashing around the bunkers of Rye with the slightly more experienced Sammy Woods would have been a rare sight. As time went by, Stoddart became a long driver. He often practised for hours on end, and it was said in later years that he was yet another cricketer to be swallowed up by the golf-course. It was written that these famous sportsmen all cheated occasionally when in the deep sandy bunkers.

His Middlesex average fell by half this year, and his first-class aggregate in 1894 was little more than half. Yet he stood top of the Middlesex aggregates. It was the county's mighty bowling attack of Hearne and Rawlin that had carried the day.

This may have been the season when "Stoddy" cut the shoulders off his bat after a series of dismissals to slip catches. The surgery had little effect on his fortunes, and he eventually gave the implement to Spofforth (another account says the Hampstead groundsman was the lucky recipient), who donated it many years later to a charity auction staged at Lord's. The "Bat of Misfortune" fetched two guineas for St Dunstan's Hostel for Blinded Soldiers and Sailors under the hammer of comedian George Robey in 1917. Just over seventy years later the bat popped up on BBC TV's

Antiques Roadshow.

William Caffyn, the old Surrey and All England cricketer, was another to put the magnifying glass on Stoddart: "I have always, for the fact of his having been so closely associated with Australian cricket, taken a peculiar interest in the career of Mr Stoddart." He considered his style to be unique: "I always think that Mr Stoddart drives more with the arms and less with the whole body than any other hitter of note that I have seen."

Caffyn was not to know that his final assessment was, for whatever reason, to be wide of the mark: "His defence is equal to his hitting powers, and his name will be handed down to posterity as one of the greatest batsmen that has ever been." Fourteen years later, in an edition of *Cricket* in 1908, Sir Home Gordon, a connoisseur of cricketers, asked whose cricket he had most enjoyed, replied: "Unquestionably Trumper's. Next to his, Ranjitsinhji's, Stoddart's and Jessop's."

CHAPTER 13

England on Top

THERE were thirteen men in this 13th English side to tour Australia (counting the two in 1887-88). And nine of them were six-footers. Early in 1894, A.E.Stoddart had been approached by Melbourne Cricket Club and the Sydney Cricket Ground Trust to raise a side to tour at the end of the English summer. He spent quite a bit of time during the season recruiting players, trying to get the balance right, persuading the reluctant, shrugging off the unavailables, glad to take on a string of acceptances. Among those who declined were Bobby Abel, who was offered £300 plus expenses but held out for £500, which was refused, and Canon William Rashleigh, who topped Kent's batting averages that summer, and the serene Somerset batsman Lionel Palairet.

On September 18, 1894 a colossal crowd at Fenchurch Street railway station wished the uniformed cricketers a back-slapping bon voyage, a crowd made up of "all sorts and conditions of men who, whilst not cricketers themselves, can get much pleasure out of seeing celebrated cricketers in mufti."

Stoddart had been given a send-off dinner at the Hampstead Constitutional Club, when the first of his many softly-delivered and slightly nervous speeches of thanks passed his lips, followed as the evening progressed by a rendition of *Tommy Atkins,* the hit song of the day. The team sailed away in *Ophir* (6910 tons; 602 passengers), which became the royal yacht in 1901, with the Melbourne-bred Honourable Mrs Ivo Bligh among the passengers. Her husband had been to Australia twelve years previously on the famous tour which resulted in the creation of the Ashes – and in their meeting and subsequent marriage.

If H.H.Stephenson and Caffyn and Charlie Lawrence, with their companions on the 1861-62 expedition, joined with Australia in the conception of big cricket in the great south land, Stoddart and his staff assisted in the delivery of a bonny child. The 1894-95 rubber, the first really great Ashes series, was to spark frenzied interest which has ever since rekindled every time that England and Australia have fought over the tiny Ashes urn. It brought a new dedication and application by the players, and the press gave the public what it wanted: detailed coverage, backed by comment from retired cricket warriors. The *Pall Mall Gazette* gave the word "test" a capital T and spent large sums on telegraphing reports across the globe every few minutes. The English, from their Queen down, loved it.

Events were to ridicule yet again some of the dim forecasts. *The Cricket Field*, for one, had stated that Stoddart's contingent, lacking several leading players, seemed hardly strong enough to play matches under the title of England v Australia. Yet we are told that the surname Stoddart derives from stud-herd or keeper of a stud, and the cricketers who set sail looked a healthy enough herd to most people – though Johnny Briggs had a battle to control his weeping wife. The last the huge gathering heard from the departing cricketers was Lockwood's shrill whistling across the water.

In Australia, anticipation and excitement were widespread. Stoddart became instantly popular as a courteous leader: his manner "contrasts distinctly with the bombastic way in which old WG used to swagger about. Stoddy moves among the crowd most unpretentiously, as if he were walking upon velvet". And his men brought in a fascinating gust of youthful dash and mature, awesome experience. The Test series was to be as gripping as any before or since, right up to the memorable battle of 2005.

The batting depended upon Stoddart, Archie MacLaren, Albert Ward, Francis Ford (whom Major Wardill, Melbourne Cricket Club's tour liaison officer, greatly admired), and Jack Brown (whose technique Major Wardill had condemned unashamedly: "He won't get ten runs in five months, and had better go home").

Billy Brockwell was a utility allrounder, and the fast bowlers were his Surrey pal Tom Richardson and Bill Lockwood, also of Surrey, with Northerners Bobby Peel and Johnny Briggs as crafty slow left-armers, and, remarkably, 45-year-old Walter Humphreys (Sussex), who bowled the long-outdated underhand lobs – very successfully. He was fairly fit, rode a tricycle, and apparently especially asked for by Melbourne CC.

Leslie Gay had been England's soccer goalkeeper the previous winter and was first choice as wicketkeeper. The rumour that "Stoddy" had never seen him in action was false, since he had played for Somerset against

The English touring team of 1894-95:
W.Humphreys, W.Brockwell, Major Wardill (liaison man), F.G.J.Ford,
W.H.Lockwood, A.Ward; seated: A.C.MacLaren, A.E.Stoddart, H.Philipson,
L.H.Gay, front: J.Briggs, J.T.Brown; dog ownership uncertain

Middlesex at Lord's that summer. The second 'keeper was Hylton "Punch" Philipson, born in Tynemouth, across the river from South Shields, and reportedly a few years later to be Stoddart's prospective brother-in-law. Miss Philipson never did become Mrs Stoddart. Life might have been longer and sweeter for him if she had. Nor, for that matter, did any of the other women whose portraits found their way into the scrapbook he kept on this tour. (One of them, captioned simply as 'M', bears a tantalisingly close resemblance to the woman he eventually married.)

The voyage was interesting. They arranged games of cricket in the nets on deck, and played a match on Colombo's Barrack Square ground against Eighteen of Ceylon [now Sri Lanka], where the outstanding local colt Raffel took 9 for 43 and 5 for 44 against them, bowling fast left-arm into a "shifting sand" pitch on the barrack square.

Stoddart's Thirteen won a highly entertaining match in which 37 wickets fell in the day. A diligent Albert Ward carried his bat for 24 not out through the first English innings of 76. The local team was a combination of Europeans and natives.

The ship behaved well in a tremendous swell, and Brockwell recorded that "Stoddy", a good sailor, was "most assiduous in his assistance to those who have suffered from seasickness".

A girl known as 'M'

The straw-boatered English cricketers line the ship's railings at departure: "Stoddy" and Humphreys are side by side in light-coloured suits.

The good ship Ophir, which conveyed them halfway around the globe

Eventually the rolling waves, the euphoric sunsets, the flying fish, and the games with the lady passengers became mere memories, and they docked at Albany, Western Australia. Then, at Adelaide, Stoddart explained that he had brought out more professionals than originally planned because he could not engage enough amateurs of the required standard. A local observer was quick to note that the amateurs and the professionals stayed at separate hotels, in the "old, obnoxious English tradition".

The players picnicked at Mount Lofty unburdened by any real threat of being recognised, and their appetites for cricket were keen by the time they made their way up to Gawler, where Albert Ward made a century first try in Australia and Stoddart made 13 on the asphalt pitch.

Now, in their white sunhats, they met South Australia at Adelaide, where George Giffen, having trained hard all winter, was bursting to get at the old enemy. Jack Brown made a century as Giffen operated inexhaustibly from one end or the other, taking 5 for 175, and Stoddart got into his stride with 66. The Englishmen totalled 477, surely a safe figure.

But the young wonder left-hander Joe Darling hit 117 as South Australia climbed to 383. Giffen now struck with 6 for 49, and his team were set only 225 to win. "Dinny" Reedman's 83 helped him into the Australian team for the first Test, and Giffen's 58 not out repaid him sweetly for the hard winter's effort with a six-wicket victory.

*Stoddart and his men in Ceylon (Sri Lanka), smart as could be in
blazers and pith helmets*

Stoddart disliked being interviewed, but one reporter managed to corner him and asked for an explanation for the batting collapse. "I don't think I could give you a reason if I tried," was the affable reply. Later, however, he is supposed to have stated weightily: "We took risks; your men took none." He hardly expected to find the crowd applauding a batsman for letting ball after ball pass him without any attempt to score off them.

He had an excellent match against Victoria, although MacLaren stole the bouquets with his 228. Again Stoddart's XI

*George Giffen, Australia's
own W.G.Grace*

made over 400, but with Tom Richardson injured the attack failed to contain
Victoria, who made 306. With a rich double of 77 and 78 (appreciated by
a little old man in a tall hat who came out and shook his hand), "Stoddy"
made sure Victoria had plenty to chase, and the home side went down by 145
runs. "Felix" (Tom Horan) and his fellow onlookers were understandably
enchanted by the MacLaren-Stoddart partnership: Horan regretted
Stoddart's downfall, trying to "send the ball to Jericho" and added his own
warm tribute to the "Stoddartian plaudits".

Further eastwards, New South Wales made a tedious 293, and
Frank Iredale secured his place in the Australian Test team with a watchful
133. But the total was not enough. The Englishmen made 394 in front of
Saturday's huge SCG crowd, J.T.Brown once again striking a century and
Brockwell, rediscovering his English form and subjugating his journalistic
and photographic duties, making 81. Stoddart continued a strange sequence
of scores with 79, this time taking nearly three hours over the runs. The
exasperated crowd often called out to him to open his shoulders, but he

The Melbourne scoreboard shows runs for the English skipper and a juicy
double-century for MacLaren

was serving notice that he had made up his mind to play purposeful cricket. The bowling was not cheap. Callaway bounced them around the ribs and Stoddart, standing, as a female columnist observed, "with quite a Piccadilly manner", stroked the ball away calmly and smoothly. His old adversary Turner tempted him with some innocent-looking deliveries but he was not to be seduced. His drives were hit hard across the grass. A chance to Callaway from a cut early on had steadied him, and the locals must have cursed the lapse as the English skipper hit Tom McKibbin three times in a row to the chains – the invective swinging to Bill Howell as he missed the third at square leg. When off-spinner Howell finally bowled him there were shrieks of excitement from the masses.

Next day, Sunday, they relaxed on Sydney Harbour. After lunch their launch moored in an inlet and Bill Lockwood, restless as ever, decided to have a swim, regardless of warnings about the shark danger. While Stoddart and Ford took pot-shots at objects in the water, Lockwood dived over the other side and began to stroke his way towards shore. But halfway across he began letting out gurgling cries. Some of the cricketers thought it was a clever, mocking impersonation of a drowning man. But England's key fast bowler was in serious trouble.

A yacht happened to be gliding past, and a lifebuoy was thrown to the thrashing figure. For a few moments only his upturned feet showed. It took some dynamic action from two of the yachtsmen to get him ashore, where brandy helped his revival. The atmosphere was ruefully and uncomfortably reflective for the rest of the day, with "Stoddy" wondering how he was going to see this bunch of players safely through to the end of the tour.

Back at the cricket ground Stoddart's men pressed on to victory in 97-degree heat, swamping New South Wales for 180 in their second innings, when Syd Gregory played *his* way into the Test side with 87.

There was a hearty banquet in Sydney, and Brockwell reported in *Sporting Sketches* that his captain made an elegant speech, stating in typically modest style that being surrounded by so many local celebrities rendered him more shy than usual.

Before they left town there came an invitation to "Mr Sttorade" to play against an aboriginal team from Shellharbour. Their secretary wanted to play on the Sydney Cricket Ground, and offered to put on a corroboree afterwards.

England in Australia 1894-95, fashionable gentlemen (and players) in Adelaide's Botanical Gardens: standing – Jack Brown, Leslie Gay, ArchieMacLaren, "Punch" Philipson, Bill Brockwell, Johnny Briggs; seated – Tom Richardson, Francis Ford, Drewy Stoddart, Walter Humphreys, Albert Ward; front – Bobby Peel, Bill Lockwood, Major Ben Wardill (Australian 'liaison officer')

The tourists almost came unstuck at Armidale, in northern New South Wales. At Stoddart's suggestion their sleeping car had been shunted into a siding to allow them some extra rest after the long night journey north. Down at the ground, they then drew lots to decide the batting order, and collapsed for 67. Ford and MacLaren saved them in the second innings, and a visit to Baker's Creek goldmine, the richest in New South Wales, gave them something else by which to remember this stop.

The Mayor and the Member of Parliament were predictably at Toowoomba railway station to meet the English cricketers. Put in to bat, Stoddart's men made 216 on another matting/concrete wicket. Toowoomba tumbled twice (113 and 105), just avoiding the innings defeat. Stoddart good-naturedly declined the offer of some extra time to hit off the three runs for victory.

Now for the first time ever Queensland faced an English team on even terms. Stoddart won the toss at the Brisbane Exhibition Ground and, batting at three, immediately showed his colours by lashing all the bowlers,

Michael Pierce (slow lobs) and Arthur Coningham in particular. The volatile Coningham was nursing an irritability that would erupt in Brisbane later in the season. Here and now "Stoddy" didn't help matters by stroking him for four, four, five, four and then a massive six out of the ground. Having had an odd reprieve on 98 when a ball from Hoare touched the bails without shifting them, he finally stepped out to McGlinchy and mis-hit to slip for 149. It was the first hundred ever made against Queensland in a first-class match. Ward made 107 in a partnership of 255 in 167 minutes, and they eventually set Queensland 494. The exasperated, persevering Coningham had 5 for 152 for his labours.

Tom Richardson now came through with a show of strength under the tropic sun. His 8 for 52 (seven bowled) sent Queensland back for 121, and Bill Lockwood, lungs now clear of seawater, stole the figures in the second innings of only 99.

Stoddart and his men now braced themselves with playing cards at the ready for the tedious rail journey back to Sydney, which took 29 hours. A truly historic Test match lay ahead of them.

"Someone will be swearing directly, Jack," Stoddart said as he watched Blackham flip the coin. "I hope it's you!"

It wasn't. Australia's captain won the toss and took first innings for his men, who had been practising for four days. Enthusiasm in Sydney was very strong, despite there being five South Australians in the side. Under a very hot sun a fair-size crowd waited tensely. Thunder could occasionally be heard but this day rain fell in other parts, where it was welcome. The sturdy shapes of Jack Lyons and Harry Trott emerged from the fairly new showboat pavilion and looked a reassuring pair to onlooking Australians, just like Colin McDonald and Peter Burge and Allan Border in later summers. And not even Fred Trueman symbolised greater menace than dark-haired Tom Richardson at the start of his run – though the latter had no time for dramatics and verbalising.

Stoddart arranged the field, and Richardson got the 1894-95 series under way with a testing maiden over to Lyons. Bobby Peel opened at the other end with his slow left-armers. Then Richardson hit Lyons's knee with an express delivery which then clattered into the stumps. Giffen came in and the score eased up to 21. Richardson now smashed the top off Trott's off stump. Joe Darling, in his first Test innings, was yorked first ball, and

Australia were staggering at 21 for three wickets. It was a powerful start by Richardson, who was expected to miss his English pitches.

Giffen and Frank Iredale now had the weight of the continent on their shoulders. The pitch was actually quite sound, but Richardson was getting the ball to rear at the knuckles and shoulder-blades. There was less danger at the other end, where runs came fairly freely off Peel and others.

Australia's team for the opening Test match, with five South Australians in the line-up – standing: Charles Bannerman (umpire), "Dinny" Reedman, Jack Blackham (captain), Charlie McLeod, Charlie Turner, Jack Lyons; seated: Harry Trott, Joe Darling, George Giffen, Ernie Jones, Frank Iredale, Syd Gregory, Harry Graham (twelfth man)

Giffen once found himself with Iredale at the bowler's end, but wicketkeeper Gay fumbled and Australia were reprieved. With the total 75, Giffen was dropped by the wretched Gay, who repeated the error a few minutes later, a pitiful performance by a man who had kept goal for England only months previously. Runs came in celebration and relief, with Giffen striking Briggs straight into the crowd for a five.

The ball seemed to be following Gay. A fast one flew off the bat's edge and was grassed. It seemed that the 'keeper had lost his nerve. It was a difficult chance, but Stoddart was starting to wonder where the next wicket was coming from. The century partnership came, and Albert Ward missed Giffen in the outfield. "Stoddy" decided to have a bowl himself. Two overs produced 18 runs. Seven bowlers were rotated in quick bursts during the afternoon, yet Australia moved strongly to 192 before the next wicket fell. Iredale was caught at mid-off by the England captain for a faultless 81.

After tea runs came faster. Syd Gregory, who had made only 100 runs against England in 10 completed innings, now clipped Peel for 14 off the six-ball over and with Giffen added 53 in only half-an-hour. The ball was speeding all over the Sydney ground like a crazy cat's cradle. Lockwood's shoulder having been ricked, most of the work fell upon Richardson and Peel as Giffen raced on well past his century and "Tich" Gregory executed one vengeful stroke after another. Gregory reached 50 and was dropped by Francis Ford at slip. With the 300 up, the sensational half-hour at the day's outset became a distant memory. Giffen rode high on 150.

In ten minutes the curtain would be dropped and the performers could rest for the night. Who knew then what feats they might perform

A keen crowd on the Hill at Sydney watch Australia's score mount, with young Syd Gregory well past his hundred. The home side seemed well on the way towards creating an unbeatable total

with strength renewed? Bill Brockwell was bowling, hoping to achieve something well worth including in his journalistic endeavours. And the drought broke. He had Giffen taken at slip by the lanky Ford for 161 (254 minutes, 22 fours and a five) his only Test century and the greatest innings of his life. Australia were 331 for five, with "Dinny" Reedman joining Syd Gregory, who was 85 by the close.

Stoddart had worries that evening, with Lockwood hurt and Richardson, though apparently tireless, not controlling the high bounce very well. Slow left-armers Peel and Briggs, such important weapons, had been very expensive while failing to take a wicket. And 'keeper Gay's confidence was in ribbons. It was as if he'd let in six goals against Scotland.

A new day, a Saturday, the SCG grass sparkling in the sunshine, and a record crowd of 24,120 eager to see what the national team could make of its cosy position. Stoddart led out his cricketers from the model pavilion.

Richardson bumped the ball to Reedman. Something interesting was bound to happen. The batsman cut towards Brockwell and was dropped.

S.E.Gregory, Australian hero

Soon Richardson struck Reedman on the skull. Within minutes the batsman was counter-attacking with a blow off Peel which lofted into the crowd, and everyone present was already thinking the journey worthwhile.

Syd Gregory was inching towards his century, but Reedman fell to Peel, and Charlie McLeod came in. Gregory, after crouching as passive witness to long periods of off theory, and seeing 99 beckoningly beside his name on the SCG scoreboard built by his father Ned, finally cut a ball and had his century. There was a tumultuous reception which lasted some time, and when it had calmed, the little chap contained himself and continued to score when chances arose.

The 400 came up, and McLeod had the base of his stumps battered by a screaming Richardson yorker. Turner, after one run in 15 minutes, was caught by the grateful Gay. Then Blackham, Australia's keeper-captain, revealed hopes of a massive total by playing studiously. There were some clean square-cuts by Gregory, and when the length was fuller he reached out and drove splendidly, or stole singles with his captain. The England fielding, Jack Brown apart, had become ragged. The match was running away from them. Leslie Gay's nightmare continued as he dropped Gregory at 131, and Blackham seemed to be run out, only to receive the umpire's blessing.

Richardson and Peel, in one of the longest spells in history, had bowled all day until lunch and for some time afterwards while 132 runs had been scored, and it was killing Richardson, whose pace gradually slackened until the batsmen were hitting him to leg hard and often.

Briggs and occasional bowler Ford took over, and in mid-afternoon Blackham snicked a ball to raise 500. The stand blistered on at two runs a minute until Australia's previous highest Test total – 551 at The Oval in 1884 – was passed.

Hearts stopped when Gregory, on 194, hoisted Ford high out to Albert Ward, who failed to hold the catch. From his next stroke Syd Gregory cut for three and secured his double-century, and the lace parasols, the handkerchiefs and the straw hats were waved and tossed in a frenzy of acclamation. The batsman's father, Ned, the SCG groundsman who had fought a drink problem and with whom Syd still lived in a cottage at the ground, lowered his head to hide the tears of joy which trickled at this glorious moment.

In the members' enclosure a collection was got up for the batsman, eventually reaching the massive sum of £106.10.0d, to which Tooheys brewery added £30. The collection was soon to be presented to the young batsman by the recently-elected State premier, the corpulent and often vulgar George H.Reid.

The applause apparently lasted five minutes. Then Stoddart, who had placed Peel on the long-off boundary, bowled to Gregory, who swung hard and this time was caught by Peel. His 201 had taken only 244 minutes, with 28 fours, the stand of 154 being a ninth-wicket record for well over a hundred years to come.

Ernie Jones, the new fast bowler, smote 11 runs off Stoddart, and only when Richardson at last whipped a six-inch breakback through Blackham were the Englishmen out of their misery. Bearded veteran Jack Blackham had made a gallant 74 in what was to prove his final Test match. His team were surely safe with 586 on the board.

In my boyhood in the 1950s, I often sat in the upper tiers of the Sheridan Stand at the SCG, watching heroes such as Ray Lindwall and Len Hutton and Neil Harvey, and sometimes gazing across at the towering M.A.Noble Stand, with the desiccated rainbow of white shirts and coloured dresses across the rows of seats. At the top of the edifice, along the steel girders, pigeons strutted or glided through the humid air. I used to thrill at the thought that these same cricket-loving birds must have watched, from their heavenly perches, the batting of Archie MacLaren and Clem Hill and Victor Trumper and this slightly mysterious A.E.Stoddart, whose acquaintance I had recently made in the records section of the match programme: whose Christian names I knew not, but whose total of Test match runs – poignantly four short of one thousand – filled my tidy young mind with sadness.

Some summers later it occurred to me that the Noble Stand had been built long after MacLaren had vacated this favourite ground of his, and his spectator pigeons had long since deserted the arena forever.

On Saturday afternoon, December 15, 1894, there may have been more seagulls than pigeons in the outfield as heavy clouds obscured the sun and diluted the colours all around, and MacLaren and Ward opened England's innings to the bowling of Turner and tearaway Ernie Jones. At 14, MacLaren played a poor shot off Turner and was caught at cover. Stoddart took guard, and while Ward scored steadily, he moved cautiously into position against both bowlers, showing that responsibility was weighing on him. There were signs of fatigue after the long period in the field. It had been noted that he placed himself where there was most work to be done.

After grafting 12 runs he offered a feeble response to Giffen, and Sammy Jones at slip held the catch.

Belligerent Jack Brown made little headway at first against Harry Trott's leg-spin, then suddenly cut a cracking four and drove another. Ward also cut strongly. Then a cardinal rule was broken: Ward called for a quick run after a misfield. Lyons recovered, and his throw ran Brown out. After so much promise England were 78 for three, and the allrounders were lining up.

Brockwell fought desperately in the fading light. The hundred came, extended to 130 by the end, Ward's 67 brim-full of courage.

Heavy rain fell that night and on the Sunday of rest, but after a shower on Monday it turned fine, and the pitch, although softened, was undamaged. Turner and Jones opened Australia's attack at noon. Ward had an early reprieve by McLeod, and soon the rain returned to hold up play. Soon after resumption Ward's vigil ended ironically with a catch on the boundary. Peel soon went, and with the weather cooling, the tall Francis Ford blazed away in his finest Lord's manner for 30 before skipping out to Giffen and missing. Brockwell fell at the same total for 49, giving Ernie Jones his first Test wicket, and England headed towards certain follow-on.

Then, during a stand of 41 by Briggs and Lockwood, wicketkeeper Jack Blackham's thumb was split by a ball from Lyons.

Briggs (57) fell to an ominous Giffen daisycutter, and with Gay managing 33, doing better with the bat than he had with the wicketkeeping gloves, England were all out for 325 as play drew quietly to a close. For the moment it was not altogether obvious just how crucial was each run. At this low ebb, Archie MacLaren apparently put the sizable wager of £4 on England at 50-1.

By the fourth day the pitch was still in good shape, but the outfield had thickened up and runs had to be earned the hard way. As the laws of the game then stood, the follow-on was compulsory if the deficit was at least 120 runs, leaving the fielding captain no choice but to lead his men out again. Here at Sydney in December 1894 it was to have amazing consequences.

Giffen, acting captain after Blackham's injury (McLeod and Reedman alternated as substitute wicketkeepers now), gave the aggressive Ernie Jones only a short burst against Ward and MacLaren before eagerly taking over himself. Turner continued to need careful watching with his variable break and changes of pace. Gradually the run-rate accelerated and the opening stand kindled some hope – until a slow ball from Giffen deceived MacLaren and clipped the middle stump. First loss to England for 44.

Stoddart made 10 extremely cautious runs before lunch, and afterwards the score ticked on, as often happens in a follow-on. Jones, naturally, dropped a few short, and both batsmen hooked boldly. Giffen was accurate and varied, but Stoddart hit him twice to the fence in one over, and Harry Trott was recalled. The hundred was posted. The captain was finding his feet, and all sorts of things suddenly seemed possible.

Then "Stoddy" took three nonchalant singles to reach 36 before lifting a ball from Turner towards cover, where Giffen caught it almost at grass level. This gave Turner Stoddart's prized wicket for the seventh time in Test matches. Jack Brown, the Yorkshire bulldog, came in.

The century stand which followed melted all the plastic preconceptions about the match. A stirring bombardment by Albert Ward and J.T.Brown took their side almost up to Australia's total. Further stiff resistance would now set the home side some sort of target after all. Giffen threw all his resources against them as the match slowly shifted axis. It was some way from inclining England's way yet, but the counter-challenge was on, turning this into an exceptional game of cricket. England ticked past 200, and Ward posted his truly outstanding century.

Giffen finally beat him on 117 as he played back, after nearly four hours at the crease, and Brockwell joined Brown, who drove Giffen to the fence to reach 50. Recalled by a later generation of oldtimers as they watched Patsy Hendren batting, Jack Brown, on 53, hit Giffen hard and high, but Jones hurtled across the outfield and brought off an astonishing catch. England were now perched indecisively on 245 with their four top men out.

Our advantage is that we may calmly examine every run and wicket wasted as destiny took its course. Peel, for instance, benefited from a critical miss by Jones five yards from the bat, and went on to be 9 not out at the close, when England were seven runs ahead with six wickets in hand. Brockwell, with so much depending on him, made 20 in the last drizzly overs.

The sky was still grey on Wednesday. But it was darker still in England, where no news had come through, and would not be coming through until the match was over. The cable delay meant that an unbelieving British public would receive the story of the last three days' play in one sensational report.

Jones did for Brockwell with a "bailer", and Peel was bowled off his foot by Giffen. So much for English hopes of a substantial lead: 296 for six, a mere 35 runs ahead.

Briggs held himself in check. No slashes just yet, no pillaging square-drives. Francis Ford ("Six foot two of don't care") had one escape, and in the cricketer's idiom of a nervous chuckle he hit a couple of fours. Briggs's caution dissolved as he slammed Giffen, then was dropped by Harry Graham, substitute fielding at square leg. The score at lunch was 344 for six.

The crowd swelled after the interval and saw some of the best from Stoddart's fellow Middlesex amateur Ford, who was hitting freely to all points of the driving compass, sharing a priceless and highly significant stand of 89 with Briggs.

Bill Lockwood also played a vital part, scoring well off the ubiquitous Giffen and gleefully snicking McLeod, who then forced Briggs to play on for 42. Eight gone for 398, and England's captain clapping every run.

Leslie Gay raised the 400 before becoming the only man to fall short of double figures. With one wicket remaining, England were 159 ahead.

Tom Richardson, heavy with flu, managed to flay 12 very useful (and what proved to be eerily significant) runs before Lockwood was bowled, leaving Australia to make 177 for victory on a good firm pitch. At 4 o'clock Jack Lyons and Harry Trott began the quest, and in only 15 minutes 25 runs were on the board to Lyons, with a single to Trott. Then Richardson hit Lyons's knee – the batsman had been distracted by three men placed square on the leg side – and the ball went on into the stumps. It was Richardson's last gasp for the day. He retired at 32 for one.

Giffen was circumspect, and with Trott "ridiculously cramped" Australia seemed to be looking towards the next day. Peel now rolled out a delivery of deceptive flight to Trott, who played at it off-line to give 'keeper Gay a catch which he actually held. Joe Darling then got off his "pair", but at 14 gave a one-handed chance to Stoddart which he failed to secure. Would this be decisive? As the clouds began to bank up, Darling started hitting in all directions.

Giffen made most of his runs from a back cut, but there was no mistaking the fact that he intended to be the anchor man. Darling raced to 44 by the close, but all that "Giff" had for his hour and three-quarters at the crease was 30 and a tender knee after a bang from Lockwood.

Australia, 113 for two wickets, needed only 64 more. It might have been a lot fewer had the Australians been a bit more positive. All the same, the Test seemed to be in the bag.

Bobby Peel: alcoholic hero

For the first time a match entered a sixth day, and the players awoke to intense sunlight. Giffen has recorded his delight at seeing the blue sky: yet only half the scene was visible. Millions of raindrops had fallen during the small hours. Somewhere the aboriginal rain-makers had exceeded the bounds of patriotic decency.

Jack Blackham had feared rain ever since the last evening, and now, his "coffee-pot" face becoming forever part of Australian folklore, he bemoaned his team's fate with Giffen as their carriage left furrows in the damp ground in front of the Baden Baden Hotel in Coogee.

For once, the Australians detested the sun's burning rays, feared their effect on the saturated cricket pitch. The job would be anything but easy now. If only another 30 or 40 runs had been banked last evening. For Stoddart's team, some of whom had "relaxed" the previous night believing the match to be as good as lost, the task still lay ahead. Left-arm spinners Peel and Briggs recognised well enough the favours awaiting them in the soggy, dark-stained pitch. Peel thought that somebody had watered it.

"Gi' me t'ball, Mr Stoddart," he is supposed to have said, "and I'll get t'boogers out before loonch." The extraction of five teeth just before the match no longer bothered him, and his captain had steadied him up after the indulgences of the previous night by ordering him under a cold shower.

Archie MacLaren was to recall that Peel and Lockwood had both arrived at the ground late, having overslept. With Blackham's gracious forbearance the Englishmen took the field late.

An 11 o'clock start might have given Australia a chance, but when the creamy-white figures did eventually spill out into the sunlight the stickiness in the pitch was obviously acute. Within twenty minutes it was cut through, churned up and as good – or as bad – as unplayable. What luck.

With only 1200 people present the ground was like "some silent cemetery" after the preceding five days of packed stands and much noise. Australia eight wickets in hand, 64 needed. Richardson, bumping the ball all over the place, opened the attack with slow leftie Peel.

A ball kept low and Giffen edged it for four. At the other end, knowing full well the urgency of his mission, Darling whacked Peel over the fence for a five. With the total 130 he tried to do it again, but Brockwell, fielding in front of the two-and-sixpenny seats, clung to perhaps the most important catch of his life. Darling's 53 was a courageous effort – in the manner of Neil Harvey's 92 not out against Tyson and company here at Sydney 60 years later. In both instances the left-hander's genius might have won the match with some decent support.

Jack Brown now missed Giffen quite badly. Was this the error that would see Australia home? Cabs and carriages were now being pulled at the gallop across Moore Park to the Cricket Ground as word spread across Sydney. Snub-nosed Briggs ceased licking his lips and took over at Richardson's end. In his first over Giffen slipped as he shaped to play, and was leg-before for 41.

Frank Iredale did all he could against the leaping, creeping ball, and Gregory, revitalised by his double-century, stroked masterfully despite the hazards. But Iredale (5) mis-hit Briggs, who held the high catch with deep relief. Reedman drove and Gregory snicked and cut. The score went up to 158 for five. Only 19 more runs and Australia would be home – on little Gregory's back.

Alas, he edged Peel, and Gay made no mistake this time. But MacLaren suffered anguish in dropping Reedman at second slip, the Lancastrian recalling years later that Jack Brown (a Yorkshireman, it might be noted) nodded his head and clicked his tongue "until both might have dropped off".

Without further damage Reedman, the South Australian, jumped desperately down the track to Peel, and was stumped. Eighteen to win, three wickets to fall. A.E.Stoddart, dual international captain, stayed calm, though his insides must have been churning.

"Observer" observed Blackham pacing up and down the little balcony in front of the Australian dressing-room, muttering "Cruel luck" over and over again; Giffen standing nearby, stunned, singlet and shirt in hands; Harry Graham, head in hands, a helpless twelfth man; Lyons sighing in vain now that his own lines had all been spoken.

Charlie Turner could bowl, Stoddart knew well enough; he could also bat, and a few well-timed blows could finish this match. The captain surveyed the field. Turner made two runs, then lifted a ball towards cover and Briggs secured the catch. Ernie Jones slogged Briggs into the outfield, and this time MacLaren held the catch. Nine down for 162, 15 wanted.

Jack Blackham, spade-bearded veteran of the original Ashes Test at The Oval in 1882, walked to the middle, damaged thumb throbbing, and took guard. A single to Charlie McLeod. Captain Blackham plays at the ball and winces from the sharp pain. Stoddart looks on anxiously. The bowlers, Peel then Briggs, saunter to the crease and dispatch the ball, not daring to pitch even as close as middle stump. Balls spit away into Gay's gloves. A single here and there. Blackham wishes so fervently that he could use both hands properly on the bat-handle. Peel in again. Blackham prods the ball back, fails to keep it down, and a half-sober Peel catches it. England have won!

They had won the match seemingly impossible to win. It ended two minutes before lunch, and the final margin was 10 ridiculous runs. Peel had 6 for 67 off 30 overs, Briggs 3 for 25 off 11. Neville Cardus, many years later, wrote that "the noise of rain in the night, surely it was heard by Stoddart, England's captain, when he was dying."

And the Australians of 1894 would have blushed to be told that well over a century later they were still the only team to have scored as many as 586 in the first innings of a Test match which was eventually lost. Nor, until the famous Botham/Willis Ashes Test match at Headingley, in 1981 – eighty-seven years later – was any Test match won by a side which

England's triumphant skipper: would the sound of that rain be with him for ever?

had followed on.

Drewy Stoddart, at the function which followed, graciously acknowledged Australia's foul fortune with the weather, but expressed the greatest pride in his "team of triers". They had fully justified his most sanguine expectations. "There'll be a good deal said about this match," he accurately predicted.

When England's amateur contingent entered the Hotel Australia dining-room that evening, 200 diners cheered them. And by a strange quirk of fate, in a nursery in the small Victorian township of Jeparit, Australia's greatest statesman, Robert Gordon Menzies, had selected this topsy-turvy sporting day upon which to make his entry into the world.

After Friday's well-earned rest, spent fishing in Sydney Harbour and cavorting in the water with a huge balloon, the touring team faced Eighteen Sydney Juniors, who rattled up 442. A youngster named M.A.Noble made a solid 152 not out, and a respectful 17-year-old called Victor Trumper scored a pretty 67. Ward and MacLaren made runs but Stoddart was caught off Noble for 13.

Christmas for the travelling cricketers meant warm, pleasant hours in the Botanical Gardens, by Sydney Harbour, followed by a traditional roast-beef dinner, with Humphreys, the lob bowler, who had recently received news of his brother's death back in England, wielding the carving knife. They did the Randwick races on Boxing Day, then found themselves in damp Melbourne for the second Test match. Among the England captain's mail intake, meanwhile, had been a lucky token from two Anglo-Indian girls who were hoping he would win the toss in the next Test.

Stoddart's hand left an impression in the soft MCG pitch, and when he pressed his foot down on a good bowling length moisture came up. All the while, according to one report, the Australians were inside choosing a leader. George Giffen finally emerged and said, "Where's Stoddy?" When he found him sitting quietly he said, "Let's look at that pitch, Stoddy, before we toss." They walked in silence to the middle, where Giffen got on his haunches and prodded and gazed at the battle strip while the Englishman stood nearby, hands behind back. The toss was made, and Giffen then went into a prolonged huddle with his seniors before issuing an irrefutable invitation to England to take first innings.

THE SECOND TEST MATCH, M.C.G.

*Second Ashes Test match, Melbourne, late December 1894: a sensational start,
and then Stoddart follows as England head for a disastrous first innings
amounting to a mere 75*

Giffen's tactic paid off, though perhaps rather too rapidly and
empathically, for England were bowled out in two hours for 75 and Australia
had to bat on a surface still a trifle unhealthy.

Bowlers dictated events right from the very first ball, delivered
swiftly by left-arm debutant Arthur Coningham in the only Test match he
was ever to play. It reared, and MacLaren popped it into Harry Trott's
hands at point.

In at number three, Stoddart was not comfortable against the sharply
kicking ball, and had to exercise great care against Coningham and Turner.
The latter struck him just above the elbow, drawing from the batsman an
involuntary exclamation which could be heard all over the MCG. Then
he opened up, as if pushing the enemy's high ladders off the battlements.
Lofting over the crowded infield, he took a couple of twos and a single,
while Albert Ward grafted. Then at 10 "Stoddy" attempted to pull a short

one from Turner and was bowled when it kept low: England 19 for two wickets.

Ward was now a Test cricketer of some stature. To him must go the highest credit for England's triumph in the first Test, and now, with runs no less highly-priced, he played sensibly, creating runs. Then Hugh Trumble came on, and at 44 England's central pillar was removed: Ward, on 30, cut, and Darling held the catch at short third. Francis Ford now found problems in the deliveries of fellow giant Trumble, but caned Turner to the cover railings. Bobby Peel made only six, and soon Ford cut and set off for a run, only to see Giffen leap across from slip and pluck the catch out of the air. England seven down for 60.

Briggs made five lucky runs, and Hylton Philipson, having taken over from the wretched Gay as England's wicketkeeper, hit out wildly. Tom Richardson, probably keen to get the pads off and the ball in his strong grasp, lashed yet another outfield catch, and they all trooped off soon after 3pm, England all out for an inglorious 75 in 115 minutes. Turner's 5 for 32 and Trumble's 3 for 15 had denied George Giffen the chance of a bowl, but the new Australian skipper was soon facing a hostile Richardson when his star hitter Lyons was bowled for two.

Billy Bruce swung at Peel and was taken at slip, and Gregory was also taken behind the bat off another Richardson thunderbolt. At 15 for three, Darling and Giffen strove to keep out of trouble by letting Richardson's bouncers fly past. Twice Darling unfurled that collector's piece the left-hander's cover-drive off an express delivery before managing to hit a fast half-volley from Lockwood over the fence for five. But a near-shooter snapped back wickedly and bowled him after a 38-run partnership (32 from Darling's bat) which was the highest stand of the day.

With Iredale in, England's puny 75 was passed, but Richardson came back and bowled him with a beauty. And at 96, Giffen (32) fell at last to a smart catch by 'keeper Philipson. Trott and Coningham saw the hundred up, but life was fleeting on this pitch and another snap catch behind the stumps accounted for the fast bowler, and Trott was run out in some confusion with Affie Jarvis.

So, as the crowd wended their way out into the world again, Australia, at 123, had a 48-run advantage on first innings. No-one could complain of not getting value for his admission fee, for both sides had displayed a complete innings in the time available. It looked as if an abbreviated Test match was in the offing.

It might have been on this Sunday rest day that "Stoddy" laughed "until the rafters rang" while listening, in a companionable group which included journalist Tom Horan ("Felix"), to the recitations and jokes and mock election speeches of William O'Hanlon, a sometime Victorian wicketkeeper who happened to have been born a day before the England skipper.

As for the lively Horan, he was so impressed by the personalities of the English touring cricketers that he wrote: "I wish they could stay with us for ever. They are the most popular team that ever came to Australia, and as for their captain, why the reception he gets whenever he comes out to bat makes me feel proud of my countrymen."

The final day of 1894, a Monday, was sunny and bright, with a cool breeze holding the temperature at a tolerable level. The pitch soon showed itself to have settled down into a batsman's strip as MacLaren and Ward began England's second innings. MacLaren played Coningham away to exorcise the spectre of a "pair", and both batsmen scored freely off him. But soon Turner knocked MacLaren's off stump out of the ground.

Stoddart started with a three, cut off Turner, and a four off Giffen. Then all was reticence as he and Ward set about investing for the future. Stoddart took a single to wipe off the arrears, and then lofted Turner grandly over the fence onto the asphalt. This seemed to encourage both batsmen, and the total reached 78 by lunch, Stoddart 35, Ward 28. "The Englishmen mean business today," one onlooker was heard to remark to his neighbour.

"Stoddy" enlivened the day with four to leg off Turner. Ward edged Trumble's faster one for three, but with the 100 up he was bowled

Stoddart warms up for one of the innings of his life: the 173 at Melbourne, highest by an England captain

off his pads by Turner for 41, and Jack Brown came in and made a shaky start.

Women made up a fair proportion of the crowd at Melbourne to watch the absorbing Test match

Stoddart was thrilling spectators and team-mates alike with his free stroking. At last he was applying his intrinsic skills to the supreme occasion. At last he dominated, and not for just several overs nor for a sunlit half-hour. At last, against the full battery of Australia's Test side – Giffen, Trumble, Trott, Coningham and Turner, especially Turner – he had the satisfaction of playing a prolonged hand when his side most needed it.

Looking back to this Test match through many years, Archie MacLaren wrote one of the richest tributes to Andrew Ernest Stoddart: "It was one of those days when he convinced you from the commencement of his innings that nothing could get past his bat, that there was no ball that could not be hit to the exact spot he selected. He stood out supremely great so often, and I experienced some of my greatest treats when his partner. A courteous gentleman, his delight over the success of any member of his side was beautiful to behold. His kindness to me was such that I always felt I could never do enough to make myself worthy of his affection."

"Stoddy" elicited much affection this day. He had the greater share of a partnership of 90 with Jack Brown, and stood 93 not out as Billy Brockwell struck his first ball to the boundary. Turner returned to the attack.

Some years afterwards Drewy Stoddart stated that this innings was "*the* century of my career. As I felt that I had contributed a small share to England's victory, nothing I have ever done in cricket gives me the same lasting pleasure to look back on as that innings."

He continued on his stylish way until the day's end, when he had reached 151. Peel had succeeded Brockwell and played perfectly to orders. The loose ball was punished but risks were shunned as England ground towards a winning total. It was even said that Stoddart's style was unrecognisable in that subdued final session. His cheerful comment: "I had to buck up for England, home and beauty."

Harry Trott bowls leg-spin to Stoddart, second Test

He was given a full-throated ovation as he returned to the MCG pavilion that evening, and George Giffen, as he clapped, knew that his opposite number had gathered the game well into his own territory with a lead of 239 for the loss of only four men. The Australians had bowled well and fielded almost faultlessly, but an early breakthrough in the morning was their only real hope.

But on New Year's Day 1895, with a much larger crowd raising dust all along the approaches to the MCG, England consolidated. In three-quarters of an hour Stoddart added only 13 to his overnight score. Bobby Peel had seldom been so restrained either. It was rather a shock when

Stoddart hit Giffen to square leg for four and next over drove another boundary.

It was to be the last jewel in this monumental innings. At 173 he chopped down at a faster ball from Giffen and played on. He had been determined, vigilant, even at times cramped, through an innings lasting five hours and 20 minutes. He had stroked three fives and 14 fours, and had become a record-holder yet again, this time for England's highest score in a Test innings, passing W.G.Grace's 170 against Australia at The Oval eight years previously. It was also to remain, for eighty years, the highest score made by an England captain in a Test match in Australia, until Mike Denness, against a depleted Australian attack, scored 188, at a greatly enlarged Melbourne ground.

As "Stoddy" left the field the crowd rose to him and the gloved ladies clapped their English hero. When Tom Horan congratulated him he was surprised to find him looking as cool and fresh enough to start another marathon innings. His effort was thought slow by some because they were used to faster runs from the Stoddart bat. But he had worn down the opposition. This was a Test match, and he had a heavy responsibility.

In 1970 a letter to Neville Cardus enquiring whether he had ever seen Stoddart bat brought a reply in the negative. But he went on to write that "MacLaren never tired of praising the brilliance of Stoddart's 173 v Australia".

F.G.J.Ford was just the man to step in to replace him now, with England 320 for five. Giffen deceived him at 24, and with Briggs in, Peel batting with uncharacteristic patience and sobriety (not having overdone the New Year celebrations), began to put some meat into his shots. He fell to Jarvis, stumped, his taxing performance of 53 containing 37 singles and not a single boundary hit in 168 minutes. This was real Test match cricket.

Australia's fielding now cracked, and they lost Turner, who had ricked his back. Off Briggs and Lockwood, first Iredale then Gregory fluffed catches. Tireless Giffen supplied the remedy: a full toss eluded Briggs's cross-bat and found him lbw: 402 for eight and the end surely in sight.

But now Lockwood and Philipson put together 53 valuable runs before Lockwood and Richardson added 20 more. With England finally reaching 475, Giffen's men needed a highly daunting 428 to win.

The huge difference (400 runs precisely) between England's first innings (75) and second was to remain a Test record for 110 years, until their 139 and 570 for seven declared (difference 431) at Durban in December 2004. In Test matches not involving England, Pakistan's bizarre 106 and 657 for 8 against West Indies at Bridgetown in 1957-58, over sixty years after this astonishing Ashes match in Sydney, had inflated this particular world Test record further.

Australia's captain had taken six wickets in 470 balls; but now, the marathon over, Giffen had to reorientate his thoughts. He decided to send in Billy Bruce and Harry Trott for a final session that could ruin everything or set up a foundation upon which to build tomorrow.

Australia romped to 86 that evening, and Bruce reached 50 off Peel's opening over next day. It was looking good for the home team, but a miscalculation against Peel stopped them short: Bruce went to drive, hit the ground with his bat, and Stoddart at mid-off took the catch off the mis-hit. Australia 98 for one.

Giffen joined Trott, and the hitting policy was maintained. By lunch the board showed 149, and with care on this first-class surface there was no reason Australia should not be able to grind their way to victory. Soon it was 190, almost halfway there, lots of batting to follow.

Stoddart called up Billy Brockwell, his erratic but often useful change bowler. He held one back and Giffen cocked up an easy catch to Jack Brown at point. Two overs later, Harry Trott, five short of a century, drove Brockwell like lightning. The bowler stooped swiftly to pick up a wonderful catch near his boots. Now Joe Darling was in, and before long Brockwell produced a suitable delivery for him, pitching leg stump and taking off. Surrey's Brockwell, to the delight of all his team-mates, had come from nowhere to crack Australia's foundations with three top wickets for eight runs. England were now back in control.

When Gregory played on to Richardson it became 216 for five. Lyons and Iredale stopped the rot momentarily, but at 241 Lyons clipped Peel into his stumps. Jarvis, Coningham and Trumble were all disposed of quickly (Trumble to a close run-out that would have warranted a video replay a century later) and Turner came in as last man, with Iredale 30 not out. The first ball all but bowled Turner, but he calmly kept the bowling at bay, and as the minutes ticked by and Stoddart rang the changes, England's frustration mounted. At one point Lockwood hurled the ball at Turner's wicket as he stood out of his ground and hit his bat. Jim Phillips rejected the appeal for obstruction, having already called "Over", but Turner was indignant and there was agitation in the crowd.

"Noss" Iredale cut charmingly, and Turner hit straight with confidence, and 61 runs were added by this pair of non-conformists. The entire cast had to report back next day, the fifth, to see the tenth and final wicket fall.

Next morning, Stoddart spoke to Peel "with the little touch of humour which would put Bobby into the frame of mind". Bobby then bowled Iredale with a straight good-length ball which kept a shade low, and England had won their Test match at last by 94 runs to go two-up with three to play.

Stoddart, the *Pall Mall Gazette* commented, had gained honours "not so much international as immortal".

The teams gathered in the Melbourne pavilion and handsome Billy Brockwell (who was to die in poverty, in a hay-shed, forty years later) was presented with the ball with which he had tilted England's fortunes, dispatching Trott, Giffen and Darling. Both captains made speeches, then thoughts turned to the upcoming third contest.

As for "Stoddy's" hero status, this was underlined by his depiction, along with several others, on the first-ever cigarette-card issue in Australia. Those little Tally Ho! cards, hardly ever sighted in the auction rooms today, are worth at least $A1000 apiece.

Having featured in the earliest cigarette card issue, in Australia, A.E.Stoddart was among the leading cricketers to feature in the 1896 set issued in Britain by Wills

CHAPTER 14

Australia on Top

AT Ballarat, Victoria's "Golden City", where Walter Humphreys, short sleeves flapping, lobbed his way to 10 for 51, they strolled through the glorious botanical gardens; they went horse-riding (Leslie Gay's mount ran off with him and tossed him to the ground); they descended into the Last Chance mine at midnight; then they moved on to Adelaide to face a much-changed Australian Test team. Perhaps by way of reconnaissance or mere curiosity, some of the Englishmen watched the later stages of the Sheffield Shield matches. As if they hadn't seen enough of him, Giffen took 16 for 186 in the match. Afterwards the visiting players had a net session.

Australia omitted Charlie Turner in view of Adelaide's faster surface. Nowhere is there a record of Stoddart's reaction, but it must surely have been of relief. Jack Lyons, with flu, was also an absentee, and Hugh Trumble was overlooked. Ambidextrous Jack Harry was selected, as was Syd Callaway and young Jack Worrall. But the most interesting newcomer was the brother whose claims Harry Trott had been promoting. Young Albert was strong and slightly wild, and he had his own method of practice. WG had his apple orchard, Grimmett his faithful dog, but Albert Trott spun the ball at some pace past a large wooden box which represented the obdurate George Giffen. And now "Albatrott" was in Adelaide to show what he could do for his country.

The enclosures were already filled as Giffen, the local idol, searched for "Stoddy" and found him out the back in the shade of a tree. Giffen flipped the coin (borrowed from Tom Richardson, who never got it back). It was a good day for Australia to win the toss: over 100 degrees Fahrenheit (38 Celsius) in the shade and 155 out of it: Stoddart wrote "108 in shade 166 in sun" in his scrapbook. The original pitch had been thought too near one side of the ground, and the revised strip may not have enjoyed sufficient preparation, although Bill Lockwood glided across it, saying it was "good enough for skating". Stoddart led his men out at 12.15pm and after five electrifying minutes Australia had 22 on the board. After this bludgeoning by Harry Trott and Billy Bruce, who wore the colours of the local authority, yellow and black (the Australian green and gold was still a few years off) all sorts of things seemed possible.

But it couldn't go on. Bruce, having been dropped on the leg boundary by MacLaren, played on to Richardson with the total 31, and in walked Giffen. Fifty appeared in only 35 minutes, and the Englishmen squinted at the fierce sun and hated its fury. After an lbw shout against Trott, Giffen called for a run. Trott, bemused by the appeal, set off late and sacrificed his wicket. His quickfire 48 could have been an inspiration to the younger brother waiting in the wings.

Stoddart brought on Brockwell, but he did not work the same trick as at Melbourne, and Australia lunched at 80 for two.

Richardson, whose sweat, he remarked, might well turn this dry pitch into a sticky, bowled Iredale second ball after the break, but Peel had to leave the field with a sprained ankle, and England's stocks slumped. Briggs bobbed in and conceded a series of singles, and excitement rose as Joe Darling showed his liking for the pull. The compact little left-hander sent the ball swirling up over the 'keeper; Philipson, recently engaged to an heiress, or so a gossip column had suggested, positioned himself and held it.

Now Syd Gregory and Jack Harry quickly fell, and at 124 for six perspiring Tom Richardson had earned four wickets as well as his captain's undying admiration.

Jack Worrall was jittery. He hit hard to Richardson at cover and streaked up the pitch, but the ball was back in Philipson's gloves even before Worrall was halfway.

Giffen raised 150 with a "quarter off drive". By now the intense heat had driven an exhausted Richardson from the field, and it was left to Bill Lockwood to chip in with a wicket, a fine caught-and-bowled off Jarvis. They took tea.

The dehydrated Englishmen, temporarily restored, set about winding up the innings. Waiting to bat was the raw recruit Albert Trott, whose teeth were chattering from nervousness. He told former premier Sir John Downer that he was "scared stiff". "Don't be so silly," said Downer, "they'll never get you out!" How close to the truth he was.

Brockwell took a valuable wicket: Giffen (58) after eight partners in almost three hours: 157 for nine. Australia's captain put a cold towel to his head and put his hot feet up, saying he had never felt so fatigued. Only Callaway and young Trott now stood between England and the cool comfort of the pavilion.

The young Australians resisted then repelled the experienced attack. Callaway cut 16 off two overs from Lockwood, and Trott picked him off his toes in the grand manner, lobbing the ball into a buggy in the driveway.

The total passed 200, and Trott miscued on the leg side, sending the ball spiralling into the blue. Richardson, back in the fray, lumbered across but just failed to reach it. Under the expanse of cloudless sky the Surrey giant now bowled again, and young Trott drove him far into the outfield, with the fieldsmen transfixed. The batsmen scampered five hoarsely-applauded runs.

Finally, Richardson, aching all over, bowled Callaway after an extraordinary last-wicket stand of 81 in 70 minutes that had hauled Australia up to 238. MacLaren and Briggs (his former coach) gathered five token runs in the final ten minutes.

There were hours of sleeplessness ahead for all of them, a night of overwhelming heat, damp sheets, throbbing heads, hopeless tossing and turning. Some of the Englishmen desperately but ill-advisedly took showers through the night. "Stoddy" was seen walking down the hotel corridor after taking shower-bath number four. All the unwitting indiscretions took toll next day as England's batting was dismembered with a certain deadliness.

Stoddart had the iron roller pulled only once up and down the pitch for fear of crumbling it, and with hopes of making 350 despite spectator Jack Blackham's sombre forecast of 200, England entered the hot cauldron and faced up to Albert Trott and Syd Callaway, both medium-fast, breaking sharply. The highest attendance of the match, 12,000 spectators, rolled up on this second day,.

Briggs soon cut Trott away for two boundaries, and Giffen readily took it as a signal to bowl himself. Callaway sent down six maidens in a row, in the third of which he bowled Briggs. Brockwell hit out at Giffen, but against Callaway there was no breathing space, and in his seventh over Brockwell tried to lift a ball clear and Jack Harry made a leaping catch. Soon MacLaren was given not out after seemingly touching Callaway to Jarvis. Then he swept Callaway to break a remarkable bowling sequence. In one hour Callaway had two for three off 12 six-ball overs.

Albert Ward, carrying so many of England's hopes, was tempted by Giffen and swept uppishly, and England were now 49 for three. "Here's that dear Mr Stoddart," a woman was heard to trill as he entered the field, having held himself back to number five. He now took a single off Callaway, and played five off-cutters from Giffen before – to shrieks from the crowd – falling to a fast, straight ball. White umbrellas danced about "like demon toadstools". There were many shouts of "Bravo, George!", and the same woman was heard to murmur "What a shame."

Bristling with confidence, Archie MacLaren sought to defeat the swarming off-side field by hitting Callaway to leg, but the ball barely rose, crashed into the stumps, and half the side were out for 56.

After lunch, Peel was bowled for 0, giving Callaway 4 for 14. A determined stand by Brown and Ford saw the hundred up, always a relief in such ominous situations; but at 111 Giffen lured Ford into getting under an off-drive. Then Lockwood lashed out and Worrall turned, ran and caught him. Eight down for 111.

Stoddart honourably rejected the suggestion that England should let the compulsory follow-on materialise in these stifling conditions. His men were instructed to strive for every run. The tail did curl up, but without any connivance. Worrall held his third catch when Richardson swiped, and defiant Jack Brown was left 39 not out, made in some style. Curiously, eight of England's wickets had fallen to the sixth and final ball of an over.

The follow-on had been averted by six runs.

With "Stoddy's" audible rallying cry of "Come on, boys", Australia went to the crease again to build on their sizable lead of 114, and Harry Trott, scoreless, touched a yorker from Peel into his stumps. Giffen and Bruce carried the score to 44, when Ford clasped a hard cut by Australia's captain. Bruce thrashed Brockwell for 13 in an over and took four, four and three off Lockwood. When Iredale struck two more successive fours it was suggested that Stoddart might have served as a statue of Melancholy.

Briggs came on as the partnership approached a hectic hundred, and Bruce, fairly worn out, hit the first alluring delivery straight into square leg's hands. It was 5.50pm and in that mood a night's rest for Billy Bruce might have set the stage for one of history's great innings. As it was, the Melbourne solicitor's slashing 80 had delighted his skipper, who feared a change in the weather.

Joe Darling failed to bridge those last minutes. Bill Lockwood, after

Albert Edwin Trott: new Aussie force

taking so much punishment, beat him. The Englishmen trooped off gratefully in the evening heat. After the Sunday rest day, a half-holiday had been granted next day, so intense was local interest in the Test match. And those of the population who went to Adelaide Oval were to savour the day. Under an overcast sky, Syd Gregory sent the ball scudding away through the cover field. Iredale went soberly to 40 before the first discordant note was sounded: Peel dropped a hard return. Soon Iredale snicked Richardson through Philipson's hands, and then split one of the accident-prone Lockwood's fingers with a cover-shot. Albert Trott, of all people, came out as a substitute for England.

Syd Gregory suffered a not uncommon fate when a ball rebounded from his foot into the stumps, and Australia at 197 for five were already ahead by 311.

Richardson bowled Jack Harry out of Test cricket, and as Stoddart swung his bowling around, Briggs accounted for Worrall. Affie Jarvis hit well, seeing Iredale to his century and eventually holing out just before lunch.

Albert Trott and Frank Iredale completed England's demoralisation afterwards. They took runs freely, and it was only a tired shot by Iredale when 140 that ended it all. A looping full-toss from Peel finished up back in the bowler's grateful palms, and neither batsman nor bowler could keep a serious face. A rumour was soon circulating that Iredale was being lured over to England to play for Surrey on a five-year contract, a mind-boggling proposal in the 1890s. Nothing came of it.

It was 347, with one to fall. And it was to be the heroism and the agony of the first innings all over again. Callaway and Trott hammered 64 runs against a weary and aching England attack. Brockwell, for one, probably yearned for a quiet corner with pen and paper where he could chronicle the day's events, reaching for a cool drink between paragraphs. Trott (an undefeated 72) did most of the damage ("Who'd have thought the kid could do it?" marvelled big brother Harry). The valiant Richardson at last got one through Callaway, the Surrey man's eighth wicket of the match.

Australia out at last for 411. For England, victory was a mountainous 526 runs away.

MacLaren and Ward set about keeping Australia in the field for an age, but the thought was a vain one, even if given weight by an encouraging start. MacLaren made a typically majestic 35 out of 52 before being caught in the longfield. Albert Edwin Trott had his first wicket, and with appetite whetted he instantly took another, and decisively at that. Ward's stump was broken from top to butt by a murderous delivery.

Philipson, nightwatchman, was bowled by Giffen, and three wickets had fallen for one run. Stoddart and Brown were watchful as the minutes grimly crept by. Trott bowled again and hurt Brown, and since the close of play was drawing near, Giffen mercifully led his men from the field, with England 56 for three.

The surface of the pitch was broken here and there but was still playing true on the whole, and the fourth day was fine as Albert Trott and George Giffen took up the attack as men might sit themselves at a lavish dinner with all evening ahead of them. The batsmen were ill at ease from the start, and before long Trott, getting the ball to kick very sharply from the off, found the stumps off Brown's pads.

Brockwell was steady, and with Stoddart looking confident there were fleeting visions of a revival. But Brockwell could not contain himself and let fly at Trott. The new boy had tasted success and no hit, however well struck, was going to escape his grasp. Peel, first ball, suffered the same fate, registering a "pair".

Stoddart tried to launch an assault on Albert Trott, but after Giffen missed him at slip off the young maestro, he was forced to go back to watchful, crouching batsmanship. After smacking Giffen into the members' pavilion, Francis Ford tipped an impossible ball into point's hands and the Trott brothers had gained a wicket for Australia family-style. Briggs went third ball, bowled by Trott, while Stoddart continued to stand firm, feeling each rapid dismissal like the lash of a whip. Lockwood tried to go after Trott, but in this match of extraordinary catches Iredale held it deep on the drive, and after a dozen aimless runs belted by the trojan Richardson the innings was laid to rest for 143 as the Surrey man edged Giffen to young Trott. "Stoddy" was stranded on 34 not out, made in 100 minutes of almost faultless technique.

But the most amazing figures, together with some clever verse, were:

A.E.Trott 27overs, 10 maidens, 43 runs, 8 wickets.

He and his captain were carried shoulder-high from Adelaide Oval.

> You didn't expect it, my sonny?
> Yet, truly, complain you must not;
> For you wanted "a run" for your money,
> And, complying, I gave you "A.Trott".

(The Kangaroo to Mr Stoddart — by "Lika Joko" Harry Furniss)

Melbourne Punch.]
THE APOTHEOSIS OF TROTT: AUSTRALIA BOWS DOWN BEFORE ITS IDEAL.

The youngster was given a great ovation for his performance, unbeaten 38 and 72 followed by those eight wickets. Boys competed to get near him and pat his back. Cash and gifts were heaped upon him, and one of the England players bet him a new hat that he'd be in the next Australian side to tour England. It defies credulity, but the Englishman did not win that hat. After his omission in 1896, and possibly with the encouragement and influence of Stoddart and Jim Phillips, the Anglo-Australian umpire and county cricketer, Albert Trott went in his disappointment to work for MCC and join Middlesex, and later to be buried in a forlorn grave in Willesden, West London, simply marked P613. An elegant headstone was later erected by Middlesex CCC. Less than a week before the outbreak of the Great War, depressed by dropsy, "Alberto" shot himself through the head with a Browning pistol. His will, written on the back of a laundry bill, bequeathed his wardrobe to his landlady. There were a few cricket team photographs, and the Coroner's office noted £4 in cash.

The Australian press at its most provocative: drink is allegedly the underlying cause of England's defeat at Adelaide (caption by Stoddart, in his scrapbook)

In 1895, all this was too far in the future for anyone to have had even the faintest possibility of predicting. The same went for England's elegant captain, who now made a post-match comment or two: "We have been beaten by a side which played vastly better cricket, and whether batting, bowling or fielding they deserved to win. I can't help congratulating our young friend Trott, and I rather credit myself for having, on the first occasion I saw him play, said he would be one of the finest cricketers Australia has ever seen . . . . I hope Mr Trott will visit England – at least I hope he will not! – but if he does come we are always pleased to welcome cricketers such as he." A few years hence they would be playing in matches for Middlesex alongside each other.

The Englishmen visited Broken Hill, where miners chipped away at the huge silver-ore faces that were so commercially important to the future of the young country that had yet to be unified. One of the cricketers spotted a chunk of worthless galena ("new chum silver") and, thinking it to be the real thing, excitedly asked "Stoddy" if he might keep it. He was drily told that he could take a pocketful if he wished.

In the match, Stoddart treated the locals to an innings of 55, and again the old deceiver Humphreys lobbed his way to a host of wickets (13 for 43 in the match). Billy Brockwell took 7 for 35 and 7 for 7, enough perhaps to have the area renamed Brockwell Hill. And wicketkeeper Philipson amazed everyone with the huge spin he imparted on the ball.

There was good shooting to be had at May Bell station. The kill included wallabies, lizards, rabbits and hawks, plus a cat shot in error by Bobby Peel, who may well have been the player alleged by one journal to have come close to being sent home by the captain for breaching the good-behaviour clause in his contract.

A special train took them into the Dandenong hills, where Stoddart was at his best with 81, the local Eighteen proudly going on to achieve a first-innings lead. Then on the first day of February they returned to the serious stuff in Sydney, where rain threatened to continue as the fourth Test match began.

To Stoddart fell the choice of innings, a decision he delayed making for a while, to the annoyance of some of the 8000-odd onlookers. The pitch would clearly favour bowlers, so much rain having fallen. Even the groundsman, Ned Gregory, described it as one of the worst he had ever seen. "Stoddy" took Peel and Briggs to the middle, perhaps to feel again the exhilaration of that fairy-tale victory here six weeks ago before asking them if bowling first would be a wise course. After further deliberation he put Australia in to bat. As reported by Brockwell, he simply told Giffen: "You will have to go in."

A.E.Stoddart thus became not only the first Test captain to declare an innings closed (Lord's 1893) but was now the first England captain ever to put in the opposition. Although it was an era in which to win the toss was to feel obliged to bat first, Australia's skippers had inserted the opposition several times previously.

England's skipper prepares to toss in the crucial fourth Test, at Sydney

Little Harry Graham, Australia's hero at Lord's in 1893, was in for his first home Test match, with much expected of him. Charlie Turner also returned to the side for what was to be his final Test – a contest that could hardly have been much shorter. Harry Trott strolled out with Billy Bruce to find out if the pitch was as bad as it looked. Peel's first ball cut a chunk out of the damp pitch, causing Trott's jaw to drop. The batsmen took a single each before Trott was caught off Peel. Richardson at the other end began to make the ball lift alarmingly, sometimes breaking twelve inches or more from the off, and, when not hooking furiously, Bruce took evasive action. Peel got him when he lifted a ball to Brockwell at deep square leg. Harry Moses came in probably ahead of schedule, and in twenty critical minutes six tortured runs crystallised, before Peel beat Giffen with an unexpected straight one, and Australia were 26 for three.

Moses was bowled for 0: 26 for four as Harry Graham took up his

The tense moments before a Test match starts. In front of the Sydney pavilion stands captain Stoddart, MacLaren facing the camera, and Richardson and Lockwood to the right of the group

Harry Graham - history-maker

position. Tom Richardson thundered in and hurled them down, rearing awkwardly to shoulder height and creating terrible problems for Syd Gregory. Graham immediately flung back the challenge with two leaping hits to the boundary then dropping to his knees when the deadly bumper roared towards him.

The sun was beaming now, slowly firming the pitch into a better batting strip as England seemed to be through the Australian batting, Gregory having been stumped by Philipson off Briggs, who then caught Iredale first ball to take him to 98 Test wickets, had he but known it. At 51 for six, whatever happened thereafter

Stoddart's sending in of Australia had paid off.

Joe Darling came in, held back to number eight. The situation was pretty dire, but the clear-eyed young man from Adelaide got straight into it: runs off Peel, then a blow over the heads of the Friday crowd and into the tennis court where the M.A.Noble stand would be built some years later. Graham became infected: flowing drives, pull shots to quicken everyone's pulse.

Stoddart brought back Richardson and swung Briggs to the pavilion end. Graham edged the ball at a nice height straight to Brockwell, who turfed it. Now Darling had to accelerate as MacLaren's return was beating him home. But Philipson fumbled at the stumps. Graham had another let-off as a steepling catch was misjudged by Briggs, running back after delivery, and receiving the forthright views of Peel, who might have taken it with ease. A tactful word from Stoddart sent Briggs back to his bowling mark, but with runs coming fast there was a creeping air of desperation about England.

Darling hoisted a ball out to long-on into MacLaren's hands – and out again. This might have been the catch that was accompanied by a barracker's cry of "Drop it, Archie, and you can kiss my sister!" MacLaren later apparently quipped that since he hadn't seen the sister he might as well have held the catch.

Tom Richardson's next ball was a horrifying loose one straight at Darling's face. It was not deliberate. The mighty Surrey man never had any nastiness about him. Darling diverted the ball into his stumps, and the exciting 40-minute stand of 68 had more than doubled the score: 119 for seven.

Australia's new pin-up boy now entered. Melbourne's *Argus* newspaper had smilingly visualised canonisation for him: "Saint Albert would look well in a coloured window." This next innings was certainly again full of vivid colour. First Richardson hit young Trott sickeningly, leaving several England fielders to work for some time to bring him round. Then he and Graham played some brilliant cricket, punishing all the bowlers on a greatly improved track.

At 192 Brockwell erred again: he might have caught Graham off his own bowling. At tea Graham was 87 and "Albatrott" had raced to 40. After the break it took Graham only a few hits to raise his hundred. The "Little Dasher", who was to die a lonely death in a Dunedin asylum sixteen years later, still stands alone as the man who made a century in his first Test innings in Ashes Test matches in both England and Australia. (Greg Blewett came close in the 1990s with second-innings hundreds.)

England captain Stoddart has a stroll around the Sydney Cricket Ground outfield

Johnny Briggs:
first to 100 Test wickets

On 105, the elated Harry Graham jumped out at Briggs once too often and Philipson removed the bails. His timely innings had Australia tolerably placed at 231 for eight, and attracted gifts galore from an adoring public: three hats, four pipes, a box of cigars, a new bat, and three suits. All the while Jack Blackham in the pavilion was remarking on how hard he had had to try to get Graham into the Australian XI.

Now Affie Jarvis edged Briggs to Philipson, giving the Lancashire spinner his 100th Test wicket, a unique achievement at that moment. Turner (22) assisted Albert Trott in a fourth consecutive abnormal last-wicket stand for Australia: 45 priceless runs. Eventually Trott was left undefeated on 85, giving him 195 Test match runs without dismissal against this star-studded

England line-up. Had he but known it, this was the zenith.

England's fielding had been "shocking", Stoddart, now at slip, alone having kept up the standard. Now his side had to survive ten anxious minutes, and almost immediately MacLaren was stumped off Harry Trott. Soon the field had emptied as rain began to fall again.

The boisterous weather continued, and there was every expectation of seeing England caught on a sticky. But another noisy deluge further damaged the pitch, and Saturday's play was abandoned at half-past-two. The 4000 frustrated spectators were given free passes for the Monday.

The Sydney Cricket Ground staff and their faithful horse do what they can to keep conditions playable

On a sunny Sunday evening "Stoddy" took a carriage out to the Australian camp near Coogee beach, and after the pleasant fraternisation, he saw rain splattering the pavements. It fell all night. Then, as if manipulated by some fiendish playwright, a hot sun came out on Monday morning, turning the unprotected pitch into an evil, gluey bowler's delight. The huge and expectant crowd of almost 16,000 was building up rapidly as Ward and Briggs of the red rose county made their way to the middle.

Lockwood would not be batting. His hand wound from a shattered soda-water bottle was still much too tender, and he sat in the SCG pavilion with his arm in a sling. England therefore had 17 wickets in hand. And they lost them all in three hours on this second day of play, in keeping with their skipper's anguished expectation. The art of batting was reduced to a lottery.

Harry Trott bowled his leg-spin faster than usual. Turner predictably looked menacing, although anything slightly short flew over the bat and into Jarvis's gauntlets. At 20 Ward made the first fatal error against Turner; then Briggs played around a ball from Trott. England stood alarmingly at 24 for three.

Stoddart was watchful, trying desperately hard to counter the drunken antics of the ball as it bounded at all angles, marking his shirt-front more than his bat. Among his recent correspondence had been an affectionate note from Gwen Thomas, who lived at 20 Bayswater Road: "Dear Mr Stoddart," she wrote, "I am a little English girl, and I want you very much to win this test match . . . I am only eight years old, and I sit in the big stand near the Governor's box . . . I hope you will make your usual big score." He surely glanced in that direction, and possibly waved.

Harry Trott bowled one short and Stoddart jumped out at it. The ball spun sharply from leg and Jarvis fetched it and stumped England's skipper for seven as his bat swung frantically through.

The post mortem: the players gather around the treacherous Sydney battlefield, which had suffered so much rain damage

"It's the worst wicket I've ever seen," he told his men, "absolutely the worst. And not only is it the worst I've seen, but it's miles the worst!" He seemed to have made his point. He felt England would not survive the day.

There was no answer. Poor Brockwell again succumbed to a miraculous fingertip catch by Darling, Ford, Giffen's "bunny", became the sixth casualty at 43. Brown, jaw set, gloomily surveyed the destruction. Peel aimed an almighty blow at Turner and gave Jarvis a third stumping. By lunch England were 59 for seven.

Giffen was cutting the ball back prodigiously, sometimes beating his 'keeper as well as the helpless Englishman with the bat. Philipson was caught close in by Graham, and last man Richardson trouped to the muddy middle. He made two runs before being mortified to see a hefty off-drive caught left-handed by Giffen. In an hour and three-quarters England had collapsed helplessly (and, in truth, to no great condemnation in the circumstances) for 65. Jack Brown, top scorer with 20 not out, didn't even bother unbuckling his pads. He and Ward marched out for the follow-on on a pitch still treacherous.

Giffen's fourth ball bowled Brown, and Stoddart made only one unproductive hit before holing out desperately to Iredale in the deep. For the last time in a Test match Charlie Turner had been his executioner. Two down for five, both last men ducks.

MacLaren had had enough of this nonsense. When Giffen gave him half a chance he hooked – but straight into Bruce's reliable hands. Three down for five, and all ducks. Britannia's trident was trembling.

Ward's turn came when Darling gathered in a lofted drive off Giffen, and Peel, stepping out to Turner, slipped on the greasy turf and was stumped for his second consecutive "pair". It was 14 for five, and the series was all but level at two-all as Ford strove with Brockwell to implant some decency into the scorebook. The total stuttered to 29, at which point Turner claimed his 100th Test wicket against England in only his 17th match.

At 47, Billy Bruce, still menacing at silly mid-on, brilliantly caught Briggs, and Ford was taken in the outfield, where most of the fieldsmen were waiting expectantly. Still the ball behaved highly unpredictably, and Jarvis drew applause for some of his saves behind the stumps. It was considered salutary that only 12 byes had slipped into England's final combined total of 137 runs.

Philipson and Richardson made the highest stand of the day with 20 for the ninth and last wicket, the latter whacking one ball into the side of the umpire's head. The carnage ended as Turner caught England's 'keeper and tossed the ball to skipper Giffen to present to a lady in the reserve.

Hats were flung in the air and cheers rang out. Australia had won by an innings and 147 runs in two days of play, and the series was level. Turner and Giffen had bowled unchanged throughout England's wretched second innings while Albert Trott, hero at Adelaide a fortnight before, had stood idly by observing it all through his oriental eyes. And with a total playing time of only seven and a half hours it was the shortest finished Test match at the SCG to this day.

Long after the end of the match a big crowd still stood outside the SCG members' gate, hoping for a glimpse of the players to "settle whether they were different to other men". Brockwell, whose home was The Oval, eyed the gathering with suspicion: "It is a demonstrative, ribald crowd that, especially the boy section of it, has so much to say in a way that is personal that even a big man like Lyons won't face it alone."

These Test matches, however, especially the ones won by Australia,

Large crowds daily filled the pavements to keep in touch with the Tests

were having a unifying effect on the budding nation. The cricketers were "no longer Victorians or South Australians or New South Welshmen, they were all Australians, and all jolly good fellows."

One newspaper gave an insight into the England captain's life away from the cricket field: "Mr Stoddart, during his recent visit to NSW, although the recipient of a plethora of hospitable invitations from his influential Sydney friends, invariably preferred the elegant comforts, the unparalleled spaciousness, and the surrounding quietude of the Hotel Australia to all the attractions of private Sydney hospitality, great and variously acceptable though they were."

Deflated at the defeat he may have been, but one item which reached him at the hotel must surely have made him smile. It was from "one Australian and two Yorkshire lassies" who wished to express their "deepest sympathy with Messrs Stoddart & Co at their misfortune in only making five duck eggs, & send the enclosed to make the half dozen. Having staked their 'little all' on the event & lost, they cannot afford to have it gilded, but trust that after the Melbourne event you will be able to put it in a golden case."

In their anguish the girls got one simple thing wrong: there were not five ducks in England's sad and soggy innings of 65 and 72. There were six.

There was almost a month between this Test match and the decider in Melbourne. Stoddart, the latest rumour linking his name with a girl from Sydney's North Shore ("his future home" miscued the correspondent), took his team up to Armidale to play against a team of 22 locals, and himself made a restorative 88 in fairly sedate style, relishing the relaxed atmosphere and the chance to practise on a fair pitch, striving to rebuild team confidence. Relaxations for Ford and his skipper before leaving Sydney included a Harbour cruise, Ford with a revolver, Stoddart with a rifle, hoping (to no avail) to come across some large prey in the water.

In mid-February 1895, at Brisbane's Exhibition Ground, England's champion, having been dropped before he'd scored a run, had reached a stylish 40 when a nasty chapter unfolded. An eye-witness described the incident: "Mr [Charlie] Bannerman, one of the umpires, gave a no-ball against Coningham. That mercurial individual lost his head, and in his annoyance deliberately threw the next at Stoddart. The English captain wisely and firmly called upon Coningham to apologise to the umpire and himself, and this the bowler ultimately did, but not for some time. The incident put Stoddart clean 'off'. Coningham's next ball bowled him off his pads."

Coningham's must be a fidgety ghost. This lively left-hander was adept at billiards, an oarsman of renown, a good shot, and as a rugby footballer probably not even "Stoddy" unaided could have caught him. Further, he had earned a medal for saving a boy's life in the Thames during the Australians' 1893 tour. And as a fast bowler he could be quite unpalatable, as he had shown on this warm February day in Brisbane.

All this seemed dull fare beside the conspiracy sensation of 1900, when "Conny", revolver at his hip, conducted his own scandalous and unsuccessful divorce case with an eminent priest named as the "other man".

The English cricketers left Brisbane at the earliest opportunity, seeking relief from the sub-tropical conditions in Armidale's pretty setting.

Drewy Stoddart gave the scribes in Newcastle something to write about with a hit for six straight out of the ground and a wicket with his first ball in a match against a combination from Newcastle, Maitland, Singleton and Muswellbrook.

During a brief stopover in Sydney the tourists watched some of the Shield match between New South Wales and South Australia – as if they hadn't already seen enough of Giffen. The NSW Premier George Reid made some pleasant remarks over tea: cricket had been greatly advanced by the visit of Mr Stoddart and his team, as had the good feelings between the two countries. He asked for three cheers for the visitors. The English skipper made a characteristically quiet and sincere response.

While back home people were skating over frozen stretches of the Thames, and across the pond near "Stoddy's" Hampstead residence, packed steamers and trains and horseback riders were converging on Melbourne for the greatest show on earth. Frenzy swept the land as the kangaroo shaped up to the lion in newspapers and over meal tables. Crowds gathered in unprecedented numbers, even for the preliminary net practices. All was set for cricket's Match of the Century.

The first great Test series reaches its climax after the Australians drew level at Sydney

CHAPTER 15

Test Match Classic

AND here we are! "Not all," *you say*? There's one – we miss him sore –
But I hear the cables clicking from the sunny southern shore:
"A Century to Stoddart"; and he knows, come best or worst,
His Hampstead pals are watching for the fate of March the First;
If pluck and captainship can win, he'll win the rub, I vow,
For Melbourne, Sydney, Adelaide, have heard of Hampstead now!
> Can't you see George Giffen asking him what Spofforth is about?
> Can't you see our Cricket Annual from his pocket slipping out?
> Can't you hear the answer, "Bowling like a waggon-load of bricks,
> He's got 200 wickets at a cost of under six!"
> And Giffen rubs his chin, and longs for Spofforth back, you bet,
> For Hampstead proves the Demon has the *devil* in him yet!

(Arthur Waugh – A Ballad of Brave Men)

Some momentous quotes have come down through the ages. "I'll never play cricket again!" exploded C.T.B.Turner when the startling news of his omission from the Australian team came through. "It's no use talking like that, Charlie," said Jack Lyons, whose position in the team was secure. "You'll have to go to England if we go next year." (They did, but "The Terror" didn't.)

Turner's replacement was Tom McKibbin, who bowled off-cutters with a suspect action, was Bathurst-born, like Turner, but was eight years younger at 24. McKibbin had just taken 14 wickets against Queensland and a further 16 wickets against South Australia at Sydney, out-Giffening Giffen. He had also bagged 5 for 98 against the Englishmen in that curious Brisbane match.

Giffen recorded his own thoughts at the start of this Ashes decider at Melbourne: "I knew that when Stoddart and I went into the ring to toss

and arrange preliminaries, he was as white as a sheet, and I have been told
that the pallor of my own countenance matched his."

On Friday, March 1, 1895,
Major Ben Wardill, Melbourne
Cricket Club secretary, escorted the
captains to the middle, linked arm
in arm with them. Looking "rather
uneasy", England's leader had Ford
and Philipson with him. As they left
the pavilion the "generous applause
of the public seemed to brighten
him [Stoddart] up a bit". The small
group stood by the hard, glossy
pitch, and as Giffen made the most
of these final few seconds free of
responsibility, Wardill could contain
himself no longer: "For Heaven's
sake, toss and get it over with!"

"Keep   cool,   Major,"
"Stoddy" soothed.

Giffen's hand was unsteady
as he flipped the coin. "Heads!"
Stoddart commanded.   But the

New boy Tom McKibbin:
bowling action not above suspicion

Australian gave a delighted little skip as it came to rest "tails". "Stoddy's"
look of despair seemed to say "It's all over" in this deciding Test match,
while the packed house cheered the home skipper for his clever spinning of
the coin. England had thus won only one of the five tosses in the series.

Reflecting the intensity of this match, Billy Brockwell wrote in his
tour diary for *Sporting Sketches* that "each one of us engaged in the encounter
with a stern resolve to uphold the cricket supremacy of Old England". He
also sympathised with Charlie Turner.

Harry Trott and Billy Bruce opened Australia's batting, the
latter having dashed down from his legal duties at North Melbourne
police court, and cutting Bobby Peel to the boundary with
typical audacity and perfect legal right. (Bruce had a strange
habit of putting his bottom hand in his pocket after striking a
boundary.) With Trott, too, punching the ball hard, especially off

Peel (who had him missed by Ford at slip), they posted 40 before Bruce was caught.

Giffen, now almost 36, hair grey as ash, walked to the middle fixing his glove. He represented the most formidable of England's opponents. Soon he was jumping out to Peel and sending carpet drives speeding into the broad outfield, and Trott began to time his leg shots off Richardson. Lockwood and Briggs took over, but after lunch, when Australia were 76 for one wicket, the pair hit strongly. Trott drove with immense power. The hundred came. Then Briggs lured Trott forward and bowled him: 101 for two.

Frank Iredale was not feeling very well, but his grace and ease, under his new white quilted hat, seemed ominous. But at 126 Richardson benefited from his short breather by coming back to crash one through off a perfect length. The last 25 runs had taken 45 minutes, and it was remarked that Stoddart "seemed to make eleven men go into fifteen places and have one over to back up".

Australia soon sustained a further setback as Peel returned and persuaded Giffen (57) to play a yorker into his stumps. The Australian innings was now perched precariously at 142 for four. It was 3.50pm when Joe Darling joined Syd Gregory and held on nervously. Ford turfed a difficult chance after tea, and Gregory celebrated with a drive and a hit to leg, both for four. Darling gave the crowd (which numbered 18,000) some sweet-sounding cuts and enchanting drives which always seem so unexpected from a small man facing fast bowling on a hard pitch with bounce. The runs accumulated as the afternoon ticked away: 200 quite rapidly posted and forgotten as the 250 was rapturously applauded. The diminutive Gregory was often up on tip-toes to the short ball. All the bowling was now being roughly handled, and Ford dropped Gregory, and Philipson missed Darling, Albert Ward worsening matters by fluffing a run-out chance given by the left-hander.

With Gregory 70 and Darling 72 at the close, Australia were set solidly at 282 for four, with odds on this decider easing towards the home team.

Joe Darling, due to be given a gold watch by his father when his century came, added only two runs next day before edging Peel low to Ford at slip. Had he but known it the paternal present would be his after all for making Australia's match top score.

The attendance of 29,123 on that Saturday was a capacity crowd and a new Australian record. How could anyone present possibly have envisaged the colossal MCG of the 21st Century? But England's quick breakthrough on the second day was not what the locals wanted.

The *Argus* man took his eyes off the play long enough to paint an enthusiastic picture: "Stoddart ought to make an excellent Agent General when he returns and looks in at the Royal Exchange and tells some of the haughty financiers of that poorly-informed institution that Australia is most prosperous, that a happier, better-spirited, better-dressed, and better-behaved crowd could not have been seen than he saw at the Melbourne ground."

The Test series had attracted a cross-section of Australian society: political figures, women in copious hats and finery, tradesmen in bowler hats, stetsons, straw boaters, along with wing collars, waistcoats and watch-chains. There were dreaming office clerks, overheated in jackets, opinionated men from the professions, seething republicans with drooping moustaches, homesick immigrants, romantic club cricketers, pilgrims from the bush, dust still on their boots, boys in knickerbockers and straw hats, militia men splendid in uniforms: they all filed through turnstiles and members' gates to watch the 1894-95 Test matches.

There was only one thing that mattered to the cricket-lovers at the MCG in March 1895, and that was the ups and downs of the absorbing fifth and deciding Test match

In faraway Britain news came a little faster than in the past, and there was one particularly eminent reader: "The Queen evinces the keenest interest in the Anglo-Australian cricket matches which are now being proceeded with, and has all the telegrams brought to her the moment they are received. It may truly be said that her subjects share her sentiments, for no cricket matches ever played have excited so much enthusiasm."

England now had the muscular Lyons to contend with. One of his drives hissed through the air and reached Stoddart in the deep on the bounce, giving him a "very nasty crack on the leg". But further excitement came next over as Gregory touched one of Richardson's rockets and Philipson completed the job. At 286 for six the match had swung somewhat.

Lyons pushed Australia up to 300, but Richardson unleashed what locals called a "clinker of a ball" at Harry Graham (6) which cut back and shattered the stumps. His place was taken by the phenomenal Albert Trott, who this time made only 10 before being caught at cover off Peel. At last "Alberto" registered a Test match average – 205 – having played a deviant shot that, it was suggested, he must have learned while recently spending so much time coaching the ladies.

Jack Lyons was aided by the equally husky "Affie" Jarvis in adding 32, but when Lyons fell for a splendid even-time 55 it was the dapper newcomer McKibbin who took his country past 400, making runs apace with Jarvis, who had a habit of stepping forward while pushing his right leg backwards and giving his partner a big knowing wink after smearing the ball. It was Australia's fifth freakish last-wicket stand in succession, the 47 raising the total to a reassuring 414, having spanned the lunch interval, much to England's frustration yet again.

At 3.10pm Ward and Brockwell set about England's reply. The latter had taken part in some huge first-innings partnerships for Surrey with Bobby Abel, so hopes were high for him. Ward took a single, then Brockwell placed Giffen away for a two and a three. But facing Harry Trott's first leggie, he advanced to hit, got it wrong, fell, and was stumped. He was later heard to remark: "Well, I've tried everything – going in late, playing steadily, hitting hard, but somehow I can't get going." It's a familiar quandary for most batsmen.

So A.E.Stoddart walked out much sooner than he would have wished, to the staccato music of nearly 30,000 clapping pairs of hands, and was soon stroking the ball away for runs. Before long, after playing Giffen to point, he looked at his bat, wondering if it was in sound condition. Finally satisfied, he began hitting to leg with assurance, and soon had 20; then he daringly late-cut Giffen to the iron railings. He settled in, and swung his opposite number to the square-leg chains, and forced the steady Giffen to falter in length. With the Australian captain wavering in accuracy, "Stoddy" won this personal duel of the leaders with strokes that excited those watching and went, otherwise unrecorded, in their memory banks to their graves. He would never have played in a more important match or before such a large crowd. Sometimes he made as if to go after runs, only to slacken the wrists and back down. Albert Trott came on, and for a while McKibbin puzzled Ward as well as his captain. Stoddart flicked several exquisite leg glances away together with some spanking leg-side shots. Ward, encouraged, ventured forward and three times achieved fours through the covers.

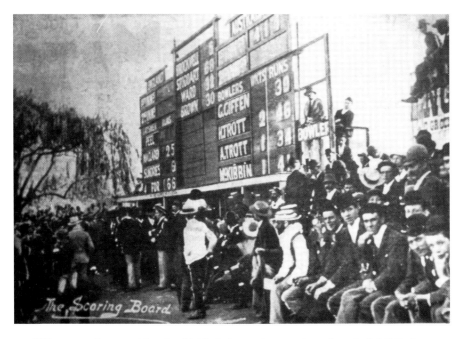

What was then considered a highly-informative scoreboard at the MGC shows Stoddart on 68 just at the fatal moment when he was stumped off Harry Trott's cunning bowling

Stoddart was master of the bowling now, so Giffen brought back

Harry Trott to tease and hope for a mis-hit. England's captain welcomed the change, unleashing a shot through the field. When he studiously played out a maiden over there was a cry of "Well played Bannerman!" and "Stoddy" displayed a gentle smile. He had fielded out often enough to Alec Bannerman, king of the stonewallers.

With 110 on the board Giffen's ploy paid off. Stoddart stepped out a pace, failed to make contact, and Jarvis stumped him. The crowd jumped to their feet with relief at this important capture. Stoddart's 68 (seven fours) had taken an hour and a half of all that was best in batting, and at a time when it could not have mattered more. He shook his head in self-recrimination for falling this way two Tests running. Moreover, this ball from Harry Trott had come in from the off, suggesting a variation off-break or perhaps a "prehistoric" googly. England were 110 for two.

"Well played, Mr Thtoddart," Jack Brown might have said as he stubbed out his cigarette and marched out into the sunlight to carry on the campaign. But almost instantly Albert Ward was bowled by McKibbin for 32, etched in almost two hours. With two new men in, Australia went for the kill.

MacLaren, who had made only 100 runs at 16 so far in the series, played Harry Trott's looping spin charmingly to leg, and 54 were added for this fourth wicket. Trott senior was then replaced by his brother, and Albert enhanced his reputation by bowling Brown for 30. The stand had promised much with its positively-made runs, but now no more wickets could be spared, and surely and safely MacLaren and Peel saw the second day out, England 200 for four, still a hefty 214 runs behind. Some Australians, mindful of the opening Test match three months ago in Sydney, feared a compulsory follow-on.

On Monday, after the Sunday of rest, MacLaren and Peel showed some fine touch in front of another large crowd, the lordly Lancastrian forcing away good-length balls, and Bobby Peel, with less of a regal air but equal authority, breezily cutting Albert Trott's fizzers. Giffen removed his imposing felt hat and took over. Peel clouted him square. And when Trott flung one down wide it bumped over the dry turf to the boundary, and a touch of anxiety and frustration was felt by the large assembly under the glaring sun. The runs were coming, but two chances went begging, one of them from Peel's whirling bat to Iredale, who tossed aside his hat, chased, lunged and failed to hold the ball, the other when the aggrieved bowler, Giffen, his sore hand a hindrance, missed a return catch from MacLaren when the Lancastrian was 69. At lunch lucky England boasted 295 without having sustained any further loss and the match was already deserving of a very high classification.

The punishing batsmanship continued, and at 322 Albert Trott came back. MacLaren imperiously on-drove him to seal his century (175 minutes), the first of five he would make against Australia. At 104 he was missed by 'keeper Jarvis, but a ball went to hand at long last when the defiant Peel (73) lifted Giffen to Gregory. MacLaren escorted Peel to the gate and returned with new batsman Lockwood. The priceless fifth-wicket partnership of 162 had almost doubled the score.

Bill Lockwood lasted only a few fidgety minutes, and Giffen dismissed Ford after he had been missed twice. MacLaren looked very weary, bending down on one knee between overs. At 364 for seven the betting in the outer was against England to equal Australia's 414, and the likelihood slumped further when MacLaren's superlative performance was finally closed when he stepped on his wicket in trying to deal with Harry Trott. It was a sad end presaged by several near misses. His 120 contained some glorious strokes, each as majestic as the many to come in the years of Ashes combat (preponderantly lost) which lay ahead.

Archie MacLaren, whose fine hundred, supported by Bobby Peel's 73, kept England in the game in the enthralling decider at Melbourne

An extraordinary catch at silly mid-on by Harry Trott inflicted on Briggs the first duck of the match, and Richardson was out (only the third lbw of the series: there were two more to follow, of great importance too) just when ten minutes more of the blacksmith treatment would have stolen a first-innings lead. As it was, England finished only 29 runs behind at 385.

There was some very determined batting in the closing phase as Australia stretched their lead by 69 for the loss of Bruce, whose 11 took the best part of an hour. "Stoddy" had led his men into the field at 4.15pm, looking curiously at the darkening sky then, and subsequently with some anxiety. The area clouded over as Giffen started batting, and while Harry Trott hit freely, the captain happened upon one solitary run in half-an-hour, Bill Lockwood's eight overs having consisted of seven maidens and two runs. The match was in the melting pot in a sense besides the meteorological.

On the fourth day a stifling dust storm caused dreadful discomfort to spectators and players alike. The awning over the Ladies' reserve was torn away, and Charlie Turner's girlfriend's parasol was blown inside out. Poor Johnny Briggs had a fit of stringhalt – severe leg twitches – and Stoddart placed him at point until the spasm passed. The roaring wind applied red dust over everything. "One looked down on a valley of dust," wrote the

The Englishmen stay tuned in the Melbourne nets

Argus reporter, "with just the roof of the pavilion and the tops of the elm trees peeping through." The rattling scoreboard needed to be secured by ropes.

The stirred-up dust may have helped Peel when Trott missed a straight one and was bowled.

While spectators chased after their hats, there was a half-century partnership between Iredale and Giffen, who drove Lockwood out of the attack. Richardson now bowled with the choking wind coming in gusts across the pitch. Iredale played on to him for 18, and Gregory saw his captain to lunch on 50 not out. At 139 for three Australia led by 168. Match very much in the balance.

Giffen eventually played over a Richardson yorker, having grafted 51 in three hours. Darling and Gregory eased the score along without the spectacular pillaging of the first innings. Every stolen run rendered England's ultimate target all the more remote, and for what must have seemed a very long time to Stoddart the two elegant little men waited for the bad ball.

Gregory finally fell for 30, bowled by the tireless Richardson, and as Lyons set out on one of the most important innings of his life he dealt some brave and thunderous blows against the Surrey giant's yorkers, seamers and occasional bouncers. England's captain exhorted his principal bowler not to flag, to draw on his innermost strength.

But it was Briggs who did the trick, flicking down a faster ball to Lyons which veered from middle to off. With Australia's Hercules gone, it was 200 for six wickets; and soon Harry Graham, aiming indiscriminately at a quick one from the relentless Richardson, was leg-before.

The Surrey giant then dealt with Albert Trott, who now frustrated statisticians then and now by making 0, halving his Test average for Australia to 102.50, in perpetuity as it turned out.

So Australia, with two wickets remaining, led by 248. Darling was still there, and with Jarvis he stretched the lead. Bobby Peel was called upon to terminate the innings, but more precious runs came as Darling cut and drove the weary Richardson. He reached a faultless 50 before being bowled as he aimed a mighty hit off Peel. That made it 248 for nine, and after McKibbin had helped Jarvis drag the score up to 267, 'keeper Philipson held him to give Richardson his sixth wicket. England needed a rather distant 297 to win the match and the series.

Tom Richardson had laboured through 87.2 six-ball overs in the Test match and taken nine wickets for 242, one of the most heroic performances in all Ashes history. Just as admirable were Bobby Peel's match figures of seven wickets for 203 off 94 overs.

The formidable efforts of these two would be the subject of some of their grateful captain's reflections in years to come. Now: would England's efforts in the field serve as a foundation for a wondrous victory? England's assignment was rather too weighty for comfort.

Billy Brockwell and Albert Ward set about it. As in the first innings, Brockwell of Surrey took five from the first over and perished to the first ball of the second, caught-and-bowled by the crafty Giffen at the second attempt. During the series Brockwell had been proverbially unlucky, but this time an indiscreet pull stroke cost him his wicket.

Nightwatchmen were not in fashion in the 1890s, and Stoddart again went in at number three. Further casualties would tilt the match. He was well aware of that. With Harry Trott twirling down his leg-spin, England's captain played cautiously off the back foot, and reached 11. By the close he and Ward (6) had taken the score to 28, and tomorrow would, weather permitting, be a great day for one side or the other. The pitch was holding. It would be a matter of whether England's batsmen could hold their nerves.

The series – this First Great Test Series – was about to be won and lost. All Melbourne, all Australia, all of the Empire was agog.

The epic entered its fifth day, a morning of fine tranquillising drizzle which conjured visions of England perhaps being trapped on a damp pitch. If anything the moisture helped rejuvenate a surface which had been slowly drying and cracking, and the light was softer, easier on the eyes. Again the attendance was large, taking the total for the five days very close to 100,000, a record.

The Australians took their time, George Giffen and Harry Trott bowling to each other in a prolonged warm-up which umpires Flynn and Phillips permitted. Returning from overseeing the rolling of the pitch, Drewy Stoddart had been heard to remark about it: "I think it is all right." Several minutes after noon Trott bowled to him, to pin-dropping silence. The opening ball went straight on, rapped the pad as England's skipper played to leg. Up went the raucous appeal, and up went the forefinger of the umpire, Jim Phillips, the Australian who played alongside Stoddart for Middlesex and was his touring umpire. England's prospects seemed suddenly to have been sliced in half as the crestfallen captain walked off, left hand to his face all the way, midst roars of delight. One report claimed that "Stoddart's face as he passed in plainly indicated that he was seriously disturbed." The gatekeeper was quoted as saying, with all the wisdom he could muster, that Harry Trott had bowled a plain, straight ball because Stoddart was so fond of hooking him.

Jack Brown now strode nonchalantly to the middle, with an immigrant in the outer section playing *Rule Britannia* on a tin whistle. The 25-year-old from Driffield, whose heart was to fail him ten years later, was about to play an innings which has been justifiably praised to the skies and listed among the very finest Test innings of them all, given the final statistics and the match situation. Under that overcast sky and with England's precious objective so very distant, he edged Trott short of slip. They scuttled two runs. Brown then flung down his challenge with a square-drive over cover's head and a sweep for four off the next ball: 11 off Giffen's first over, followed by a stream of red-blooded strokes all over the MCG.

Jack Brown from Driffield: one of the greatest innings ever seen in a Test match. It secured the Ashes

Rule Britannia continued to float across the ground as the solidly-built Yorkshireman chopped the ball through slip, cut it hard through the cover area and stirred even his opponents with short-arm pull shots: he had 26 after 12 minutes, 35 after 18, some hits scudding across the turf, some airborne. Brown was severe on McKibbin, who tended to be wayward, and it is to be regretted that the precision of modern record-keeping was not then available, for Jack Brown smashed his fifty in what is now agreed to have been 28 minutes, although it may well have been quicker still. He himself believed the board showed his half-century in 27 minutes, and he said so in a letter to his parents back in Yorkshire. Over a hundred years later it remains the fastest fifty in Ashes history. (And it would have been even faster had Albert Trott not made a wonderful interception at cover just before the landmark.)

On he charged, with Albert Ward supporting him as almost a dumb partner (five runs while his runaway associate smashed that half-century). The bowling was switched frequently, but Giffen, Lyons and both Trotts, untidy McKibbin and Bruce all came the same to J.T.Brown. If the weather was to be a factor, England seemed determined to beat it. And all the while the musicians in the crowd played away: *Daisy Bell* followed by *Sweet Marie*.

England's captain: seated in the vice-regal box, applauding both teams impartially

Soon after one o'clock the hundred came up (Brown 60). Now Ward, born in a village named Waterloo, with all its dramatic implications, took equal billing, particularly with some beautiful cuts as England's total climbed to 145 by lunch. The chatter now was all expectant of an English victory. Ward seemed to edge to Jarvis, but Phillips, unsighted, had to reject the appeal, and soon Jack Brown had scorched to his glorious century. It came in only 95 minutes with a big four off Harry Trott's leg-spin, followed by an all-run four and a square-leg hit. In the 100 years that followed, that time was to be bettered in Ashes Tests only by Jessop (75 minutes), Joe Darling (91 minutes) and Trumper (94 minutes).

The momentum was now with England. The Australians were frustrated by Brown's reprieve on 125, just after Ward had lifted a ball from Giffen into the crowd for a five. Had Giffen kept himself on too long yet again? To any such criticism he made it clear that Harry Trott had encouraged him to continue.

By now Mr A.E.Stoddart was seen sitting in the vice-regal area alongside Lady Hopetoun and applauding both sides impartially.

A new overall Test match partnership record was established when the Ward-Brown stand passed the 207 put on by Billy Murdoch and "Tup" Scott at The Oval in 1884. But when it stood at 210 (in only 145 minutes), having been dropped by 'keeper Jarvis when 125, Brown steered McKibbin to slip, where Giffen was able to spare his puffed-up right hand by taking the catch in his left. Jack Brown's 140 contained 16 fours, and was rewarded with a heart-warming reception by the audience of over 14,000, as well as by the Australian players as the muscular little Yorkshireman made his way back to the pavilion. This phenomenal performance would remain his only Test hundred, and the greatest innings of his life, notwithstanding the two triple-centuries for Yorkshire which came later.

Now, with only 59 needed and seven England wickets in hand, MacLaren joined Albert Ward, whose century was in sight. But at 93 he was yorked by Harry Trott after a coolly-crafted, heroic 3½-hour innings, with only a handful of boundary hits. It was said that even his opponents felt sympathy for his shortfall from three figures. (Trott further recalled, with no great enthusiasm, that the band had played *Sweet Marie* that historic day.)

Bobby Peel had taken the winning wicket for England in the first Test match, at Sydney, and also in the second, at Melbourne. He now sealed a distinguished (and probably unique) hat-trick of conclusions in one series by hitting the winning runs in this fifth Test, whacking Harry Trott's weary full-toss through the off side at 4.12pm.

England had made 298 runs in only 215 minutes from 88 six-ball overs, winning by six wickets to wrap up the first great Test series.

When the news reached Ballarat Stock Exchange, an Englishman unfurled a Union Jack and burst lustily into *Rule Britannia*, at which the Southern Cross flag was hoisted and his Australian colleagues attempted to drown him out with *The Men of Australia*. They all ended up singing *God Save the Queen*.

Newspaper offices had been jam-packed all afternoon as people studied the progress boards while Ward and Brown built their historic match-winning partnership. Nowadays enthusiasts would be glued to their radios or television sets or mobile phones, missing out on the fervid group excitement and togetherness on the pavements.

George Giffen's emotions almost got the better of him as he shook Stoddart's hand: "It's hard to have to congratulate you, Stoddy, old boy." He apologised for the hesitancy in his words, but he had written a victory speech.

Melb. Punch.]

THE TEST MATCH.

1. *The Victorious Stoddart to the Defeated Giffen.*—"Well, old man, I've won, but I'm glad it's over." *Giffen (feelingly).*—"And so am I."
2. Richardson gets fairly on to a fiery wicket.
3. *Old Sol.*—"Well, neither side can blame me this match. I've been very impartial."
4. Harry Trott catches an easy one.
5. George Giffen makes a left-handed catch.

Newspaper and magazine artists had much fun during the 1894-95 Ashes series

The crowds besieged the pavilion for some time, calling loudly for the England captain, who eventually appeared at the window and bowed and smiled.

Peel gave his bat to Charlie Turner, whom "Stoddy" thanked for helping England . . . by not being selected. But the greatest prize, the ball itself, ended up in Tom McKibbin's joyful clutches, although his figures of 2 for 120 in the match hardly made him a key player.

Stoddart would have treasured it, and he enquired of Jack Blackham: "Do you think there is a possible chance of getting that ball? I'd give my very soul to get it, upon my word I would."

Australia's erstwhile wicketkeeper probed the possibilities, but young McKibbin told him: "The ball's very valuable to me. I prize it greatly." But a look at "Stoddy's" eyes was enough: "If you give me your photo," he relented, "I'll give you the ball."

So the dressing-room transaction was completed and England's captain showed delight at "the nice way in which McKibbin met him". Stoddart held the ball aloft and said, "I'm glad Turner hadn't the handling of it!"

That cricket ball, a sort of early present for "Stoddy's" 32nd birthday five days later, should have had a preservation order put on it, but it seems to have gone the way of all things.

George Giffen, in recognition of his efforts across this famous summer, received something rather more useful: 400 sovereigns from the adoring cricket public of Australia for his services to cricket. Lord Hopetoun, a popular Governor of Victoria who was to become Australia's first Governor-General when the Commonwealth was created on January 1, 1901, presented bats to Joe Darling and Jack Brown for top-scoring. After his speech, Frank Grey Smith thanked everyone on behalf of Melbourne Cricket Club, and complimented England's leader on his victory and on his "consummate tact and sportsmanlike conduct".

England's leader made a typically modest, serene and heartfelt reply, but poor Giffen was still struggling with his emotions, generous remarks mixing with patent disappointment. His players weren't Englishmen but "they were sprouts of a magnificent old trunk".

The most absorbing Test series to date and for many years to come was over, and the last frantic and expensive cable dispatched. Over in England, *The Times*, with Victorian restraint, announced ENGLISH VICTORY IN AUSTRALIA. Melbourne's *Argus* told the tale as succinctly as any: "Two for 28; three for 238. The one satisfactory point to Australians is that they will be able to say long years hence that they were at the match and saw that partnership [Ward-Brown 210]."

"Felix" speculated that this may well have been "the greatest performance on record".

In *Cricket* magazine, the Reverend R.S.Holmes wrote: "Well, England won the rubber. Yet it may be open to question whether on the whole our men did as well as the Australians in the test matches. True, the luck was against us in the choice of innings; Stoddart won the toss only once [in the catastrophic two-day fourth Test at Sydney], and then he was foolish enough to put his opponents in, with the result that England lost that match by an innings and 147 runs. I wonder if it ever pays to do this?"

The question hauntingly echoes down the decades.

Another Australian interpretation of the England captain's fortunes; one of several in his tour scrapbook marked 'For Book'

Let me offer my sincerest congratulations to A.E.Stoddart and his gallant band," he concluded. "In a letter to myself before leaving he spoke in the highest terms of the fibre of his men; they have deserved all that was said. The captain has never played better, perhaps never so well when we take into account the burden of responsibility he has borne throughout in an office to which he was almost a stranger."

To modern eyes it could seem that "Stoddy" was born expressly to govern this fabulous series of Test matches. Nothing in his life before or after seemed so important and significant.

Now, though, it was time to let the hair down. It was almost as if Shakespeare were there:

> Upon a chair in that big banquet hall
> Sate Stoddart, England's captain; he did heartwarming
> That sound the first amidst the festival,
> And whispered in a portly waiter's ear,
> To fill Brown's glass who sat so thirsty near,
> Humphreys' and Ward's: he knew that Peel, too, well earned

Liked it, preferring it to muddy beer;
And so the aforesaid waiter he did tell
To put a magnum near, on which he promptly fell.

Douglas Moffat

Johnny Briggs was pitched out of his bunk on SS *Coogee's* turbulent sea crossing to Tasmania, where the touring team played two matches against odds, the first at Launceston, where Stoddart made 73 not out in the drawn three-day match and the local girls surprised him with a birthday cake; and the second in Hobart, six hours away by stagecoach through mountainous country, some of it ablaze with bushfires. The cake, iced in team colours (as of Melbourne Cricket Club), was greatly appreciated by this warm and gentle man who was so many miles from home and relatives.

"OVER!"

Mr. St-dd-rt, Captain of the English Eleven, with Mr. G-ff-n, the Australian Captain, sing in harmony—
"THE LION AND THE KANGAROO | THE LION LICKED THE KANGAROO—
FIGHTING FOR THE C——

The lion and the kangaroo were becoming popular cartoon symbols

This second match was marred by the weather, Mount Wellington being lost in mist, and some of the amateurs going missing too, which did not impress the locals. "Stoddy" top-scored with 21, having had to get the carriage to return to the hotel because he had forgotten his boots, which were drying out on a hot stove and might well have set light to the hotel. He later agreed to play on through the rain, and paid for his sportsmanship with a nasty chill.

The gossip columns still oozed with theories about the English cricketers' romances, and an enquiry into the status of the English amateur contingent resulted in the following par: "Stoddart and Philipson are the only ones with any money at all, each possessing an income of five or six hundred a year [a very comfortable sum]. The former is a stockbroker in London, and the latter does nothing."

They re-crossed the turbulent Bass Strait without "Stoddy", whose chill persuaded him to remain in bed for a while. He followed them back to the mainland later aboard *SS Parramatta*, and missed the Victoria match.

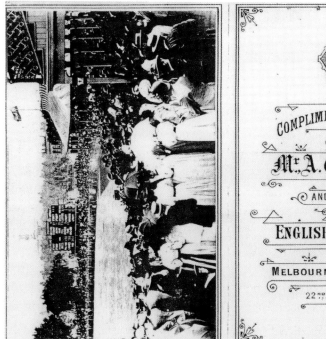
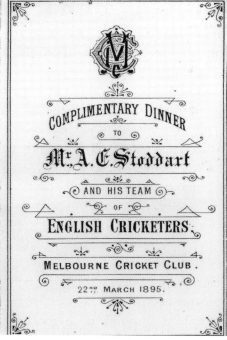

Menu for the lavish farewell banquet laid on by Melbourne Cricket Club in honour of the English cricketers

Philipson was asked to bat by Harry Trott, and the Englishmen really lost a poorly-attended match on the first day with a total of 131, the Victoria skipper ramming home his decision by spinning an 8 for 63.

The action on the 1894-95 tour was now almost done with. A farewell banquet was thrown for the team in the MCG luncheon room, with Stoddart pudding among the entremets. Mr Justice a'Beckett proposed the toast to Our Guests, recalling that everybody had followed that final Test match as a father would watch over the progress of a seriously ill child. Bulletins had been handed up to him at the bench. Such excitement might even have interfered with his understanding of what the witnesses were saying!

England, he said, had won esteem for their steadfastness in an uphill battle and for the affability with which they had accepted defeat. The Australian people were saying farewell to thorough sportsmen, and although they may have to wait for Federation of the Australian States, federation in sport was an accomplished fact.

For They Are Jolly Good Fellows! boomed around the room from 150 throats. The liquor flowed, and the cheering was prolonged. When the cheers had faded away, the chairman commended the English professionals for their "uprightness of conduct" (what exactly had Australia expected?), and their fine play. Drewy Stoddart then rose to respond.

He had to wait some time for the cheering to subside, and was clearly moved by it. In his soft voice he thanked Melbourne for its kindness. Their lot as cricketers had been a very happy one from the time they set foot in Australia, and he felt certain that all his players regretted most sincerely that it was almost time to leave. As a member of Lord Hawke's team (1887-88) he had thought the trip near perfection. Lord Sheffield's tour (1891-92) was also most enjoyable. But the hospitality extended to them on the present trip eclipsed all else.

And the cheers rose again.

In thanking the Melbourne and Sydney cricket authorities for the delightful venture, he could not help mentioning two of the best fellows it had ever been his lot to meet: Major [Ben] Wardill and Mr [Phil] Sheridan. Australian visits did much good for English cricket. He said he would like to see a tour every two years. Moreover – diplomatically – he hoped it would always be under the auspices of the Melbourne and Sydney authorities. Australia could congratulate themselves upon having three of the best umpires in the world: Jim Phillips, Charlie Bannerman and Tom Flynn [cheers] and he acknowledged the great service rendered his team by Phillips.

Finally, he could only hope that the next English XI would have half as good a time as his team had experienced. If only he'd known how chillingly real and literal would be the reality of this equivocally uttered wish.

"Stoddy" was to paste the menu from the banquet into his tour scrapbook as a tender souvenir of a memorably warm and friendly occasion, with even Johnny Briggs, Archie MacLaren, Francis Ford and Hylton Philipson making speechlets. With songs and recitations following, the very special event drew to a close half-an-hour short of midnight.

A dance was staged at Prahran Town Hall, then they piled onto a train at Spencer Street station bound for Adelaide. The final match of the tour, against South Australia, was fittingly sensational. Again Stoddart remained in the wings nursing his cold, and this time his side piled on the runs. Clem Hill had celebrated what was thought to be his 18th birthday with a wonderful 150 not out, and the Giffens made runs. When an English fieldsman chased a hit into the outfield with the stride of a tired emu, the band played 'E Dunno Where 'E Are as the batsmen scampered five runs.

But the Englishmen dwarfed the South Australian 397 with an innings of 609 in just under eight hours, and George Giffen, with Jarvis having been badly injured when thrown from a carriage, must have wondered how he might have offended cricket's Great Puppeteer. Clem Hill kept wicket for some hours.

Francis Ford made an entertaining hundred, Brown carried on from his Melbourne delights with 101, and Ward made certain of his century this time, and after six hours at the Adelaide Oval crease he had converted it into 200. Tireless Giffen wheeled down 87 overs to take five wickets for (could this be right? - the scoresheet says so) 309 runs. This was a record until Arthur Mailey's hilarious 4 for 362 in 1926-27.

Hill made another fifty, but Richardson, Peel and Briggs had them out a second time for 255, and Brockwell and Ford chased 44 for victory in the remaining 20 minutes. It took them seventeen.

On the eve of departure from Australia the Englishmen were entertained by Governor Sir Edwin Smith at The Acacias, and Stoddart exclaimed that, much as he disliked speechifying, he almost regretted that this would be the last of the many occasions on which he had got to his feet.

Major Wardill, their "escort" throughout the long tour, spoke with some feeling, remarking on what a splendid time had been had and how he would miss the players. He and the rest of Australia's cricket authorities would have been dancing with glee at the tour profit of £7000. Weary George Giffen simply wished the opposition all God speed.

The English professionals, prompted by "feelings of love" as well as respect for their skipper, privately presented "Stoddy" with a silver tobacco jar as a parting gesture, and he was too choked to say more than a word or two in thanking Johnny Briggs. He himself had given each of his players a diamond scarf-pin.

A couple of years later, K.S.Ranjitsinhji caught Stoddart off guard by asking him who were his favourite touring cricketers. "Well," he told Ranji, "I never want to meet three better fellows or more pleasant companions than Tom Richardson, Albert Ward, and Brockwell." Almost certainly he felt acute embarrassment when he saw his words in *The Jubilee Book of Cricket*. Bobby Peel understandably failed to get a mention. It was thought that he stood alone with the number of fines he had sustained for being unfit to play.

The small launches taking them out to *Ophir* were caught in a rain squall which drenched the players and showered possible foreboding on A.E.Stoddart, A.C.MacLaren, Johnny Briggs and Tom Richardson, who were all destined to return three years later.

Back in London at last, the bronzed captain, banjo conspicuous among his luggage, was greeted by cries of "Well done!" and "Bravo Blackheath!". He was soon visiting the Hampstead ground where, oddly enough, a match against Stoics (his 485 victims nine years previously) was in progress. And of course Albert Craig, The Surrey Poet, was not slow in saluting England's captain:

> Honour our Stoddart, a prince amongst sportsmen,
> Honour our lads who proved loyal and true,
> Prized by the Queen, and esteemed by her people,
> Long live our colours, the Red, White and Blue!

The jubilant aftermath of the amazing 1894-95 tour lasted a full month.   Brown received a tumultuous hometown reception in Driffield. Members of the House of Commons collected £100 for equal division between him, Peel, Ward and Richardson.   The bat with which Brown made his grander-than-fiction 140 was displayed in Wisden's window in Cranbourn Street, London, and for a time was kept in the Wisden museum, where the batsman sometimes cradled it in his hands once more, recalling his extraordinary Ashes-winning innings.   This historic long-handled lightweight bat, together with many similar, was eventually sold, and Brown's has for some years been in the author's collection.

One editorial asserted that the 1894-95 tour had made cricket the question of the day for over four months: "Politics local and Imperial, the war in the East, currency tangles and municipal corruption in the United States" had been "cast in the shade". "Nothing, in short, has been able to withstand the avalanche-like progress of the Stoddart combination."

As for Andrew Ernest Stoddart himself, the celebrations culminated later that month in a highly memorable banquet in the glittering splendour of the Cafe Monico in Piccadilly Circus. W.G.Grace, having just notched his 100th first-class century, was present, as were Sir J.M.Barrie and the Reverend R.S.Holmes (indulgent towards the vast array of bottles and magnums): "We had the usual loyal toasts and much singing one could have dispensed with, good though it was. But we had come to hear Stoddart and WG; and we were getting impatient at the interval between their speeches, although a recitation entitled 'The Cricket Club of Red Nose Flat' brought down the house, and the editor of the *Pall Mall*, along with the Honourable Justice Stephen from Sydney, were well worth listening to.

"But Stoddart and WG bore off all the honours. It was more than generous for WG to hurry off from Bristol to do honour to a brother sportsman. What a reception we gave him as he rolled in a few minutes late, as fresh as a new pin, and as brown as a berry, although I would have preferred to see him in flannels rather than a swallow-tail."

Another report remarked on WG's failure to freshen up before his dash straight from the cricket field to Bristol's Temple Meads station to catch the train for London, and how noticeable his recent exertions were to the noses of those who sat near to him. In his ghosted autobiography he recalled jumping into the carriage and seeing a kindly old lady as the only other occupant as he switched to formal attire: "She made some objection, but when I explained that I had to be at Stoddy's dinner, she smilingly agreed."

Holmes continued: "Stoddart's speech was modest, and very happy. I couldn't help wondering how this singularly quiet, mellifluous talker could be the mighty smiter we all know him to be. He assured us that two factors made his stay in Australia the happiest eight months in his life. The first was the loyalty of his team; the second, Australia's boundless hospitality. He thanked his old club, the Hampstead, by whom the banquet was given, for the introduction it had given him to first-class cricket, and he perorated by a very appreciative note of thanksgiving to the enterprise of the *Pall Mall [Gazette]* and the services they rendered to his team and the cricket-loving public at home. WG's speech was like his cricket, entirely devoid of all meretricious ornamentation. It was the man, and was effective just because it was guilelessly natural."

The Champion spoke of his past association with "Stoddy" in England and in Australia, and referred to the sensation the recent Test matches had created.

"Who else was present?" Holmes wrote in conclusion. "Well, I forget, or rather I saw only two persons out of the company of nearly 300, and their names were A.E.STODDART and W.G.GRACE. Other names I heard mentioned, or read them in the paper on Monday." There had been "a heartiness and spontaneity about the proceedings which those who were present are not likely to forget."

One lasting piece of imaginative verse ought forever to commemorate the man at the centre of The Greatest Test Series (greatest perhaps at least until the vacillating Ashes battle of 2005). This poignant verse appeared in *Melbourne Punch* magazine at the conclusion of the 1894-95 series. The twelfth line even gave this author a title for the 1970 [prototype] Stoddart biography:

> There went a tale to England,
> 'Twas of the Test Match won,
> And nobly had her cricketers
> That day their duty done.
>   They didn't fail like funkers,
>   They kept up England's tail,
>   They kept their pro's from off the booze

And knew they could not fail.

Then wrote the Queen of England,
Whose hand is blessed by God,
"I must do something handsome
For my dear victorious Stod.
   Let him return without delay
   And we will dub him pat -
   A baronet that he may be
   Sir Andrew Stoddart, Bat."

Another unsigned poetic tribute reached beyond the England skipper to acknowledge the efforts of a few other key players:

The Queen at Windsor heard the news,
And hied her straight to town.
"Make Stoddart Duke of Hampstead Heath,
A baronet of Brown,
   KCMGs for Lancashire,
   To show how proud we feel,
   Knight Richardson of Surrey side –
   Arise, Sir Robert Peel.
Of England's worthy sons today,
The bravest, boldest batch
Are Stoddart and his merry men,
Who won the Great Test Match.

CHAPTER 16

WG's Year

AND the score is running up as the rays are running down,
"Old Grace" is at one wicket, and "young Stoddart" at the other;
And they both have got their eyes in, and the bowlers are done
brown,
Grace has hit ten fours already, and by Jove, there goes another!

(E.J.Milliken)

The year of 1895 was the Year of Grace. The 47-year-old monarch of
cricket enjoyed a second wind which amounted to something of a whirlwind:
a thousand runs in May, his 100th century (an innings of 288 to make quite
sure before the champagne corks popped), nine hundreds and well over
2000 runs in a summer not without its damp pitches.

But it had its moments for "Stoddy" too as he left the excitement
and tension of the Australian tour behind. This year he was honoured
by having his life-size likeness installed in Madame Tussaud's waxworks
exhibition, a public drawcard situated not so far from where he lived. It
seemed natural that his effigy should be alongside his friend W.G.Grace's.

WG's formal assessment of his younger batting partner is of special
interest. Allowing that the Grand Old Man was a "singularly inarticulate
man", according to Arthur Porritt, who ghosted his autobiography, WG's
view of "Stoddy" seems not only to have been as well informed as anyone's
but supremely complimentary: "As a rugby three-quarter back he has never
been excelled; as a cricketer he is brilliant in all three departments . . . He
is a graceful, spirited and finished batsman, a rapid scorer under almost
any conditions. He always acknowledges – especially when his bowling is
being punished – that it is my 'fault' that he became a bowler, and I am not
disposed to resent the soft impeachment; indeed, I congratulate myself on
introducing so good a change bowler to the cricket field. His fielding is so

sure, and his picking up and return so clean and rapid, that a bowler has no anxiety when he sees a ball go in Mr Stoddart's direction."

Early in this 1895 season they opened together for the Gentlemen against Cambridge University, having travelled together by rail following the gala dinner in London. They raised 100 in an hour, Stoddart going on to 84. At Oxford, H.T.Hewett dealt out the punishment in company with "Stoddy". The hard-hitting Somerset left-hander made two speedy centuries that week.

England's finest two cricketers in wax effigy

So things initially were looking good for A.E.Stoddart. But it turned out to be a year of frustration. Time and again he appeared well set only to get out unexpectedly. He bowled a good deal, but without penetration, and each wicket for Middlesex cost him over 30. His followers needed to be patient and wait for the luck to run.

He had been out of form at net practice after the long sea voyage home, and withdrew from the MCC match against Yorkshire. Indeed most of the tourists suffered reaction and performed modestly for at least the first half of the season.

There had also been an unwelcome contretemps with Lord Sheffield, whose tour of Australia three years previously he had so enjoyed. Just before "Stoddy" left Australia after the most recent tour His Lordship had cabled him to ask if he would bring his English team to Sheffield Park to play the next Australian team when they toured England in 1896. Stoddart was not in a position to accept because he was unable to check on the long-term availability of Francis Ford, who was returning home late via Japan, Leslie Gay, who had gone to Ceylon, and Archie MacLaren, who had stayed on in Melbourne (probably to be with the girl of his dreams). Back home in England the triumphant (and ever-courteous) captain planned to call on

Lord Sheffield to explain the dilemma, but, as historian Roger Packham has discovered, His Lordship was so incensed that he terminated all friendly contact with Stoddart. "It was said that the sympathies of leading English cricketers were entirely with Stoddart who, they pointed out, was the last person to give offence." When Sheffield chose his team for his 1896 match against the Australians not one member of the 1894-95 touring team was invited to play.

The first match Middlesex ever played against Essex saw Stoddart bowled fourth ball by Walter Mead, but he made up for it in the last innings with a 67 that brought victory.

The next match went down boldly in the annals of cricket. Gloucestershire came up to Lord's on May 30 with WG needing 153 runs to become the first person ever to make a thousand runs in May. The Old Man won the toss and took advantage of a good-looking pitch upon which "Nipper" Nepean's spin troubled him most. He sweated through the crisis and settled down as the afternoon wore on. Hearne and Rawlin in particular were difficult to score from, but WG was watchful, taking every chance to drive and cut with that old authority. He was equally determined not to fall to his old friend "Stoddy" either.

His hundred came after three watchful hours, and the pressure was renewed as the four-figure prize drew nearer. At last, near the end of this long day, palpably fatigued, WG swept a long-hop away for his 1000th run, and the ever-attentive crowd stormed acclaim. The members stood as champagne was brought out to the middle.

It rained heavily that night, and Middlesex toppled twice for around 200, with Stoddart managing only a couple of runs each time. Gloucestershire then lost five men chasing the 43 for victory, but so long as the mighty Doctor waited in the pavilion there was little serious anxiety.

Like WG, Stoddart had a valuable propensity for high scoring in cricketers' benefit matches, and this time it was to Tom Mycroft's advantage. There had never been such a crowd at Lord's before on a Whit Monday – over 16,000 paid – and the Palairet brothers of Somerset captivated their audience with centuries. Middlesex, however, passed their total of 337. Stoddart needed only an hour to reach 50 and a further hour and a half to reach his century. Vernon Hill missed him twice at the Nursery end because, he claimed, ginger beer bottles were tossed at him. But finally the fans had to pencil reluctantly on their scorecards that Lionel Palairet had trapped Stoddart (150) leg-before, such a rare mode of dismissal in those days, when the ball needed to pitch between wicket and wicket for an lbw.

Somerset nearly made 300 again (Sammy Woods 109, in a purple patch) and Middlesex needed 259. Now the bowlers had their way. Stoddart was again in wonderful form, making 56 (once more lbw) but the innings subsided and it was only courageous tailend resistance that held Woods and Tyler at bay.

Middlesex 1895: - umpire Burton, J.E.West, J.T.Hearne, J.T.Rawlin, G.Thornton, umpire Tuck, umpire Draper; seated: M.E.Pavri, H.B.Hayman, A.J.Webbe (captain), A.E.Stoddart, T.C.O'Brien; front: G.MacGregor, R.S.Lucas

That Saturday, "Stoddy" was back at Hampstead, making 52 against Granville, who had the promising young spinner F.G.Bull (playing this season for Essex). In 1897 he would be in line for a place in Stoddart's team to tour Australia, but his days were played out in the leagues (his bowling action considered suspect), and in 1910 he was to become yet another of cricket's tragic figures. His body, weighted with stones, was washed ashore at St Anne's. (Only weeks prior to this, Arthur Woodcock, the Leicestershire fast bowler, had taken his own life with poison.)

The words of "An Old Cricketer" come back: "Uncertainty can be very depressing as well as glorious, and it makes men moody."

When Stoddart failed twice against Yorkshire on a crumbling Lord's surface, his admirer the Reverend R.S.Holmes perceived by way of his own analysis that he had "all too quickly gone into his shell again – that beastly Australian trip again I suppose". Not that the "beastly" tour had affected J.T.Brown: he hit 62 and 47.

But there were runs aplenty at Hove. He made a quickfire 41 before leaping out at his tour compatriot Dick Humphreys, the underhand bowler, and missing. O'Brien (202) and R.S.Lucas (185) went on to thrash the bowling of Alfred Shaw, Humphreys and others in a stand of 338 in 200 minutes, a display that would have dwarfed anything that modern Twenty/20 cricket might offer. On that peach of a pitch Newham, Brann, Bean and the new sensation K.S.Ranjitsinhji all made runs as the inevitable draw was registered.

Middlesex beat Kent by an innings at Tonbridge (AES 28), then I Zingari marked their jubilee with a match against the Gentlemen of England at Lord's later in June. Here Stoddart came good with a swashbuckling 92 in IZ's second innings, and the Gentlemen needed 172 to win. An hour and three-quarters later it was all over by ten wickets: WG 101 not out, Sellers 70 not out.

Middlesex resumed their quest for the Championship, with Surrey now the visitors (and in the course of winning their eighth title in nine years). Mighty Tom Richardson took 290 wickets this season, 10 of them in this match at Lord's, including Stoddart both times caught by Bobby Abel for 30-odd.

They beat Lancashire at Old Trafford, Stoddart going in lower down and making second-top score (33) of the match for his side, Hearne and Rawlin setting up victory with 17 wickets. And as July blossomed forth they took on Surrey again at The Oval. It was a match to be remembered. During its progress a simple but eloquent placard was set up by the entrance to Monument station:

MIDDLESEX v SURREY
STODDART

The crowds needed no urging. Over 25,000 paid to enter the friendly old ground for this battle of the Thames – this on a Monday, Tuesday and Wednesday. They were entertained royally.

A remarkable incident was the "stumping" of Stoddart at 25. Wicketkeeper Harry Wood clipped the stumps firmly and the umpire raised his finger. Then it was noticed that the bails had refused to budge, and the decision had to be reversed, allowing him to make another 50 runs.

The Gentlemen XI, Lord's 1895: back – G.J.Mordaunt, T.C.O'Brien, J.R.Mason, N.F.Druce; seated – E.Smith, G.MacGregor, W.G.Grace, J.A.Dixon, F.S.Jackson; front – A.E.Stoddart, C.B.Fry

In the second innings Stoddart and Hayman put on 67, and again there was an extraordinary escape by the senior man. "Surrey" Smith enticed him into playing a ball quite hard into the stumps, but the bails held fast, and "Stoddy" went on to 67 before Abel pocketed a lofted cover-drive. The declaration left Surrey 270 minutes to make 386, a task beyond most sides. At a final 303 for four, match honours eventually divided evenly.

The cream of cricket now assembled at Lord's on July 8, 1895 for the Gentlemen v Players match, the showpiece event of the summer. There had been what some chose to refer to as a long drought, and the pitch was fast and fiery, especially when Richardson and Mold set about the destruction of the amateurs after the Players had made 231.

W.G.Grace and A.E.Stoddart walked out at 5 o'clock, and for half-an-hour it was mainly The Champion who was hit about the arms, occasionally ducking with surprising agility. Gradually the runs came as the ball was hit up the slope and down the slope with increasing authority. The fifty came in even time, and at the end of a momentous afternoon the Gentlemen were 137 without loss, Dr W.G.Grace 64, Mr A.E.Stoddart 61.

Painting by Dickinson of the 1895 Gentlemen v Players grand match at Lord's: Albert Ward exchanges a pleasantry with his recent tour skipper Stoddart as W.G.Grace walks to the batting crease. J.T.Hearne and George Lohmann are the two other professionals depicted

The stand reached 151 before Stoddart, who had once driven Richardson into the pavilion, fell to him for 71. It had been a delectable innings: glorious strokeplay blended with judicious defence against as hostile an attack as any captain on earth could unleash.

WG moved on to 118, and O'Brien's 21 was the only other double-figure score apart from the 22 kicking, flashing byes. The Players, at one stage half out for 61, finally set the Gentlemen 336 to win. This time neither WG nor Stoddart was at ease, and the partnership broke up at 34. By 5.30pm the score stood at 231 for nine. Then Ernest Smith and newcomer C.B.Fry smashed 72 runs in 35 minutes before Fry was stumped for 60. It was a match to be revered for its colourfulness and its character.

Ranjitsinhji stroked a century at Lord's for Sussex and Fred Tate had a grand match: 10 wickets and a steady bat at the right time. His haul included Drewy Stoddart twice, something to celebrate while bouncing new-born son Maurice on his knee when he got home.

Archie MacLaren was in the spotlight at this moment after making 424 for Lancashire in a siege of Somerset at Taunton which triggered among the pile of telegrams one from WG which had been urging him to exceed his own 344, and another from "Stoddy" laying his 485 on the line. "Am speaking to everyone of my <u>friend</u> Archie," he wrote. "Well played, hope this will find you not out and going strong. Stoddart." When MacLaren was finally out, another wire went off from his recent England team-mate on the Australian tour: "Heartiest congratulations. Wish I had seen it. Must have been ripping. Was rather anxious about my record though. Stoddart."

So "Stoddy's" "second-class" record remained intact, for the moment at least, the highest innings of them all.

Rawlin and Hearne slaughtered Nottinghamshire on a dodgy Lord's pitch at the end of the week, then for a while the big action was done. As July drew to a close, Stoddart hit 62 not out for Hampstead after taking nine wickets. Then it was the western tour with Middlesex, and frustration from rain at Clifton and Taunton, where they may have been some private amusement as Sammy Woods "castled" his pal Stoddart for 38.

Woods' peculiar sense of humour was once demonstrated at dinner at Stoddart and MacGregor's shared digs at 30 Lithos Road, in Hampstead, when his first move upon entering the room was to switch off the light and chase his companions round and round in the near-darkness, over chairs and stools, and brandishing a carving-knife.

Grim times now befell "Stoddy" on the field. After top-score of 19 against Essex, he failed at Trent Bridge, where O'Brien's amazing century stole the show, and at Leeds he was "never less like his old self than when facing Hirst".

He took a compensatory century off Hampton Wick at Hampstead, but back at Lord's Middlesex were steamrollered by the high-riding MacLaren with the bat and Briggs and Mold bowling unchanged through both dreadful innings.

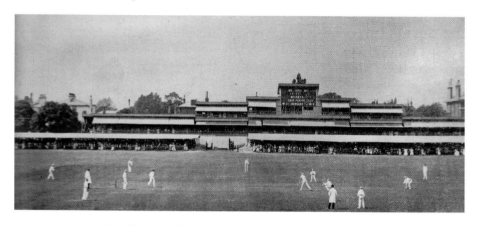

Lord's ground 1896 – before the developers got to it

So it came to the final county match of 1897, and Kent made 208 against a lively Jim Phillips who, abandoning his umpire's coat, had jumped down from the bench into the courtroom, so to speak, to lead the prosecution. This Australian who had recently been umpiring Ashes Tests in his homeland took 8 for 69 to allow Middlesex the best part of two hours' batting late on the first day, and MacGregor went in first wicket down and helped Stoddart put on 138. "Stoddy" was at his very best during this partnership of the flatmates. There was breath-taking power in his strokes, and the treatment dealt out to Bill Bradley, then a promising young fast bowler, might have broken a lesser man. Continually he forced good-length balls to the off boundary. His hundred came, and he went on crunching the bowling to all parts of the Lord's ground, now his own personal domain. At last the toiling Bradley earned some reward: a lusty hit ended in long-off's hands and the chanceless 131 was complete.

Middlesex made 412 and rolled Kent up a second time for 190.

On Lord's Ground, in the fading light,
I watched the leather's rapid flight,
And very pleasant was the sight
Of Stoddart scoring rapidly.

"Century"

He made a lot of runs at Hastings early in September, in front of large crowds: 68 and 71 for South against North, with a stand of 150 with WG in only two hours. (This was the eighth and final century stand for the first wicket between these two, and the third this season. Only elder brother E.M.Grace chalked up as many hundred opening partnerships with the Grand Old Man during WG's 44-year career.)

Then came the long-awaited contest between A.E.Stoddart's victorious Australian XI and the Rest of England, a match perhaps a shade irrelevant at this late date, but it did attract a capacity audience.

The touring team fell before Mold and Woods for 217, the captain holding the fort with 55. Then WG was bowled by Tom Richardson for a duck and the Rest were in bother until Walter Read and Woods hit 95 blistering runs. Stoddart's men eventually conceded a lead of just three runs on first innings.

Now Stoddart weathered another storm as his companions collapsed against Woods, Martin, Mold and Pougher. In 100 minutes the captain strung 10 fours together in a 59 that ended in bad light when Mold sent a stump cartwheeling.

Francis Ford and Lockwood swung the match on the final day. The outcome was a matter of some importance for all involved, and this stand of 169, unbroken and of "merciless severity", left the Rest to get 287 upon Stoddart's declaration.

Richardson and Peel, the outstanding bowlers during the Australian campaign, bowled unchanged and sent the Rest packing for 68. The fielding was superb and all the old tour spirit was there, the spirit which had swept them from Adelaide to Brisbane and back. In fact Stoddart's band, after their parlous posture of the previous evening, had, as somebody recorded, "finished up with a display of batting, bowling and fielding that made it easy to understand how harmoniously they had worked together and how they had won so many good matches in Australia".

Friendly gathering at the 1895 Hastings festival: G.F.Vernon, W.G.Grace, C.L.Townsend, A.E.Stoddart

A Mr Grace sent "Stoddy" some photographs taken during this match at Hastings in September 1895, and the cricketer duly replied by letter: "So very many thanks for the splendid photographs, it was awfully good of you to send them. They will just form a most charming finish to my scrap book of the Australian tour. I am certain Ford will be delighted to receive some, his address is the Old Rectory, Hatfield, Herts."

The rest of the letter is historically revealing: "I have decided not to go to South Africa thinking that after my glorious tour in Australia and the hard keen matches it might perhaps fall flat." That sounds logical enough. As for "glorious", this should surely be seen as acceptance of the general view, for "Stoddy" was nothing if not modest.

Another end-of-season letter took the form of a testimonial to batmakers Nicolls. He asked for two more Patent Number Ones, indicating preference for a bat of light weight. "I want 2 lb 3 or 4 oz." Either before or after this communication he allowed his name to be put on a Slazenger bat, which boasted "Superior cane and whalebone combination handle

– First Selection 15 shillings". Any suspicion that he was paid for this endorsement would have had the purists tut-tutting again.

Further precious photographs taken at Hastings by Mr Grace:

Tom Richardson, W.G.Grace, Stoddart, and umpire Bob Thoms

Bill Lockwood, MacLaren (on the ground), Stoddart, Francis Ford (on his captain's lap), and a thoughtful Bill Brockwell

More Hastings 1895 snapshots:

Hylton Philipson, "Stoddy" in an unguarded moment, and Archie MacLaren

Perhaps the most informal photo ever taken of Drewy Stoddart: MacLaren on the ground, Brockwell to the right

More conviviality at Hastings: Bill Lockwood, "Punch" Philipson, "Stoddy", Francis Ford, Billy Brockwell; in front: Archie MacLaren and Johnny Briggs

A bat signed by Stoddart fetched £2580 all in at a London auction in 2006, and another, darkened by the years and from oiling, inscribed "From A.E.Stoddart May 10th 1899", is in the author's collection. It has a long handle with a blade stamped with the maker's mark of Nicolls Patent Automatic Handle, and it sits well with a bronze paperweight cast in "Stoddy's" image from waist up, created in 1898 by Albert Gilbert ARA, whose major works included the world-famous Eros statue in Piccadilly Circus.

The 1895 season could hardly have ended on a more satisfactory note. "Stoddy's" personal output was 1622 first-class runs at 37.3. His bowling had often been clouted,

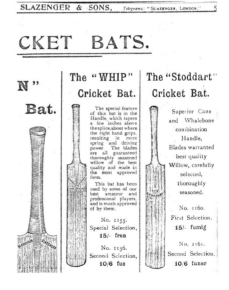

One of several Stoddart bat endorsements

which fact seems not to have worried him. He never did consider himself seriously to be an allrounder. It was WG, he was known to say, who encouraged him as a bowler.

Seldom now did the crowds see him drop gracefully onto one knee to field the ball at mid-off and in the deep. He had developed a liking in Australia for fielding at slip, and now functioned there most of the time.

Thus an exciting summer receded into the mists of time, to be written about for ever afterwards, most of the pages embossed with the great bearded figure from Gloucestershire.

Stoddart paperweight
by Albert Gilbert

CHAPTER 17

◆◆◆

Shamateur?

HAMPSTEAD saw little of her champion during the busy 1896 summer. He batted only twice for them and took 122 off Teddington and four off Stoics, whose relief must have been evident following his five wickets, all bowled. The annual dinner was, as always, a splendid affair: numerous lush courses, witty speeches, and music, often from the charming Kennerley Rumford, former school friend of "Stoddy's" and husband-to-be of the celebrated Clara Butt and a pop star of the day who sang for the Queen at Balmoral.

Harry Trott's Australians of 1896 were greeted by Stoddart and a welcoming party upon their arrival in England. They set up headquarters at The Cricketers pub in Mitcham, and in the bitter April air the practice nets were rigged up on the Green and a cluster of curious mortals edged eagerly forward to identify the "Cornstalks".

Ernie Jones, the Merv Hughes of his day, although bowling within himself, was obviously going to activate many balls and bowels before the summer's end, and Tom McKibbin moved the ball a lot on the admittedly imperfect surface. Another who caught the eye was the giant Tasmanian barrister Charles Eady.

The month of May brought

Kennerley Rumford; school friend and crooner

forth unexpected joy for Stoddart this year. For MCC against Lancashire he and de Trafford made a dashing 103 at Lord's, Stoddart striking a memorable blow off Willis Cuttell that came to rest among the critics in the holiness of the pavilion.

Against an Oxford University side containing three future England captains, he followed his 51 with 5 for 38 and caused one reporter to dwell mistily on the thought that he was "a much better bowler than he himself seems to think".

This was a purple period for him. Yorkshire came to Lord's and toiled a long time before the spectacular Stoddart-Hayman first-wicket stand was broken at 218, the batsmen reaching centuries within minutes of each other. Cricket reflected on how "correct, powerful and attractive" AES's batting was.

Middlesex actually lost that match because Jack Brown hammered a double-century, and after rain Bobby Peel mopped up the Middlesex wickets. Brown and Tunnicliffe then belted the 146 runs required in a mere 80 minutes.

But A.E.Stoddart was in top gear too, and when Somerset came up to Lord's he made another hundred. It was "Turkey" Rawlin's benefit match, and 17,000 people crammed into Lord's on Whit Monday to see the local pride play a textbook 121. He jumped out at Tyler's slows and hit him hard along the ground; he cut tearaway Woods cleanly and probably exchanged a joke or two with his old rugby colleague; he stroked to leg in a manner that had the throng cooing and made such an impression on little Billy White that, as Pensioner William H.White, he was to find some joy seventy years later in reliving those strokes one morning as the same old sun shone down on Chelsea Hospital for Pensioners. It had been the only time he ever saw "Stoddy". For a schoolboy the choice had been astute.

Stoddart, having stroked 84 and taken seven wickets in MCC's two-day match against Royal Artillery at the start of the month, walked into Lord's again later that week for Middlesex's match against Nottinghamshire. It needed an exceptional delivery to dismiss him at this point, and Dick Attewell produced it, surprising him at 16 with a ball that shot as he played back. Middlesex continued their triumphant passage with another win after rain, Hearne and Rawlin taking 19 of the wickets.

Then on June 11, for MCC against the Australians, he took part in another match earmarked for all-time notoriety. The pitch was difficult, and

WG soon departed, followed by the rising star K.S.Ranjitsinhji. Stoddart and F.S.Jackson then demonstrated how to bat on a dodgy pitch, resisting all the wiles of Trumble and Giffen and the unpredictable movement of McKibbin. "Stoddy" smashed one ball into the Tavern assembly: as always there was the problem of applauding with one hand gripping a glass of beer.

Finally he ran out at Trott and missed. Jim Kelly took the bails off, but to everyone's astonishment umpire W.A.J.West, perhaps enjoying the batsmanship, gave it not out. Ever-decent, Stoddart stepped out to the next ball and kept walking to the pavilion. His 54 was top score in MCC's 219.

J.T.Hearne began the bowling from the pavilion end. The first nail was driven in early when a ball kept low and sped through Harry Graham (4). Harry Trott made 6 before Hearne bowled him too, and on that sporty pitch Jim Kelly (8) was the only other Australian to break his duck. He had opened the innings with Graham, and the remaining eight Australians all registered ducks, with Darling remaining not out and Giffen "absent ill" - although "A Country Vicar" simply believed that he refused to bat on such a spiteful pitch.

Jack Hearne had 4 for 4, but the really dramatic figures belonged to "Dick" Pougher [pron. Puffer], the Leicestershire fast-medium bowler who was on MCC's ground staff. After Kelly had thumped Attewell for four WG immediately replaced him with the droopy-eyed Pougher, whose ears were as prominent as Charlie Turner's and moustache as flowing as any of his generation. He bowled a wicked breakback on any helpful pitch, and here he instantly held a smart return catch off Kelly. With his next ball he bowled a bewildered Clem Hill.

Hearne bowled Iredale, then Pougher, whose second over had been a maiden, forced Trumble to play on. The next ball skittled the giant Eady, and for the hat-trick he had McKibbin caught at mid-on.

Australians all out 18, the last six wickets falling for nothing. Sweet revenge, some thought, for Spofforth's and Boyle's carnage in 1878 when MCC fell for 19. Pougher had 5 for 0 off three overs, Hearne 4 for 4, with better to come.

The follow-on innings was almost as disastrous as the first. The sixth wicket fell at 33, giving Hearne 6 for 15 to date. The surfeited bowler then missed Giffen at slip, and on an improving pitch the score climbed out of the rubble to 62 before Gregory was out. Eady and Darling then added over 100 runs. Hearne got Eady at last and had Darling caught off a skyer by Stoddart at third man for a skilful 76. Australians, second innings, 183; Hearne all nine wickets (Giffen absent again) for 73 off 50 overs. He would be back at their throats in a few days, during the first Test match.

For the time being John Thomas Hearne had his 100th wicket of the season on June 12, a breath-taking performance. There was to be another hat-trick next month, and 257 wickets in all this season.

All was now set for the first Test match of the 1896 series, starting at Lord's on June 22, a Monday. Only WG and Giffen remained from those who had played in the historic 1882 Ashes Test, and new faces were now plentiful: Jim Kelly, Charles Eady and Clem Hill were appearing for Australia for the first time, and for England, Tom Hayward, "Dick" Lilley and Jack Hearne all made their debuts.

The conspicuous omission was K.S.Ranjitsinhji, considered by the MCC authorities as "unqualified". Such sentiments were not to inhibit the Lancashire committee for the second Test match, when Harry Trott also generously welcomed his selection.

THE NEXT AUSTRALIAN ELEVEN.
THE NEW BOYS.

The next Australian generation. "And we have to play these little boys?" says W.G.Grace. "Don't make any mistake," warns Stoddart. "I've played against them."

Lord's creaked with a full house of 30,000, some encroaching upon the playing area, some exhibiting a rowdiness that would have reminded Stoddart of some of the Australian audiences which had upset him. Many of them saw hardly any of the play that day, so dense was the hedge of straw boaters and caps, peppered with solemn bobbies casting a steadying eye.

Tom Richardson bowled with the pavilion behind him, then WG tossed the ball to George Lohmann, who bowled an immaculate maiden. In the fourth over Harry Donnan was run out.

The crowd were still buzzing when Giffen edged his first ball low to Lilley. Australia two down for three, captain Harry Trott in to repair the damage. At the other end Darling took a single, and Trott, still scoreless after a troublesome time against Lohmann, lost sight of the ball and was bowled by Richardson. He later condemned the absence of a sightscreen, the background of members in their dark suits having rendered the ball almost invisible.

With Trott gone the innings hung sickeningly at 4 for three wickets. The slaughter abated temporarily as the score drifted slowly to 26. England's mighty captain had a word with Richardson, and the field settled: Lilley standing back, Abel, Lohmann and Stoddart closely grouped in the slips. Richardson bowled a very fast delivery to Syd Gregory, and the wicket was shattered. Then Harry Graham went first ball: Australia half out already for 26.

Minutes later Hill played back to Lohmann and helped the ball into his stumps, and Eady strode out to assist the doughty Darling – who fell at last, bowled by Richardson for 22 made in nearly an hour. Trumble and Kelly went too, and Richardson let Ernie Jones have a shortish ball that kept low and hit the stumps, giving him 6 for 39 off 11.3 overs, all his victims bowled. "We'd better pack up our traps and go home, boys," Giffen gloomily and part-jocularly told his team.

W.G.Grace and A.E.Stoddart set about responding to Australia's miserable offering of 53. The members were startled by Ernie Jones's first delivery. Surely the man was throwing? The alarm receded as WG placed a short one through slip for two, and then a bye brought Stoddart to face the muscular miner from South Australia. He bustled in with the pavilion behind him, the same backdrop for Richardson's destruction earlier in the day. "Stoddy" took a four and a two through the slips, and although discomfort was in the air, Australia's pathetic total was already on the way to being overtaken.

Jones hurled a yorker at Stoddart, and as the bat fell hurriedly down on the ball somebody relieved the taut atmosphere by calling out: "Another minute and he'd have been too late!"

Now, when Donnan's hand was damaged, who should come out as substitute but Albert Trott, who had been overlooked when the touring team was chosen. It was a classic irony.

After lunch Eady bowled a shooter at Stoddart. Playing back, he almost clamped down on it, but it was through and he was gone for 17: England 38 for one.

Bobby Abel found Jones problematic. Balls which came up to WG's armpit were flashing past Abel's nose. It seemed certain that England would soon be two down. But the little Surrey man held on.

Australia's score was doubled, almost trebled, before WG skyed Giffen after batting for two hours for 66, passing 1000 runs in Tests and setting his side well along the road to victory. Jack Brown made two agreeable hits before Jones got a fiery delivery through and England were 152 for three. Little Abel consolidated with lofty Gunn. Then F.S.Jackson came in to force the bowling military fashion. And Abel, though taking a bruising from Eady, batted on gamely, lamely.

Nearing 6 o'clock England's lead reached 200, and Abel's hard-earned century neared. But the courageous little man hit over a ball from Eady when 94, leaving Surrey team-mate Tom Hayward to commence his Test career.

Stanley Jackson now lofted Giffen into the deep, where Darling was impeded by some of the spectators on the grass. The batsman was aware of what had happened, and deliberately hit the next ball in the same direction, where Darling this time held the catch, a "pretty piece of quixotism" as Percy Cross Standing saw it, although Wilfred Rhodes has insisted that "Jacker" was never so misguided as to throw his wicket away in a Test match.

Dick Lilley became another "first-baller", and Lohmann lashed out unsuccessfully so that England rested at 286 for eight.

A "more gentlemanly company" of 15,000 filed through the gates at Lord's next morning and saw England quickly dispatched. In Australia's second innings, with great suddenness, Joe Darling's middle stump was plucked out without a run posted.

Richardson soon had another wicket, his 50th in only seven Tests, as Eady touched one through to Lilley. Australia again were two down for three. Giffen and Trott set about clearing up the mess. The captain was troubled but Giffen's form was excellent. He escaped a chance to Lohmann, but the fifty came up rapidly as Trott made four, four and three edgily to leg off Richardson, who eventually split the pair at 62, touching Giffen's off stump.

"Tich" Gregory bravely attacked Richardson, and the hundred came after only an hour and a quarter, the same time-span of the previous day when they had been entirely dismissed for 53.

Rather belatedly Hearne was called back and the scoring rate slumped against his accurate, well-concealed variations. Then the umpires had a controversy on their hands when Trott edged to Hayward and the close fieldsmen were amazed to find the appeal rejected.

England XI at Lord's, 1896, and every one of them a household name: Standing – Dick Lilley, J.T.Hearne, William Gunn, Tom Hayward; Seated – Tom Richardson, F.S.Jackson, W.G.Grace, George Lohmann, A.E.Stoddart; front – J.T.Brown, Bobby Abel

The bowling was changed, the runs continued to come, and at lunch the Australians were a resolute 152 for three wickets.

The 200 came in 150 minutes, and WG was taking the spasmodic tug at his beard and pondering on which bowler to use next. There was criticism of his failure to use Stoddart.

Trott on 99 saw Lilley drop him, and soon he was scurrying for a 100th run that had scarcely been there. G.H.S.Trott, captain of Australia, had made a duck and a century in a Lord's Test.

Syd Gregory wiped off the arrears, and finally cut to the ropes to bring up his own hundred.

Soon Trott was in trouble again as Stoddart threw a sharp return to Lilley. The 'keeper fumbled and all was well – until Lohmann caught a low-flying snick from Gregory.

Gregory and Trott had put on 221 in 161 minutes, the highest stand for any wicket by either side to date, and a fourth-wicket Test record until Bradman and Ponsford compiled 388 together at Headingley in 1934.

Australia were now in with a chance. But Trott now hit out at Richardson, and Hayward this time took a legitimate catch at deep mid-off. His 143 had taken him 3½ hours, and now the tail needed to wag with all the lustiness of a King Red.

Clem Hill, 19, fresh-faced, was furious at being bowled off his legs for five. Harry Graham was yorked by Richardson. It was left to Trumble and Kelly to resist and defy for 20 minutes while only four runs accrued. (These two outstanding cricketers had been born in the same month and were to die within hours of each other in the Australian spring of 1938.)

Lilley accounted for Trumble and Ernie Jones was caught in the deep, where a fast bowler ought to be caught. The lead was only 79 when Donnan came in last, hand bandaged, to add 29 with Kelly. Australia's five-hour innings of 347 ended on the stroke of six, leaving England 109 to win. By the close they were 16 for the loss of Abel in poor light against Jones at his fastest.

The sound of rain on the rooftops must have interested the Australians that night and inflicted some anxiety into English hearts as it persisted during the morning. It let up at 11.45 and the burly umpires Phillips and West announced a noon start. WG ordered ten minutes of the heavy roller, and everybody sat back expectantly.

The pitch was hard underneath, but the soft top caused the ball to kick, and Ernie Jones thundered in and enjoyed himself with several bumpers that whistled clean over the batsmen's heads. In seven tense overs WG and Hayward advanced England's score by four runs.

That was as far as they went for the moment: W.G.Grace was taken by Hill off bat and pad and showed great surprise at the decision, and with two good wickets taken the Australians sensed a chance of pulling it off.

Brown strode out and narrowly escaped injury as Jones greeted him with a hot blast. Four leg-byes helped the cause, and then the Yorkshire terrier on-drove a four. Another virile hit almost had him caught, then another drive found the boundary.

The run rate eased off. The field tightened around Hayward and Brown. The pitch was worsening, and with only 26 made in three-quarters of an hour and the sky dark, it became a matter of whether the runs could be got in time – if they were to be got at all.

"Stod": stroked winning runs at Lord's

Jones forsook his lethal short stuff for a while and flung a fast one through Hayward's defences, leaving England 42 for three, 67 still required. A.E.Stoddart walked to the crease.

For a time he was subdued, leaving the runmaking to Brown, whose vision was now adjusted. "Stoddy" was shaping queerly at Jones and Trumble, but he got one away nicely to the leg boundary to raise England's fifty. Then fortune smiled : wicketkeeper Kelly missed him.

Brown was leaving the short flyers alone but taking full toll of the driveable deliveries, while Stoddart, reprieved yet again, at slip by substitute Iredale, hooked Jones twice for four, once magnificently off his face.

At last Kelly caught Brown for a 36 which he actually regarded as his finest innings in view of the conditions, and no less satisfying than his famous

Melbourne 1895 effort. Four down for 82, and the extra-tall Billy Gunn in.

Stoddart now played some beautiful cricket. He ran four to leg and cut Giffen exquisitely to the boundary. Gunn twice drove Trumble for four, and suddenly all the English apprehension seemed laughable. Harry Trott stepped out his run, came in and bowled, and Stoddart cut his first ball for four to win the match. Moments after the cheers had gone up, a deluge was sweeping across the ground.

It was to be a further 38 years before the crowds could assemble again before the pavilion to applaud an England victory over Australia at Lord's – and then a further 75 years before the next Ashes victory at "the Home of Cricket" was witnessed.

The scoresheet at The Oval next match bore a sad double entry for Stoddart's fans:

Mr A.E.Stoddart   b.Hayward   4   b.Richardson   5

However, at Old Trafford, a happy ground for him, he returned to the headlines with a superlative 78 and 109 against Briggs and Mold as Middlesex recorded a palpitating victory.

With a few days now at his disposal he watched the Varsity match at Lord's, where WG's son was opening for Cambridge. A match immortalised by E.B.Shine's deliberate no-balls to the boundary (to eliminate the compulsory follow-on) also had a poignant human touch. WG junior was out twice for nought and his illustrious father took it badly.

WG, not usually a fastidious dresser, was decked out in a new grey frock-coat and tall hat. Stoddart was sitting with Billy Murdoch and George Brann at a table in the pavilion when the Doctor entered. With mock gravity "Stoddy" received him: "Pardon me, would you tell me whom I have the honour of addressing?"

"Ah, you old rogue!" WG retorted gleefully as they all made for the refreshment room. "There will be one or two here that I shan't be knowing later on." It seems probable that at this point his son had still to bat a second time.

After a fishing holiday ("he thinks that even in cricket one can have too much of a good thing") Stoddart's next cricket was the Gentlemen v Players match at Lord's, then more important to some than even the

Ashes Test match. One of the greatest amateur batting line-ups set about dismembering the bowling combine of Briggs, Lohmann, Hearne and Richardson. The amateurs' batting line-up was attractive enough to drag businessmen from their offices and schoolboys to their grandmothers' funerals: W.G.Grace, A.E.Stoddart, K.S.Ranjitsinhji, L.C.H.Palairet, F.S.Jackson, A.C.MacLaren, T.C.O'Brien, S.M.J.Woods, A.O.Jones, E.Smith, G.MacGregor.

Stoddart was not seen at his best this time, and when the England team for the second Test, at Old Trafford, was discussed some felt that he might no longer be worth a place automatically. But the Lancashire committee wanted him. They also invited Ranjitsinhji, whom they considered a drawcard, and their own Briggs and MacLaren. The Australians, strengthening as the summer advanced, went quietly about the task of levelling the series.

Harry Trott won the toss again on a gloriously sunlit day, and Frank Iredale put Tom Richardson away for four between slips fieldsmen "Stoddy" and Ranji first ball of the match; three to leg, and four to open Joe Darling's score, and the first over had produced 11 runs. The Australians were probably unaware that only a fortnight earlier Richardson had taken seven wickets in seven balls playing for Andover against Basingstoke.

The total soon ran up to 41. Then Dick Lilley pouched Darling, and Giffen almost lost his wicket trying to make his first run. The hundred blossomed in a mere 80 minutes, and WG stepped in to quieten things down with his cunning. But at lunch Australia were 130 for only one wicket.

Immediately after the interval Giffen fell to a return catch to Richardson for 80, and with Trott in, Iredale sailed elegantly on. F.S.Jackson was called back into the attack, and Stoddart himself bowled tightly – six overs for nine runs – his first Test match bowling in England. Iredale hit away a full-toss from him to raise his hundred, but Briggs got him for 108. Gregory came in and added 52 with Trott before WG's bizarre tactics paid off: Lilley removed his pads and bowled. Soon Trott, lunging at a wide one, edged to Brown, who shouted exultantly as Lilley took his one and only Test wicket. WG thanked his 'keeper and told him to put his pads back on.

Now Gregory tried to smack Briggs to leg and Stoddart at slip held the edge: 294 for five. England had more success when Richardson yorked Donnan, and Hill was caught for nine. The last three wickets then added 87 invaluable runs, and at the day's end Australia rested in comfort on 366 for eight, with England's fielding display being roundly condemned.

　　Australia's total was finally raised to 412. Then the old firm of Grace and Stoddart embarked on the reply. "Stoddy" faced Ernie Jones (who was not completely fit) and played out a maiden. In a flash of inspiration Harry Trott took the second over himself and tossed up some teasing leg-breaks. WG stumbled as one ball spun away, and Jim Kelly stumped him. A few overs later Stoddart (15) was also stumped, though it was a near thing. Both opening batsmen stumped in a Test innings also seems a rare thing.

　　Ranjitsinhji and Abel had 90 up by lunch after an hour of pure charm from the Indian, but soon afterwards Abel was caught off McKibbin. And although Ranji had a word with the umpire when Trott clutched a catch at point, he too had to go. Australia were on top again: more so still when F.S.Jackson was run out and MacLaren fell to a juggling catch by Trumble before scoring in his first home Test match: England 140 for six.

K.S.Ranjitsinhji: glorious Test debut

　　With Jones now out of action, Trumble, Giffen and McKibbin carried the attack, and wickets continued to tumble. Only when Hearne and Lilley linked forces did a real resistance materialise. The wicketkeeper, with a beautiful 65 not out, made up for his first visit to the Test crease at

Lord's a month previously, which had taken only a few seconds. Richardson brought further support, but England finally managed only 231 and had to follow on.

WG failed a second time, and Ranjitsinhji came now to play one of the finest innings imaginable. Stoddart was also looking good at this stage, hitting Jones freely, stroking all the bowling with ease. Yet every ball carried a hazard, a risk that the graceful hook might misfire and go to hand, or Ranji's favoured leg glance, newest and most pleasing of strokes, might somehow fail.

Bat met ball faithfully and powerfully. For forty bewitching minutes Stoddart and Ranji kept the scorers' pens scratching busily. Then, with England's total 76 and his own score 41, Stoddart was bowled off stump by McKibbin. Had it but been known, this was to be the final time he would leave the batting crease in a Test match in England. There was to be no farewell tour, no fanfares and eye-misting consequences. His home crowd were simply to be denied the chance of showing their appreciation.

Abel made 13, and Jackson (1) became Giffen's 100th Test wicket. So England were listing badly by the Friday evening.

Manchester's sky was grey and bulbous on the Saturday, and only 5000 people considered it worthwhile witnessing the coup de grace as Ranji and Jack Brown set out to ward off an Australian attack which had not conceded a century so far in their twenty matches. Now Brown became another disappointed candidate as Iredale held him at slip off Jones.

Little Ranji's masterly fifty came after some watchful batting punctuated by some inimitably daring strokes, and MacLaren held on while almost 50 runs were added. Ranji tamed Jones with hooks and wristy drives, and onlookers yearned for some solid authority to support him, from, say, a Gunn or a Hayward. Then there might have been no telling . . . .

Trumble lured a fragile MacLaren into hitting too soon, with England still two runs behind on aggregate, while Ranji continued on his lucid way, flicking to long leg, snappily cutting the fast-rising ball with computer precision. Fifty-three runs were made before Australia's leader, Harry Trott, held Lilley at the second attempt.

Johnny Briggs stood guard as Ranji continued his life-saving epic, and the score reached 268 before the popular Lancashire cricketer was stumped. Ranji was now into the 120s, and England would have a chance if only somebody would stay with him. Hearne did his best. The 300 came up, but he and Richardson were flushed out and England had to settle for 305. Ranjitsinhji was left with a famous 154, the only visible sign of his battle royal being a trickle of blood from his ear-lobe where an Ernie Jones bouncer had eluded his magical bat.

Australia required only 125 to level the series.

After an hour the innings was not proceeding very well at all. Richardson, in a fabulous bowling performance equal in terms of heroism to Ranji's superlative innings, bowled Iredale and forced fatal edges from Giffen, Trott and Darling. Australia four down for 45: 80 still wanted.

Jack Hearne at one stage had bowled 11 overs for four runs, while Richardson continued to thunder in like a man inspired. As Briggs replaced Hearne and strove to keep the tide moving against Trott's men, Richardson sweated and strained on and on, ignoring the protest in his muscles. At 79, Ranji held Gregory at short leg, and at 95 Donnan became Richardson's fifth wicket. The hundred came up almost by way of apology, and Richardson struck once again, Hill giving Lilley another catch: 25 to win and three second-class wickets to fall. Harry Trott, nerves in tatters, went off in a hansom cab.

Trumble and Kelly took a whole hour to make those 25 runs. The moment of destiny came when Kelly edged to his opposite number. Poor Lilley caught the ball, but the jarring of forearm against knee sent it toppling to earth, an unhappy phenomenon which he was to omit from his autobiography.

And so, just before 6pm, the players ran to the pavilion, the series levelled by virtue of Australia's first Test victory in the Old Country for eight years. It was no great way for W.G.Grace to celebrate his 48th birthday.

Tom Richardson lifted his pint with slightly trembling hand, scarcely able to believe that his three-hour effort had failed. Figures for once have a value: he bowled 554 balls in the match (including one wide: did the aching muscles get a word in there?) and his reward was 13 wickets for 244 runs. Cardus, who was eight years old at the time and unlikely to have been at Old Trafford, visualised Tom standing in the middle after the match had been lost, bewildered and numb with exhaustion, and needing to be led off. Another account suggested that the Surrey colossus was the first into a pint.

It seems true, however, that he was never again *quite* able to maintain such prolonged hostility, and it was thought that only an exceptional financial lure secured his services for the next tour that Stoddart led through the hot and humid cricket centres of Australia just over a year later.

The hero with black ringlets, born in a gipsy caravan in Byfleet, the honest fast bowler who had stolen much of Australia's glory in victory in Manchester, Richardson was at Lord's two days later for another important match: the return between Surrey and Middlesex. Surrey ran up 300, and the man who took the bowling figures was Drewy Stoddart. In 25 overs he bagged Abel, Holland, Hayward, Lockwood and G.O.Smith, and he caught Walter Read. But his 5 for 78 wasn't followed up.

His 4 and 5 at The Oval were now weirdly followed by 7 and 8 at Lord's. Middlesex fell for 159 (Richardson, refreshed, 5 for 82) and had to follow on. This time it was even worse: 83 all out, the damage again inflicted by Tom Richardson with 5 for 37, bowling unchanged with Bobby Abel of all people (4 for 36), and finishing the local derby on the second day.

Stoddart now captained MCC and top-scored with 61 as they almost doubled the score of the Australians. His opening stand of 96 with MacLaren greatly pleased the crowd. Clem Hill came good in the visitors' second innings, when a slow rearguard action drew derisive chants from the audience. "Stoddy" gave William Gunn a bowl and the enterprise paid off with three wickets, but only a draw could result at that late hour. Nevertheless there was another smooth innings (59) from MCC's skipper as they ran to 99 for three at the close. He caned Jones with fierce cuts, slashing off-drives and (in one over) a "clinking pair of fours". He also held four catches in the match.

The Times remarked this year, when he was thirty-three, that Stoddart had developed even more strokes recently and was no longer predominantly a driver.

Hearne and Rawlin administered a thrashing to Sussex at Hove, where Stoddart, opening with Plum Warner and making 20 before his young partner had scored, found runs easy to come by. And he continued to add catches to an impressive bag.

As July drew to a close the Australians went to Bexhill-on-Sea to play Earl de la Warr's XI, a fixture "Stoddy" had scribbled expectantly into the rear of his *Wisden*. The mighty Hearne and Pougher were the scourge of the Australians again, chopping them down for 80 and 138, and the Earl's champions won by four wickets, Stoddart having topped the lean innings with 26. It seems that the visitors cared little about losing this one.

At Taunton, returning to county cricket, Stoddart was caught twice by his rugby pal Sammy Woods, while a few miles away W.G.Grace was making a triple-century against Sussex at Bristol.

But the Grand Old Man was unable to reach double figures when Middlesex dropped in later in the week. Stoddart made 48 and 2. He was due for another substantial score, and The Oval might reasonably have first expected it as the third and final Test match rolled around on this busy calendar. Although a number of critics, both armchair and professional, were attracted by some of the newer names which cried for attention with some high scores during these warm weeks, the selectors chose Stoddart, and the [imaginary] photographer evocatively did his stuff:

> Sit in the middle, Mr Grace,
> For you're the captain bold,
> The Doctor made a funny face,
> And did as he was told.
>   And Mr Jackson by his side,
>   Yes, you can hold the ball;
>   No! Mr Ranji, not the pads,
>   That will not do at all.
> Now Richardson can stand behind,
> And also J.T.Hearne,
> And Captain Wynyard, here Sir, please.
> And do not look so stern.
>   Yes Mr Stoddart, on the ground,
>   That's where you'd like to sit,
>   And Mr Ranji, if he likes,
>   It matters not one bit.
> And now we want two more to stand,
> For two alone look silly,
> So Peel can stand by Richardson,
> And next to Hearne – yes, Lilley.
>   Ah! This part will not do, I see
>   That place looks very bare,
>   Abel and Hayward you can come,

And put yourselves just there.
That will do nicely, gentlemen,
And are you all quite ready?
I'm going to take the cap off now,
So keep your faces steady.
  Yes, thank you, Sirs, that's very nice,
  Ah! Hearne, I saw you smile,
  Do try to keep your countenance,
  Just for a little while.
First one and then the other laughs,
There's always one mishap,
And Mr Stoddart drops his pipe
Just as I lift the cap.
  I think I have you all at last,
  So please look at your best;
  But Abel, turn your head this way,
  And never mind the rest.
One minute now, while I count three,
Then you can have some fun,
And laugh and talk just as you please,
For this job will be done.

"Century"

A shock-wave reverberated when Stoddart withdrew from this Test match at The Oval just before the start, igniting wild speculation around the ground. England were to win a damp contest following a professionals' revolt before this match began. Many of the paid men felt they were underpaid while the so-called amateurs (W.G.Grace the most obvious) were being paid laughably high "expenses". Surrey players Abel, Hayward and Richardson eventually agreed to play now for the £10 originally offered, and for the glory of retaining the Ashes. The other Surrey man, the great George Lohmann, remained unshiftable and never played for England again, having taken 112 wickets at 10.75 in 18 Tests. William Gunn too refused to play, although this would not be the end of his Test career.

Why, then, had Mr A.E.Stoddart pulled out? Archie MacLaren, writing in *The Cricketer* in 1921, stated that he had withdrawn because of the surplus of invited players and so that he (MacLaren) might play. It had been reported that Stoddart was suffering from a cold, a very heavy one which was still in evidence a week after the Test match. Alternatively or additionally, he may have had some sympathy for the protesting professionals who were threatening to strike over pay. There can be no arguing against the fact that he felt affronted by the hints of underhand payments.

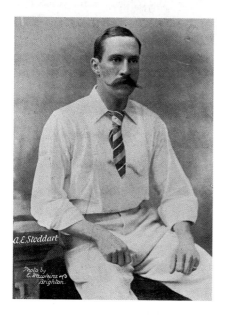

A.E.Stoddart: mystery withdrawal

E.G.Wynyard, who seems to have been the beneficiary of the dispute, coming in for a Test debut, claimed years later that WG had told his batsmen that he wanted them out in half-an-hour on the final morning: "I must be bowling at them [Australia] by 12.30 at the latest." Stoddart (not playing, of course) protested, according to Wynyard, although in vain: "You can't do that, Doctor, you want every single run you can get," said the man who had withdrawn emotionally from the Test match but apparently stayed to watch play.

By far the most likely reason for his withdrawal was the recently published suggestion that he was being paid far more than simply expenses by the Oval authorities. This had a disturbing echo of the insinuations of the rugby tour eight years previously. *The Morning Leader* had run a rather bitter, facetious sketch of him, with scathing criticism of his alleged back-handers.

The same "Rover" [Alfred Gibson] was referring to him a few weeks later in saccharine prose (completely misplaced as far as his name went) as "Andy" when he scored 127 against Kent. "Rover" was later to claim that when pressed on the matter of why he withdrew from the 1896 Oval Test match, Stoddart had snarled, "Archie [MacLaren] needed the money." He certainly wasn't the snarling type. But the thread of the story touches credibility.

Midst a storm of correspondence, "Stoddy's" fellow amateur

W.G.Grace had the Oval authorities issue a statement clarifying his expenses, and eventually decided to play. Not so Mr A.E.Stoddart, who would never play another international on his native soil. It was a deeply poignant way for such a wonderful career to end.

The dreaded Arthur Mold got him twice for miserable scores in the following county match, but at Bradford his finest talent shone again as he and James Douglas began the contest with 178 for the first wicket against a very strong Yorkshire attack. "Stoddy" just failed to make a hundred before lunch – or at all when Wainwright had him caught for 94.

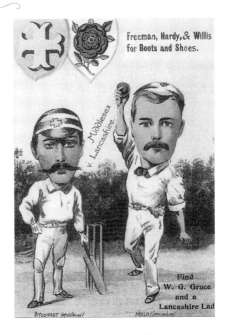

Stoddart and Mold on an advertisement postcard: were they paid?

The pair did it again at Trent Bridge: "Middlesex 132 for nought" was the lunchtime score which excited readers of the early edition. At 158 the first wicket fell: again it was A.E.Stoddart and again he was deprived of his century: b. Attewell 93. On the third day he made 41, but no-one scanning the sports pages really cared, for Gloucestershire were being annihilated for 17 by Trumble and McKibbin, and Ranji was stroking two centuries in one day for Sussex against Yorkshire.

Back at Lord's, A.E.Stoddart's home with its celestial sitting-room hung with portraits and its garden of green stretching down to the Nursery, he made only six against Sussex, and on Thursday he walked into the garden again, only to be dismissed from the sunlight by Martin of Kent without scoring. He did hold an astounding catch to get rid of Jack Mason, holding the ball at the third attempt despite colliding with the hefty Rawlin, and he hit with some force in the second innings. Once again he and Douglas were on the rampage, and for the third time in a fortnight they had 150 up. This time "Stoddy" got his hundred, an innings that had the journalists wallowing in nostalgia. This was their Stoddart of old, the man who could deaden the dangerous ball with masterly ease and stroke it along the turf and wide of helpless fieldsmen who could only wait for the young spectators to toss the ball back for some more.

He was caught late in the day by 'keeper Huish, and when Plum Warner offered congratulations he received encouragement in return: "Thank you so much. If you play as you did tonight you'll get a hundred, too, tomorrow."

This was Stoddart's fourth century for the county this summer, and there were the two nineties besides, all taken off powerful attacks. But although he had made 1100 runs for Middlesex, it was equally a story of what might have been. The representative matches have always mattered that little bit more, and in the ultimate of fixtures – England v Australia, with all to play for – he had not quite made it. These were the conflicts that live on. Drewy Stoddart *in England* left many thousands in unfulfilled hope.

September already, and the Australians made their final appearance. The rain, which had respected cricketers' wishes for most of the summer, intruded at Hastings and helped the bowlers, especially Hearne, whose 6 for 8 knocked the tourists over in their final innings for 63 (Lohmann 4 for 45). "Stoddy" opened with WG for the South of England and failed in both innings, McKibbin the bowler.

Harry Trott's men, all bachelors bar two, sailed away with a proud enough record even though they had failed to regain the Ashes. When an English team next visited their shores some of the youngsters would be ready to play a mature role in regaining the urn.

The final first-class match of the season was South v North at Hastings, and with rain as his ally Hearne again was taking wickets almost as fast as the scorers could record the deed. For those who appreciated classy batsmanship Stoddart stole the show with a stirring 43, the innings of the match, made against four tough, uncompromising professionals in Attewell, Wainwright, Mold and Hirst.

After being bowled by Tom Richardson for 16 in the Gentlemen of England v Surrey match at Reigate (were there smiles all round?) "Stoddy" eyed a calendar that afforded three blank months before his winter venture, which this time was a trip to the West Indies.

He was golfing in Sheringham, Norfolk when Ranji's complimentary dinner was staged, so he had to write apologising for his absence and praising the Prince's "mighty achievements".

Then it was farewell to all the cogitation and backward glances of an English winter, and full steam for the Caribbean. The people of those leafy islands were about to see the greatest cricketer so far to have stepped ashore.

Putting demands all the
concentration of a keen sportsman

C.L. Townsend and "Stoddy"
watch as their companion tees off

CHAPTER 18

Calypso Cruise

H.D.G."SHRIMP" LEVESON GOWER, a member of Lord Hawke's touring party which reached the West Indies later than the first English group – Arthur Priestley and his men – wrote that upon their arrival he was "awakened by a Negro with a beaming black face putting his head through the port-hole of my cabin and shouting: 'Mr Stoddart got a duck!'"

Nothing in the records of that tour shows a Stoddart duck in Barbados or anywhere else (the author has the original scorebook). Although Hawke's party had slightly the better record, no-one in either team came close to matching "Stoddy's" tireless consistency with Priestley's team. While Plum Warner notched four hundreds for Lord Hawke, Stoddart played in all sixteen matches for Priestley, stroked 1079 runs, including six centuries (at least one on each island they visited), and took 104 cheap wickets. This prodigious one-man show had *Cricket* magazine suggesting that "if he had passed the winter in England, West Indian cricketers might perhaps have thought that English cricket was on the downward grade." He certainly cast a spell over the local population, many of whom waited outside the hotel to catch a close-up of him.

In three early matches against Barbados at Kensington Oval, Bridgetown, Stoddart fell five times to Clifford Goodman, a burly fast-medium bowler who took 36 wickets in those three contests with the visitors. A story in the 1992 celebration of 100 years of organised cricket in Barbados embellishes Goodman's recurring success against "Stoddy": some rum-swigging planters were standing beside the Anglican Bishop of Barbados and getting rather excited when Goodman did it again. With a slap on the episcopal shoulder-blades, one of them exclaimed, "Be Jesus Christ, 'Bish', Clifford's bowled him! Let's fire one on that!"

A contemporary account, in the rare book on this 1896-97 tour by A.B.Price, conveys the picture vividly: "Stoddart played the first ball of Goodman's ninth over. Then the 'demon bowler' sent down one of his 'changed pace' deliveries, with some work on, which Stoddart allowed to get past him and recline his off stump. Then followed a scene which beggars description. Round after round of tumultuous applause went up from thousands of excited men. Hats and sticks were thrown into the air, and for a long time the cheers crashed from the enclosure followed by a clamour of thousands of voices as men excitedly congratulated their neighbours on the happening of the unexpected." In the third match "Stoddy" did at least slam Goodman onto the top of one of the stands.

The St Vincent match, also played in Bridgetown, saw Stoddart make an unbeaten 153 and take 6 for 29 in the second innings, his old friend Billy Williams having taken 8 for 20 in the first. Crossing to Antigua, Stoddart hit another hundred and took seven wickets, and at the St Christopher Club, St Kitts, having creamed 133 runs (47 singles), he bowled a local chap named Stoddart for a duck in the locals' second innings of 29, finishing with 6 for 8. The native "Stoddy" toiled through 36 overs for figures of 4 for 117.

The real "Stoddy" continued to enjoy the tour with runs (with the odd reprieve in the field) and wickets galore, numbering H.B.G.Austin among them, a major figure in West Indies cricket in the years ahead. Against United Services, a mixture of British military and naval personnel, all officers bar two, Stoddart dismissed Lieutenant de Roebeck, who would one day command the naval assault on the Dardanelles, and become MCC president in 1925.

Invitations to dances and parties fell thickly upon the team. The cards invariably bore the promise "TWBF" (There will be fun). And there usually was.

They sailed over to Trinidad, where Stoddart hit another century, the Queens Park club being captained by Aucher Warner, brother of Plum. Next on the card was a match against "All West Indies", also at Port-of-Spain. Learie Constantine's father, Lebrun, made runs in both innings, and the haunting Clifford Goodman had Stoddart caught in the critical second innings. The Englishman might well have been wondering if facing Charlie "Terror" Turner wasn't so bad after all. The locals' jubilant victory by three wickets on the third day would have given much inspiration to the region, and was the forerunner of so many thrilling Anglo-West Indies encounters in the decades to come. It had seemed all over when, seeking 141 for victory, the West Indian combination had slumped to 41 for six.

There was a further boost for Caribbean cricket now when Trinidad beat Priestley's team, who were routed for 33 and 141 on the St Clair ground, Stoddart under the weather and offering little with bat or ball. The damage was done by Wood (or Woods) and Archie Cumberbatch, who would both soon impress on West Indies' 1900 tour of England. Lebrun Constantine played in this one too, but the other star performance came from D'Ade, who made an unbeaten 140: further encouragement for the Caribbean cricket community, even if it was the only hundred scored against "Skipper" Priestley's team.

After a break, which took in "Stoddy's" 34th birthday, they sailed to Jamaica, and earned an innings victory over the locals at Sabina Park as the final leg of five matches began, all of them won. Sammy Woods, troubled throughout by rheumatism, continued to serve his own special cocktails before breakfast, which seems not to have had any adverse effect on the players.

Arthur Priestley's team in the Caribbean: standing – C.A.Beldam, F.W.Bush, Leigh Barratt, R.P.Lewis, S.M.J.Woods, White (umpire); seated – R.C.N.Palairet, A.E.Stoddart, A.Priestley, W.Williams; front – C.C.Stone, H.T.Stanley. Missing from the group were Dr G.Elliott and J.J.Leigh. The name Packer hanging from the scorer's box is an eerie pointer to cricket's future

The 1897 Barbados team: standing – P.L.Cox, C.E.Goodman, R.Browne, A.B.St Hill (umpire); seated – H.A.Cole, A.Somers-Cocks, D.McAuley, P.Goodman, C.Browne, H.B.G.Austin; in front – C.H.Packer, G.B.Y.Cox; absent – T.W.Roberts, E.C.Jackman

Wickets clattered before Stoddart's offcutters and spinners at the rate of eight per match, and he made further hundreds in the second and third All-Jamaica matches, allowing H.T.Stanley only 18 runs in a fourth-wicket stand of 100. England's star player signed off in that final game with 143 and bowling figures of 7 for 67 and 3 for 10. By now he must surely have put the upsets of the 1896 season out of his mind by virtue of the pleasures of touring this idyllic territory and by the sheer weight of his achievements on this pioneering venture: 1079 runs at 56.79, with six centuries, nine single-figure innings in his 23 starts, but no ducks; and 104 wickets at 7.83. Nine of the matches were rated as first-class, and his figures of 416 runs (27.73), with two centuries, and 53 wickets (9.81) topped the lists.

The name "Stoddy" was reverberating around the islands. On the cricket grounds the crowds had often beaten sticks on the galvanised palings and chanted "Steady, Stoddy!" every time he looked like collaring the bowling, and probably as many babies were named Andrew later that year as were called Patsy after England's 1929-30 tour.

Regrettable though it was that both Hawke and Priestley toured the Caribbean at the same time, the abundance of fixtures was still inspirational to the peoples of the West Indies. The only previous English cricket tour, two years previously under the captaincy of Stoddart's Middlesex colleague R.S.Lucas, had resulted in ten victories in ten matches, so local strength seems to have been on the rise. Today, with cricket seemingly in decline in the region, perhaps cricket should tip its hat to those 1896-97 fun-loving pioneers from England, and not least to Arthur Priestley, a life-long bachelor and adventurer, future Member of Parliament (Liberal) for Grantham, and knighted in 1911, who must fervently have wished to be a better cricketer than he was. A popular hanger-on during Stoddart's next tour of Australia, he was gratified to take the field in two minor matches. He seems to have been the sort of chap who would allow no-one else to pick up the tab after a session of drinks.

CHAPTER 19

Distractions

THERE was the usual tingle in the air in the spring of 1897 as Arthur Priestley's suntanned players arrived home. The young cricket writer J.N.Pentelow reflected the feelings of a cricket-starved public in April: "It will be delightful to see once more the Indian Prince [Ranjitsinhji] on the warpath, to see our dear old WG again piling up centuries, and Mr "Andrew Ernest" back from the Indies, browned and more sunburnt than ever, to see them all troop out from the pavilions once more, batsman, and bowler, veteran and youngster, 'Bobby' Abel and 'Tom' Richardson, Murdoch and Killick. 'Cricket on the hearth' hath its charms, but, by your leave, gentlemen, surely cricket on the good greensward is best."

"Stoddy" didn't necessarily think so at that moment. He had been ultra-productive for almost a year non-stop and there was the prospect of an even longer span ahead, with an Australian tour at the end of the summer, linking the English seasons of 1897 and 1898.

At the Hampstead club nets, with MacGregor and Hayman, he provided something worthwhile for the locals to ponder, but he reserved his energies during May, playing hardly at all as the spring showers disturbed the balance between bat and ball. There was too always the business to be attended to in the City, at an office near Copthall Court. Another of his letters to survive is to the Hampstead club's "Daddy" Besch. It is undated, but may have been written this spring: "I am sorry to say I find on my return to England my mother very seriously ill. Consequently I haven't quite the heart to perform with the 'Hampstead Coons' otherwise I should have been delighted."

On May 19 he unleashed himself with a hundred against his old foes the Stoics. Then, for A.J.Webbe's XI at Cambridge, his 16 and 51 satisfied most that his form was intact, although he was thirty-four now, and one writer was recording with sensitivity that the brilliancy of former years seemed to be absent. He should have seen him in Jamaica.

It was a depressing year for Middlesex. Not until the middle of August was a match won. By then Stoddart was out of the game with a knee injury and immersed in the concerns of tour organisation.

Warner and Hayman opened for the county this year, with Stoddart usually batting first wicket down. They went under to Lancashire on a bad Old Trafford surface, and he did nothing against Nottinghamshire. Yet another draw took place at Lord's as Yorkshire exceeded 400, so that by the time Middlesex went in, they had been fielding out to one side or another from 5.30pm Tuesday till lunchtime Friday. Still they managed over 300, Stoddart being stumped off Peel for 26. In the follow-on his 57 pleased everybody.

On June 21 the stars and stripes flew at Lord's when the Philadelphians played. Francis Ford's sensational one-hour hundred hurried the match to its conclusion, the second day having been kept free for Queen Victoria's Jubilee Day: for sixty years she had graced the throne. Stoddart, after his Philadelphian duck, took the opportunity to score 103 for Hampstead against London and Westminster Bank.

There was only moderate success for him at Tonbridge and at The Oval, although his 28 in the last innings was described as being as valuable as any hundred. Against Sussex at the Saffrons, Eastbourne he made 13 in both innings. Ranji, more memorably, made a delectable century on the perfect pitch.

At Lord's a strong Players side beat a strong cast of Gentlemen. Shrewsbury made a century, others made runs enough, but Stoddart, after a swift 51 with WG, missed his chance again. Jessop, man of the hour, played another of his unique innings, hitting Tom Richardson contemptuously and warming up for his performance against Yorkshire later in the month when he conjured a century in the equivalent of a lunch interval duration.

"Stoddy" began working to something of a pitch by the next match, which was against Surrey. This time he kept out Richardson, who cut down thirteen batsmen in this encounter. He made 91, a popular innings, though again causing some to lament that he wasn't quite radiating the dash of former years. The unmistakable style was there, but youth had evidently flown and responsibility was tightening him up.

He relaxed again during the Hampstead Cricket Week, so rich in memories. He took 127 off Richmond, and against West Herts Club and Ground he thundered to 113. Days later his season was cut short in

Taunton, after he had made 109 off Somerset, including a hit over the cottages beyond square leg. He had some luck, but those ever-eager critics noted with satisfaction that his batting still contained many of the exciting elements of his younger days. They seemed to be cherishing already the memory of the svelte Stoddart who rose to the top of the pack in the late 1880s. The injury occurred in the field on the second day. His knee was strained and he took no further part in the match.

W.A.Bettesworth evaluated his 1897 performance by saying that "although Mr Stoddart had an average of 30, he was not the Stoddart of former days; it is possible that playing cricket pretty nearly all the year round has proved too much for him, strong as he is."

After a golfing holiday in Sussex, and still limping, he was probably glad to board ship and head out into the clear and lively waterways that led to Australia.

A.E.Stoddart leads out the Middlesex amateur players

By the end of 1897, 54 centuries had been recorded for Middlesex since 1878, and A.E.Stoddart had made thirteen of them. In F.S.Ashley-Cooper's opinion he was the best batsman the county had ever had. Now the sportsmen of Adelaide and Melbourne and Sydney were looking forward for a fourth time to renewing his acquaintance.

As in 1894-95, he was at the centre of a whispering "shamateur" rumour, a figure of £1000 for him from Melbourne Cricket Club and the Sydney authorities being enviously bandied about. In retirement he would write to a newspaper explaining the financial structure of his Australian tours. Travelling costs and hotel bills were covered, and he was left a discretion in ordering champagne. "With the weather we experienced there this was almost a necessity, and the discretion was exercised by me freely, but wisely, in the best interests of our health and cricket."

He believed that no amateur finished the tour less than £100 out of pocket.

The chief English complaint was that, by contrast, the Australians pocketed a considerable chunk of tour profits themselves when they toured the Old Country.

In 1897 there was again inevitable complaint at the composition of the English touring team. There was surprise at Stoddart's invitation to Attewell, who was 36, and relief at Attewell's inability to accept. E.G.Wynyard was ready to go, until he received orders from the War Office. Letters have survived. From the tour skipper, 30 Lithos Road, August 15, 1897: "Dear Wynyard, I was very pleased to hear that the War Office had given you leave and that you accept the invitation to join the team. I feel certain you will enjoy the tour immensely and I shall be glad to do all in my power to make things happy for you. Yours ever A.E.Stoddart".

A further letter, probably also to Wynyard (the preceding page is missing: each player must have been sent something similar), covered some of the arrangements: "colors [sic] the day we leave England. I enclose a tie and hat ribbon, also you will find an order for caps & coats which please have made in plenty of time, all the other things in the shape of colors I will look after. I have arranged your berth Cabin 43 & 44. it is an inside cabin but very comfortable . . . ."

A week after the first letter to Wynyard, "Stoddy" wrote with sadness to the Hampshire batsman and Army officer: "My dear Wynyard I cannot tell you how sincerely sorry I am to get the news of the War Office cancelling your leave. I was looking forward with the greatest pleasure to having you with us and can only tell you that I am almost as disappointed as you are. Possibly you may be able another year to visit Australia with a team but this is no consulation [sic] to me. About the inconvenience caused please don't let this add to your trouble I can easily get another man, I had intended to take 14 but now I think that if Briggs takes your place that will be enough. I only wanted another good bowler to add to the 13 which appeared in the papers to have a rare side As my object in accepting

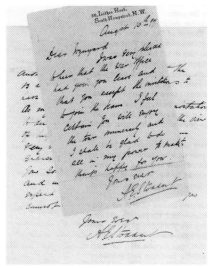

Knight's Auctions

Plaintive correspondence

your invitation to dine with you was only with the view of helping you re the tour, and I am very much busy I will ask you to excuse me. I shall hope to see you somehow before we leave and in the meantime can only repeat how sincerely sorry I am you cannot join us. Yours ever A.E.Stoddart".

In truth, Wynyard's absence may have been a blessing, for he was a cantankerous individual. During a Hampshire-Sussex match, Ranjitsinhji was sampling some hothouse grapes unaware that they had been placed on the pavilion table for Wynyard's benefit. "Teddy" was furious, "his wrath unquenchable". Fixtures between the two counties were reportedly cancelled (if true, they were reinstated in time for the 1898 season). "Then Stoddart took a hand. He pointed out that he had invited both Wynyard and Ranji to be members of his side to Australia and that he must cancel the invitation if Teddy did not apologise." Wynyard's friends concocted a letter, which he was induced to sign. But a happy ending was aborted by War Office orders.

Further insight into the mechanics of arranging an Ashes tour in that era comes from the contract that "Stoddy" gave each player to sign. George Hirst's (now in the author's collection) has details filled in by Stoddart and is dated August 16, 1897, which indicates that it was signed by Hirst during the Yorkshire v Middlesex match at Bramall Lane, Sheffield. Stoddart had travelled north in spite of the knee injury sustained at Taunton that kept him out of this match, Hirst's signing, together with Wainwright's and Peel's, surely being the object of his journey.

The agreement was between each player and the Melbourne Cricket Club coupled with the Trustees of the Sydney Ground. These authorities, it is confirmed, have an arrangement with Andrew Ernest Stoddart to bring a team of English cricketers "for the purpose of playing a series of Cricket Matches in the Australian Colonies (or in New Zealand) during [1897-98]." The New Zealand option is interesting and slightly puzzling.

Hirst's fee was £300 (equal perhaps to £30,000 today), £25 payable before departure and the balance at the end of the tour. His travelling expenses from home to London and back again after disembarkation were not to be covered. The married professionals certainly needed to leave some funds for their families before setting out on the odyssey.

Johnny Briggs had delightedly accepted his invitation on the spot. It would be his sixth trip to Australia, a record. Among amateurs, Stoddart himself was creating a record with his fourth trip.

An irregular problem surrounded Ranjitsinhji. The New South Wales government proposed a deterrent tax of £100 on coloured persons entering the colony. "Australia for the Australians" was the rallying cry. But the cricket fraternity were longing to see Ranji, so any suggestion of a restriction was waived. The lithe little man was, after all, commonly designated as the world's finest batsman.

One Friday morning in September 1897 the cricketers settled into their cabins as the ship's engines throbbed. Another great cricket venture was about to unfold. Three shuddering, echoing blasts on the fog-horn and their England in its autumn was receding slowly into the fond distance. Within hours the only view was of grey sea, with sperm whales spouting.

CHAPTER 20

◆◆◆

An Ill Star

THEY were a band of only thirteen once again: A.E.Stoddart, A.C.MacLaren, K.S.Ranjitsinhji, J.R.Mason, N.F.Druce, T.W.Hayward, G.H.Hirst, E.Wainwright, W.Storer, J.Briggs, J.H.Board, J.T.Hearne and T.Richardson.

The party, of which only four had been to Australia before, were bade farewell by C.E.Green, a shipping man with strong Essex cricket connections, and "in a somewhat nervous reply Stoddart, assisted by shy glances at the marginal notes on his shirt cuff, disclaimed any pretensions for his men to be considered an all-England team". He regretted his inability to invite the 1894-95 stalwarts Brown and Ward, but felt it was *reasonably* representative of English cricket (Hayward, Wainwright and Hirst had all achieved the 1000 runs/100 wickets double in 1897). Perhaps with a tinge of apprehension he expressed a hope that they would be warmly welcomed home, win or lose.

The magnetic personality, the mystic, colourful figure the crowds all sought, was Ranjitsinhji, "The Lion that Conquers in Battle". The diminutive Indian joined them at the Naples stop-over, to the clear relief of his skipper. Young Jack Mason wrote in a letter to his family that "Stoddart is very nice to us".

Two passengers were taken off at Port Said, one dying from consumption and the other with typhoid. However, there were the usual festivities and sports on board the Orient Line steamer *Ormuz* (commanded by Captain H.E.Inskip), including cricket in the nets, with Stoddart's knee holding up well as he straight-drove his side to victory over the ship's captain's team. And he became quoits champion: solo, and then with a Mrs Calvert in the doubles. Another lucky lady, Mrs Todd, helped him win at bull-board. He'd had one bad episode during the journey, becoming very ill, forbidden to leave his bed even if he'd wanted to.

Jack Hearne, the Middlesex master seam bowler, kept a diary for most of the tour, and noted that his captain had suffered a bad bout of neuralgia. Hearne's journal is full of keen observations: the streets of Gibraltar stink; Bill Storer thinks the ship's foghorn blew the fog away; filthy people in downtown Naples, half the men walking around with their flies undone; chats with his team-mates to while away the hours; socialism the topic with Tom Richardson and Jim Phillips; Ranjitsinhji told "talk English and I'll understand thee" by someone referred to as "old Kaye"; Stoddart monopolising the deck games; locals disappointed in Ceylon when the English cricketers didn't play there; Ranji unwell; poker in the evening with Stoddart and others; lunch with Western Australian cricket folk in Albany, where the locals expressed disappointment that the Englishmen would not be playing in Perth. The financial demand of £1500 was too great.

Stoddart, in straw boater, boards for Australia for the last time

On deck with the Honourable Ivo Bligh

Captain Stoddart and some of his men while away the hours reading on deck

After some uncomfortable days of high seas they were greatly relieved to berth at Adelaide, where the big shake-down began, the task of loosening limbs and presenting a civil countenance to the numerous receptions to come. Archie MacLaren greeted them, having sailed ahead of the team because he had a wedding to a Melbourne lady pending. "Stoddy" hit a topical note in his speech at Adelaide Town Hall by stating that "Australia will not be Australia without Giffen", and they set off to absorb the views at Mount Lofty and at the Zoo and Botanical Gardens. In the evening they went to see *Maritana* at the Theatre Royal. And the popular impulse to versify was unleashed:

> Mr Stoddart, we greet you,
> We're happy to meet you,
> We hope you feel fit for the tussle;
> May your Ranji and Storer
>   Soon worry our scorer
>   And give us a taste of their muscle.
>   May Long Tom and Mason
>   Not fail to get pace on,
> Nor their trundling of wickets be barren;
> May Briggs ne'er be wayward,
> But stonewall with Hayward
> And pile up the runs with MacLaren.

Australia's champion, George Giffen, had slipped into semi-retirement at 38 because "popularity will not keep me". It seems that while he played cricket all summer, the juniors in the Postal Department were moving above him. He was named in the South Australia side to play the Englishmen, but the match had to proceed without him.

Jack Hearne was impatient at the local Ranji frenzy: "Enormous crowd waiting to get a glimpse of Ranji. All Ranji – nobody else thought of (absurd I think with such men as Stoddy, Tom, Tom H. etc)." He wasn't impressed with the professionals' hotel either: "No gas and no bells in there; if you want anything must wait till somebody comes, or fetch it."

Stoddart had looked very good in the nets, where as many as 3000 curious locals came to watch. But on the second day of the match the skipper was ordered to rest as his temperature registered the first century of the tour. Bill Storer's tour diary reveals that the skipper was actually very ill and forbidden to leave his bed. Influenza had been rife aboard *Ormuz*.

Clem Hill partially erased the memories of his poor 1896 tour of England with each hook, cut and thumping drive as he made a wonderful 200. But the English team took heart in passing South Australia's 408, largely owing to Ranji's 189, for which an old miner presented him with a small gold nugget. (Hearne thought this a "deuced insult". But then bowlers have seldom been rewarded on the same scale as glamorous batsmen.) Luck had been with the Indian. He had been dropped after scoring a single, then five more times after reaching his hundred – and all off the suffering Ernie Jones.

The Englishmen left the match drawn in order to be at Flemington in time for the Melbourne Cup. Back in Adelaide, where thirsty people were guzzling "Stoddart" tonic ale and "Ranjitsinhji" ginger beer (what might they have been

Clem Hill: coming good

paid for these commercial deals?), Jim Phillips' no-balling of Ernie Jones for throwing was still being debated with some feeling. "Keep that arm straight, Jonah," Phillips had urged during the tough guy's 54 six-ball overs, which brought him 7 for 189. Jack Hearne considered Jones's bowling action as "the most outrageous thing I have ever seen".

In Melbourne, where the amateurs stayed at Scotts, the professionals at the White Hart, MCG ground developments now kept the ladies out of the pavilion reserve. "Stoddy's" men had a good two-wicket win over Victoria after all had seemed lost. Bill Storer, the Derbyshire utility player, contributed two valuable innings, and Kent's J.R.Mason made a businesslike, match-winning 128 not out, with only six fours. Hearne, who hit the winning runs, was again sensitive to the bias of the onlookers: "Shows how the colonists crave for victory," he wrote after seeing the cool response to the English success.

For Stoddart, his health still uncertain, there had been only 26 and a duck. The official reception was followed by a gala fancy-dress ball at Government House, and the players were invited to the Princess Theatre to see *The Gay Parisienne*.

In their "brown serge sac suits" the English cricketers took the night train to Sydney, leaving Victorian columnists to compare Tom Richardson's appearance with that of an Italian baritone and suggesting that Stoddart, with his "fresh English face", might be using curling-tongs on his moustache. Poor Richardson had just received news that his home back in Thames Ditton, Surrey had been burgled; and there was nothing he could do about it from so far away.

Archie MacLaren stroked 142 and 100 against New South Wales, breaking two bats in the second innings; and Ranji also made another magical century, while Storer scored well again and Richardson took plenty of wickets, including young scoreless Trumper's in the second innings, when he snapped the top off his off stump with a huge breakback. The youngster could at least reflect on his running, diving catch to dismiss Tom Hayward, than which there could never have been one more spectacular.

Since "Stoddy's" previous visit to the SCG it had undergone much change. A new Ladies Stand and a stand for smokers had risen, and at the Randwick end the notorious Hill was starting to swell. The encircling cycle track was now tinted green to eliminate glare.

With the elevated onlookers watching closely, Stoddart, putting himself in at No.8, had made only one run when Tom Garrett gathered an apparent bump ball. The veteran, unnerved by prolonged heckling, moved deliberately for the "catch" and held it, and Stoddart walked off to the pavilion. But Bill Storer, the other batsman, wasn't happy, and after appealing to the umpire he ran after his captain to call him back. The question of Stoddart's return to the crease led to a good deal of moralising. Right or wrong decision, his batting now was reckless, and M.A.Noble bowled him off stump for 32. Earlier, MacLaren had questioned Noble's bowling action, which enabled him to flight the ball curiously; but Stoddart allegedly replied "Rats!")

Another English win ensued, and after a relaxing cruise up Middle Harbour, a banquet at the Hotel Australia (George Hirst came away still hungry), and a reception at the impressive town hall in George Street (where Stoddart and Ranjitsinhji sat either side of the mayor, the skipper speaking briefly and courteously as ever, the latter stirring it up by referring to the "poll tax" that Indians had to pay to enter Australia), the tourists moved on to Newcastle.

There "Stoddy" lost his fourth consecutive toss. The locals batted valiantly, and then Stoddart got into his stride with 116, putting on 240 with George Hirst in only a couple of hours in front of a subdued gathering. It became a match more to be remembered for the plague of flies, mosquitoes and flying ants. The skipper discovered an uncured bird-skin, alive with insects, under his bed, and his hands and face were, as Ranji beheld them, "globular" from swelling from the bites. Hearne thought the crowd ignorant, and wondered why they had bothered to come. Ranji had been the centre of attention at Lake Macquarie, where he shot several musk-ducks from 150 yards.

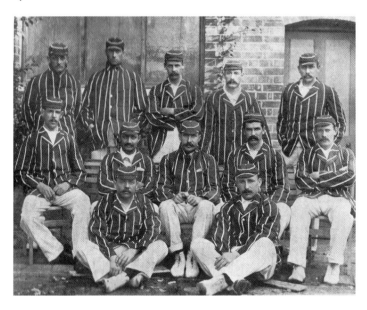

The 1897-98 English touring team (minus Archie MacLaren): rear – N.F.Druce, J.R.Mason, T.W.Hayward, J.H.Board, J.T.Hearne; seated – E.Wainwright, K.S.Ranjitsinhji, A.E.Stoddart, T.Richardson, W.Storer front – J.Briggs, G.H.Hirst

Welcome to Brisbane: Stoddart is robbed

The English cricketers were jolted out of their sleeping-bunks when the train struck a horse near Werris Creek, but when they reached Glen Innes the township was agog with excitement. The cricketers' visit was an event of truly historical value, and a banner above the entrance to the primitive ground proclaimed "New England welcomes Old England".

When the touring team inspected the matting-on-concrete pitch, Stoddart looked at the join halfway down and teased his star batsman: "That'll kill you, Ranji!" Here "Stoddy" bowled deceptively and took 5 for 10 and 10 for 39 as the local Twenty-two, gloveless and in brown pads, trekked a sorry procession across the pebbly, dusty, grassless terrain to the middle and back again. Stoddart's clever slower ball was referred to thereafter as "the Glen Innes pusher". Having drawn lots for the batting order (Ranji, by special request, going in at first drop), the tourists had smacked almost 400 quick runs, Hayward getting his first hundred on Australian soil. Unhappily this stopover was overshadowed by the local belief that the amateurs had behaved rather snootily in failing to attend the concert staged in the team's honour.

All the way to Brisbane they were greeted noisily by crowds eager to catch sight of them, often forsaking courtesy in the attempt. Jim Phillips recorded that at Toowoomba the locals were extremely demonstrative, while at Ipswich they were nothing short of offensive.

A massive crowd turned out for them at night when they reached Brisbane, where porters and policemen were helpless in the fearful stampede. When the hubbub had died, Stoddart's watch and chain – of great sentimental value – were missing. Although it was later reported from South Brisbane Police Court that a pickpocket had whispered to his female accomplice: "Don't you Jerry anything to the John about Stoddart's watch!" the police were unable to recover it for him. At the official reception next day the English captain eased local embarrassment by stating that he thought none the worse of Queensland for his loss. Indeed, the thief might easily have been an Englishman!

Misfortunes were starting to pile up. Next he lost his keys between the racecourse and the hotel (the Queensland Club, where the amateurs were staying). He took the trouble to offer £1 for them in the Lost and Found columns.

Then a piece of luck came his way: he won a toss at last. This was in Brisbane, where the Woolloongabba ground had sprung up out of wasteland. It was the Gabba's first international cricket match, and the dressing-rooms weren't even finished. Against a combined New South Wales and Queensland XI he once more hid himself in the lower part of the batting order, giving his new men every chance to acclimatise. They did this to the extent of 636 runs: Norman Druce 126, Archie MacLaren building his reputation even higher with 181. For old time's sake as the home team played out a draw, Stoddart dismissed a diminished 35-year-old Charlie Turner, who was now living in Gympie.

Ranji, in keeping with the unfortunate off-field trend of the tour, developed a chill that was to bother him for weeks. With a touch of ingenuity, they left the Brisbane hotel this time disguised as a wedding party, the proprietor showering rice over them and crying "Good luck!" with admirable duplicity.

At Toowoomba, where the local Eighteen stood up to them well,

Stoddart and MacLaren went off shooting, narrowly escaping death on the road during the drive back. These rural Queenslanders wore white pads, which elevated them in the eyes of the Englishmen after the brown pads worn by the Glen Innes cricketers. However, Hearne noted, the mosquitoes here were as big as butterflies. He had a moan about Phil Sheridan, who was supposed to be looking after the touring cricketers' every need.

At Armidale, New England, where Ranji's quinsy intensified, the tourists were dismissed for an unprepossessing 141 on another matting surface after drawing straws for the batting order. Nine bags of sawdust had been needed to make the ground playable. That night they stayed late at a dance put on in their honour, then in the morning took the train down to Sydney with several days in hand. They were days of destiny.

On December 8, 1897 a cable was delivered to Drewy Stoddart informing him that his mother had died. He was grief-stricken to the point of collapse, and as the expressions of sympathy began to pour in, he withdrew to the sanctity and solitude of his room, while the rain crashed down on Sydney town.

The weather posed a separate problem, urgent and pregnant with controversy. The Sydney Cricket Ground trustees had postponed the start without consulting either captain, even though the umpires had pronounced the pitch as being fine. They explained that their chief consideration had been that the pitch should be fit for play, and also (with an eye on takings, no doubt) that perhaps the extra day might enable Ranjitsinhji and perhaps even the captain to recover and play in the Test match.

Stoddart, first hearing of the postponement when one of his players spotted a newspaper placard outside a pub, was in no state to become embroiled in such a muddle. Probably after conferring with MacLaren and others, he sent a letter of protest to the SCG trustees, a protest that was never dealt with, although expressions of condolence and regret came back. The trustees had refrained from consulting the England captain in consequence of his bereavement. Then, a trifle ungraciously, they explained that even if he had been drawn into the discussions, his opinion would not necessarily have guided them.

By the Sunday night, Ranji, his quinsy burst at last, was speaking of playing. Drewy Stoddart, from the moment that cable arrived, was hopelessly unfitted.

Elizabeth Stoddart, fifteen years a widow, had died in The Quarry Close, the home of a niece, Harriette Dallas. She was buried in the parish churchyard in Radford, Coventry, no great distance from her husband's hunting lodge. A monument of pink marble was set upon the grave. (It was removed in the 1980s, having suffered damage first during the Luftwaffe raid on Coventry and later from vandalism in the churchyard.) Any man who is absent from his mother's funeral is likely to be left with troubled thoughts.

Francis Thompson, the pathetic young poet who wrote *At Lord's,* probably cricket's most celebrated and sad piece of verse, referred to Stoddart as "that Son of Grief" in his review of A.E.Housman's *A Shropshire Lad* this very year, 1898.

The Census of seven years previously had listed Mrs Elizabeth Stoddart, then a 58-year-old Leicestershire-born widow, as residing in Quarry Close, Radford, probably the home of her daughter Averal (Minnie?), 37, and her husband Montague, 43, a solicitor, who had two children and two domestic servants.

For Drewy, the loving son who spoke of his mother quite frequently, the cricket tour on the other side of the world had lost all meaning.

MacLaren won the toss in this "pro-Test" match and chose to bat on a beautiful pitch. The Australians, like their opponents, wore black mourning arm-bands, and, after all, lacked Giffen, who would never play for his country again. Stand-in skipper MacLaren stroked a cultured century, and substantial innings from Tom Hayward, Bill Storer and George Hirst lifted England beyond 400. But it was the almost supernatural powers of K.S.Ranjitsinhji, held back to fifth wicket down, that ensured a winning total. Batting against mounting exhaustion, he charmed his way to 175. After having written a condemnation of Ernie Jones's action, incurring the crowd's wrath, this was stirring proof that he feared no bowler, not even the Australian express. As for "Jonah" himself, he freely paid tribute to the diminutive Indian: "he's too good; he's a wonder."

The Australasian had something rather more pointed to say about this glorious performance: "Ranji must either have wonderful recuperative powers or his illness was exaggerated, for to come almost straight from his sick-bed and play as he did was a marvellous thing."

There is surviving film of Ranji batting in the nets by the encircling cycle track at the SCG, just a few casual slaps towards cover, a sequence that does him less than full justice and yet which remains a jewel among cricket's early moving images. Other film was shot during this tour, of the English and local teams taking the field, but shameful indifference and carelessness, worthy of the modern age, caused it to be lost many years ago.

Tom Richardson gained immense enjoyment in helping Ranji add 74 for the last wicket, taking England past 500 for the first time in a Test match. And that 551 seemed mountainous as Hearne and Richardson disposed of Australia for 237. There had been a traumatic incident for a number of the Australian cricketers on the second evening of this Monday-to-Friday Test match. Outside their lodgings in Coogee Bay a runaway gig threw its female occupant into the roadway. She was dead by the time some of the players reached her. It was something that would stay forever with those who were closest to the tragedy.

There was sterner resistance in the follow-on (which was still compulsory). Joe Darling and Clem Hill, who dominated the series like very few pairs of left-handers before or since, made 101 and 96, Hill falling when within a boundary hit of 100 on the first of five occasions in Test matches against the Mother Country.

Australia made 408, but not before another unpleasant incident. Charlie McLeod, being rather deaf, left the crease when Richardson bowled him, but "no-ball" had been called. Bill Storer, ever alert, took the throw from Druce at third man, pulled out a stump and appealed, and Jim Phillips had to give McLeod run out. It would be erroneous to suppose that it was never played tough in those days. Years later E.J.Metcalfe wrote in *The Cricketer:* "Dear old Stoddart [who must have been sitting in the pavilion or guests enclosure] did not like it and wanted him to come back, but it was no use, out he went." The row apparently lasted a week, and when "Stoddy" asked his friend and umpire Phillips for an explanation he was told that it was "not my business if a batsman's deaf".

England eventually needed 95 to win, and MacLaren was again in sleek form, steering them home on the fifth morning and freeing them to hurry to the Rosebery Park races before spending Christmas fishing and shooting in Victoria's Gippsland Lakes area, where Stoddart, slowly recovering his vivacity, killed a stag at 250 yards with a Colt repeater. Overall the Englishmen bagged very little on their hunting excursions, though Tom Richardson did once find himself eye-to-eye with a huge black snake.

For England the emphatic triumph in the opening Test match was a glory and a satisfaction not to be repeated. As the tour progressed, all the promise shown by the Australian batsmen and bowlers came to fruition, and the tide turned with bombora force. The first symbolic sign was the rising of the mercury over Christmas. The earth was parched, thirty-five lives were known to have been lost to excessive heat in two terrible days, and all humanity was reduced to languid disinterest. Even such hardened local warriors as Frank Iredale, Jim Kelly and Syd Gregory were known to have been grilled into a state of near-collapse.

They recovered their senses sufficiently to take their places for the second Test, at Melbourne, where Stoddart's team was in some distress. Ranji, tonsils squeezed clear of pus, was still ailing, and the skipper was plagued by bouts of melancholia. He first included himself in the team, then withdrew when he saw that Ranji was responding to treatment.

Between the first and second Test matches they had played a three-day match in Bendigo, the gold-mining town which had been asked for £125 as the fee for an English visit. Twenty-five members of the local cricket club put in £5 each, and the three-day match, played in ferocious heat, together with a concert yielded an overall profit of £62, a tidy sum. Stoddart and the amateurs (one of whom, Jack Mason, scored 128) stayed at the City Family Hotel, as did the professionals. Hearne and others desperately searched for a drink at four in the morning, but had to wait until the bar opened at 7.30am.

As Melbourne crackled in the heat, Harry Trott had the luck to win the toss, and relentlessly through the day the Australians set about constructing a mammoth total. Charlie McLeod ground out a century, and Hill, Gregory, Iredale and Harry Trott all made a lot of runs, with debutant M.A.Noble scoring 17 at No.7, as New Year's Day 1898 gave way to a Sunday of convalescence before a hot and inevitable Monday in the field for MacLaren and his toilers.

Ranji had an abcess removed from his throat during an interval and was cheered when he returned to the field. He was the most talked-about cricketer in the land, and his name was being exploited ever more widely: appended to bats, matches, cricket shoes, hair restorers, heavy metal cigar-cutters, even sandwiches, in a wry portent of commercialisation to come. Ranji brooms became a particularly popular product.

Johnny Briggs, pleased at having bamboozled fourteen Bendigo batsmen and surprisingly buoyant in the sultry conditions, took three top wickets now, but it was a very tired England that set out on that Monday evening to reply to Australia's 520 (the highest Test total without a leg-bye for well over 100 years, until England's 528 against Pakistan at Lord's in 2006). Some were still smarting at the vulgar attempts by spectators to distract Tom Richardson as he shaped for a high catch off Kelly.

The relationship between Ranji and his captain was the source of curiosity among some Australians

Ranji did not fail them. The slightly-built Indian made a fine 71, and was supported by the rugged Bill Storer (51). It took a longish stand by Briggs and Druce, however, to carry England past 300, and the follow-on on that dry, crusty pitch was a formality. Jim Phillips, not merely umpiring but acting as Stoddart's general assistant and talent scout for certain counties, and correspondent for a newspaper group, was earning his fees. He found it necessary to no-ball Ernie Jones again for throwing – the first instance in any Test match – although it seems to have worried no-one unduly so long as it was confined to the very occasional delivery. At this time only the bowler's umpire was empowered to call a no-ball, but Phillips was already advocating an amendment: if only the square-leg official were allowed to pass judgment, he promised to "sort out" several other bowlers.

Master bowlers Trumble and Noble did the damage now on a broken Melbourne surface, which, according to Storer's tour diary, had some cracks which were an inch and a half wide. England's batsmen had no answer and were bundled out for 150 early on the fourth day to give Australia an innings victory to level the series.

During the match, Charlie Bannerman had wandered past as Drewy Stoddart was batting in the nets. The scorer of Test cricket's first century later stated that he had never seen anyone bat better at the nets in his entire life. During play, "Stoddy" had had a bird's-eye view of it all from the dressing-room over the members' reserve, a vantage point private only briefly as one set of beautiful eyes after another was turned towards his "fine face at the window", shooting "sympathy and invitation to the desolate but favourite cricketer".

The society columns through the summer were suggesting he was looking for a wife. "Whose wife?" enquired one impertinent journal. Another publication irritably demanded to know why Australian girls almost without exception wore boutonnieres in England's colours.

Spectators rushed out to take souvenir scrapings from the pitch, which would not have pleased the groundsman. According to "Short Slip" it looked as if fine wool had been scattered over it. It would have been interesting to have seen England's professionals bowling on it if the follow-on had been averted. As it turned out, it was the most gilded of fleece for Australia.

Archie MacLaren, in his loser's speech, expressed the hope that in future the pitches might be longer-lasting, which sparked an attack by "Mid-On" (H.W.Hedley), among others, on the "inexperienced" views of, to start with, MacLaren and Ranjitsinhji.

After a month out of the game, Stoddart resumed playing at Ballarat, having pasted into his scrapbook an apparently irrelevant but evidently mesmeric cartoon of a "tired pessimist" committing "fish suicide". With the rifle muzzle in his mouth, fishing line tied to the trigger, the pessimist waits for a hungry fish to do the rest. It is the only item non-sporting or non-romantic in the entire book of cuttings.

He now encouraged, and perhaps surprised, his colleagues with a sparkling comeback innings of 111 against Eighteen of Ballarat. Yet the anxieties continued, with Ranji's asthma still troublesome, and the insufferable heat (113 degrees Fahrenheit) in the next match on the grassless arena at Stawell (Stoddart 44 and two wickets) causing the Englishmen to consume an estimated 400 drinks during the game. Here they stayed out of town at Kirkella, Duncan McKellar's pleasant country residence, and shot about 300 rabbits around the estate..

On their way to Adelaide the team passed through Horsham, where in the early hours they were awakened by excited townsfolk yelling "Come out and let's have a look at ya!" The response from the bleary-eyed Englishmen went unrecorded.

The blazing nightmare continued as the third Test got under way on the greenness of Adelaide Oval in front of 10,000 people. Harry Trott met Drewy Stoddart outside the England dressing-room, and Stoddart called "Heads". But almost as if to mark the death that day of Lewis Carroll in faraway Guildford, Surrey, the coin bounced and turned over with Mad Hatter caprice. The disappointment plainly showed on Stoddart's face. It would have made his worst enemy "– if he has an enemy – feel sorry for him" as one paper put it. At the end of the first hot day Australia had amassed 310 for the loss of McLeod and Hill.

As ever, Tom Richardson was the main man on whom all England pinned its faith, but, bothered throughout the tour by rheumatism, he could make no impression here against watchful Australian batsmen. The adjustment in line against the left-handers seemed beyond him. Joe Darling hit him about from the start. Then Briggs's turn came as Darling hoisted him into the crowd at square leg. Jack Hearne steadied things, but Darling still reached 50 in an hour. Hirst came on, but he was never the same bowler in Australia.

Briggs finally got one through McLeod: Australia 97 for one. Then joy became unbounded as Clem Hill built up a huge stand with the other South Australian, Darling, who, dropped by Ranji at point on 98, reached his hundred in spectacular fashion, hitting Briggs clean out of Adelaide Oval, the first time this had ever happened. The applause was tumultuous for the young man's dashing show of strokeplay: 104 out of 157. No-one had ever scored more than one century in a Test series thus far.

Soon the 200 came up as the afternoon's heat reached its peak. Stoddart juggled the bowling, and at last the perspiring Richardson broke through: Hill, having made a chanceless 81, was caught at the wicket by Storer after a stand of 148.

Gregory filled the breach as England tried for one more success that evening. Briggs had tired more than Darling, who battered 18 off two overs as the shadows lengthened protectively

Perhaps Saturday would bring renewed strength to the toiling bowlers.

There was misleading early success as 17,000 spectators crammed into Adelaide Oval. Richardson had Darling caught before he had added to his overnight 178, and Briggs returned to his tantalising best with four maidens in a row. But when Gregory, on 32, hit him to mid-off, Stoddart, possibly fighting distractions, dropped the chance.

The Australian score touched the upper 300s, Briggs working like a beaver, conceding a mere five runs in 13 six-ball overs. Then English spirits slumped as Tom Richardson left the field.

At 374, Gregory was at last caught (by Storer), and with Richardson back after lunch the Englishmen tried to dissemble the remaining batting order before it was too late. Harry Trott soon went, and Noble entered. But England's next stroke of misfortune came when Hirst had to retire with a strained stomach muscle. The 400 came, and soon Iredale had his fifty as the flagging attack was used to the best of Stoddart's intelligence. He asked Storer to remove the pads and bowl, Druce taking over behind the stumps. Three Storer overs produced 16 runs.

Richardson had another turn, and bowled Noble with a slower off-break. Enter the tall Trumble, a number eight always difficult to dislodge. Ranji now left the field with a dislocated finger (no W.G.Grace around to put it back in place). Tom Richardson laboured away, striking again when Iredale played on after a patient 84. There was to be no flamboyance now. Kelly took twenty minutes to make a run, then applied himself vigorously as Australia passed 500, the first Test side to do so two innings in succession.

At last Stoddart gave himself a bowl – and bowled Kelly as he aimed a huge drive. Ernie Jones, tearing the pitch with his spikes as he turned between runs, was eventually run out, leaving Australia 552 for nine as the umpires mistakenly lifted the bails eight minutes early. There was no objection from the Englishmen. Seldom had a rest day been more welcome.

The innings climbed to 573 on the third day, and now MacLaren and Jack Mason started off against those uncomplicated men and testing bowlers Bill Howell and Ernest Jones. Jones made the first incision, bowling Mason for 11. It was proving to be a frustrating series for the young Kent batsman.

Ranjitsinhji, fingers strapped, was greeted by the crowd cordially enough. But they had had their Hill and their Darling. They were not to have KSR this day. Trumble had him caught at mid-off and cheers rent the air as patriotism surfaced.

Following lunch, MacLaren was bowled by off-spinner Howell, and as Tom Hayward, seemingly at home, stood helplessly at the other end, Storer was also trapped by the Penrith bee-keeper. At 42 for four Stoddart still held himself back, and when Druce mistimed a drive off Noble, it was Hirst who went out. The score eased to a much sturdier 172 before Jones bowled Hayward for an immaculate 70, and now the careworn captain went in at number eight. There were no further casualties before stumps were drawn with England 197 for six, Hirst 50, Stoddart 11, and perhaps giving a reflective and encouraging thought to his first-ever Test century, made on this Adelaide ground half-a-dozen years before.

The fourth day was sultry, with a dust storm blowing at the start reducing visibility. There was to be no building of hopes this day. Stoddart, facing Howell, aimed his first big hit and Jones, finest mid-off in Australia, secured a marvellous catch: 206 for seven, last man 15.

Briggs thrashed merrily for 14, Howell bowled Hearne for 0, and Hirst batted bravely on, often in agony from his injured side, finding support as Richardson held up an end. They put on 54 for the final wicket before Hirst, in sight of a dramatic century, gave a slip catch on 85. England were out for 278, nearly 300 runs behind, and the compulsory follow-on came next.

After lunch Mason was dispatched by Noble for a duck, and there now developed the partnership many had been waiting for. Ranji opened with an exquisite cut, and he and MacLaren settled in against concentrated bowling and fielding that conceded nothing, if Darling's lapse in the outfield be excepted. And the people of Adelaide would have excused Darling anything

Ranji's injured finger was an inconvenience, but the batting at both ends remained very correct. The hundred came. They both passed 50, and the tempo increased. Ranji drove and cut with boneless wrists and pulled anything short with time to spare. Archibald Campbell MacLaren batted like a master, too, off-driving in the grand manner. Soon it was 150 for one.

Then Charlie McLeod struck. Ranji, trying to steer him away, lifted the ball to Trumble at slip. Hayward was the victim of a brilliant caught-and-bowled, and Storer failed again. McLeod's three quick wickets towards the end had crippled England's cause, although MacLaren (70) remained, and perhaps Stoddart could play a protracted hand.

The cricket was slow next morning. The innings was almost

four hours old when the 200 came up, and at 208 Monty Noble bowled "Chubby" Druce via his pads. At lunch England were still 70 behind as Hirst supported MacLaren (99).

MacLaren's hundred came, his third against Australia, but the other end continued to prove vulnerable. Hirst was leg-before, and Stoddart came in at number eight, a travesty no other captain would have allowed. Instantly he showed some authority, hopeless though the outlook seemed. The score rose to 262, when MacLaren's wonderful and always stylish resistance came to an end. His 124 had taken 5¼ hours of rigid defence and imperiously confident strokeplay that alone had kept air in England's lungs. He was received resoundingly at the pavilion.

Stoddart now began to hit out, but for the second time in the match Jones caught him at mid-off, this time for 24. That was it: Hearne and Richardson were soon out and England, with 282, had failed by 13 runs to evade the innings defeat. Australia stood one-up with two to play, with – it had to be confessed – strong prospects of winning the next two as well. As for the England skipper's dismissal, umpire Charlie Bannerman shook his head as he branded it an innings thrown away.

The teams took wine with Sir Edwin Smith and received an apology for the behaviour of some of the crowd, particularly towards Ranji, who, it seemed, had been misrepresented in some of the newspapers. Stoddart emphatically denied that there had been any friction between Ranji and other members of his team; and personally he got on very well with him.

Now, in January 1898, he found himself once again having to choose his words carefully with regard to Australian cricket crowds. Meanwhile, Ranji was declaring that he wished never to play in Adelaide again. And a local paper vented its opinion on him: he would be "greatly improved when he has more time to study and realise the advantages of discretion in speech as practised by that most popular of all English cricketers, A.E.Stoddart".

"Stoddy's" turn was soon to come.

There was only a short breather before the fourth Test, and at shivering Hamilton "Stoddy" took eight wickets in a narrow victory, with Briggs up to his usual comedy tricks. Then, after a day's postponement, there commenced in Melbourne the 50th Test match between England and Australia. It was also to be A.E.Stoddart's final international, by his own decision, and perhaps not altogether an inevitable decision.

Eight times he had captained England at cricket, and here for the sixth time Australia won the choice of innings. A few hours later it didn't seem to matter.

Stoddart's final toss of the coin, Melbourne, January 29, 1898

The Australian crash began when Hearne hit McLeod's stumps. The batsman left the field "looking all broken up and crippled in spirit". He soon had company as Darling snicked Richardson deep to Hearne at slip. Then Gregory failed to deal with his first ball from Richardson, a lethal yorker. At the other end Iredale, also without a run, was held by Storer, and Australia wobbled at 26 for four. Giving the new ball to Jack Hearne had been a profitable ploy.

At 32, Noble returned a ball low to Hearne, who scooped up the catch, and in came the skipper to investigate the fuss. The tension was sky-high. Harry Trott and Clem Hill steered safely to lunch, but Hearne had Trott straight afterwards: Hearne now 4 for 20, and Australia six down for 58 on a surface that was true if slow at one end. They needed the sort of styptic seventh-wicket stand that would last as a record for many decades to come. They got it. In almost 2½ hours of exhilarating strokeplay, with chances going begging, Hugh Trumble made 46 and helped Hill add 165 precious runs, a stand that completely swung the compass of this contest.

Hill unwrapped some breathtaking drives and took vicious toll of anything outside leg stump. The stand was punctuated several times by Bill Storer, firstly when his Derbyshire roar against Trumble met with hoots and hisses from the crowd, then when he dropped Hill on 65 and Trumble on 34. Finally the miserable 'keeper was asked to discard the gauntlets and have a bowl. Druce took over (and also kept for most of the second innings when Storer was found to have broken a finger). Hill, well past 100 now, thrashed him.

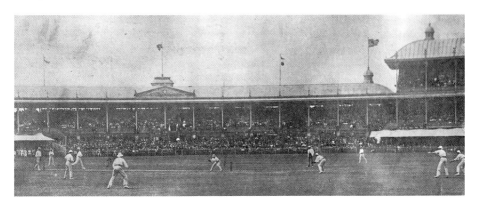

Clem Hill swishes at an off-side delivery from Tom Richardson before a packed house at the Melbourne ground

Stoddart then surprised everyone by coming on and bowling lobs. Nine came from his first over, and he bowled a wide; but "Felix" (Tom Horan) thought he should have had a more extended spell (he finished with figures of 6-1-22-0 in what turned out to be the last of his Test match appearances). "By the way," Horan wrote, "at lunchtime someone wished to speak to A.E.Stoddart, and AE said, 'Excuse me just for a few minutes, will you? I must look after my tired bowlers.'; and, glancing at the large bottle of Pommery under his arm, he passed into the dressing-room."

Storer took Hearne's end and broke the stand at last, Mason catching Trumble at square leg: Australia 223 for seven. Jim Kelly, a road-digger, shovelled Storer to the leg-side pickets, as fresh resistance was mounted. Hearne no longer seemed to be posing problems, and after Hill had taken 11 off an over he gave way for Wainwright, the Yorkshireman bowling for the first time at 257. His form was unswervingly ineffective here at the MCG as it had been on other Australian wickets.

By the close Australia had surprisingly salvaged the innings to 275 for seven, Hill a superlative 182 not out.

On Monday, following the welcome day of rest, smoke from bushfires enveloped the ground and the temperature was well over the century, prompting Ranjitsinhji to write that Australia was the only country that would set itself alight just to win a Test match, a remark not seen by all Australians in the humorous light intended. The sleepless English cricketers were distressed again by the heat.

The air became steamy from recent rainstorms, and the smoke made the haze so dense at times that distant fieldsmen were reduced to "white streaks moving about with ghostly strides".

On Saturday evening Clem Hill had tried to dodge the photographers because it was a superstition of his, photogenic though he was. Now, after adding only six runs, he was caught at slip by Stoddart off Hearne for 188, and Australia were 283 for eight. A further valuable 20 came from the heavy bats of Jones and Kelly, then another 20 came for the last wicket before Hearne took his sixth wicket, and Stoddart led his men from the field with 323 their first-innings target.

It had been a worthy fightback, and now, on a perfect pitch, England needed to respond in such a way that the series might be levelled. A repeat of the grand finale of 1894-95 would be much to everybody's taste.

But it was not to be. Trott enterprisingly opened the bowling with Bill Howell and himself, spin at both ends, and MacLaren, one of England's major hopes, floundered and was bowled for eight by Howell's wicked breakback.

Ranji accompanied makeshift opener Wainwright after lunch, and within minutes the luckless Yorkshireman was England's second casualty, spooning Trott to point. Hayward then pressed on with Ranji, and gradually the score mounted to 50. At last the bowling was changed: Noble and Trumble for Howell and Trott. And in mid-afternoon Trumble gained the wicket all Australia hoped for: Ranjitsinhji, caught Iredale, 24.

Without addition to the score Hayward, driving at Noble, was caught, and Storer, handicapped by that busted finger, lasted only a short time. With England 67 for five, Druce and Mason saw their chance to become heroes – a chance that passed them by. Their resistance showed some promise as the hundred came up, and Ernie Jones, belatedly brought into the attack, seemed to pose no threat. But at 103 Druce was trapped in front by "Jonah" and the innings lurched.

Drewy Stoddart came in at number eight, to a genuine, heartfelt reception. Jack Mason, upright and dignified, stood guard at one end while the skipper picked up runs as best he could. But again Jones crushed any hope of revival. The captain, when 17, launched into a big drive and was caught off the edge by Darling at short third man: 121 for seven.

Briggs, perhaps remembering his only Test century, made on this MCG thirteen years earlier, helped add 27: then Mason's innings ended, bowled by Jones, for a top-score 30, Hearne went second ball, and Richardson struck a few defiant blows. England were all out for 174 on a blameless pitch. It was marked down as their feeblest effort of the tour.

This time Wainwright and Briggs opened England's innings, 149 behind and following on (compulsorily) for the third Test running. And for the second time that day Wainwright failed, driving at Jones in hazy light described by one observer as being as bad as a London fog, and seeing McLeod tumble and hold the catch: England one down for 7 on Monday night.

The umpires alone (Bannerman and Phillips) had been unmoved by Stoddart's claim that visibility was too poor that evening. "If that light was too bad," asserted Phillips, "then cricket had better be given up entirely at Bramall Lane or Bradford."

That night, an old man attempting to walk to Melbourne to watch the Test match was found dying at Moonee Ponds Creek – one Australian deprived of the sweetness of victory, although the progress score whispered to him as he died should have sent him on his final mission with a cricketer's contentment.

The heat was again overpowering next day as MacLaren and Briggs set about restoring their country's battered image. They were seldom in difficulty, and as the score grew, "Pommies" in the Melbourne gathering gripped their benches in desperate hope. When Briggs was caught off a Howell long-hop for 23, hope intensified as England's finest twosome came together.

Ranji was seeing the ball clearly, but now Hugh Trumble and a patriotic Australian fly struck simultaneously. MacLaren was to claim – midst much local mockery – that his vision was blurred when the insect navigated itself past his eyelids. Iredale picked up the catch at short leg, and the score dropped to 94 for three.

Hayward played calmly, and the hundred came up. Soon, as the sun scorched down, the 150 drew near. Ranji secured his fifty. This, perhaps, would be the big stand England so desperately needed.

Again, it was to be written otherwise. Noble forced Ranji to play on, and at 147 for four England still needed two runs to stave off the innings defeat. Jack Brown and Albert Ward, where were you?

"Stoddy" walked out to play what would be his final Test innings.

At 157 Trumble held a return catch from Hayward, and Druce managed a dozen runs, by which time Stoddart had picked up five, looking carefully at this bowling attack which had cut his side to pieces with its variations and relentless innovation. He began to punch the ball with more verve and a touch of the authority of old.

A.E.Stoddart: final Test innings

There was no radio and there were no live-wire statisticians to point out that when the axe finally fell he had needed only four runs for his thousand in Test cricket. Jones bowled rather wide and he cut at it, fetching the ball back into the wicket, scattering the bails. He had made 25.

England, 192 for six, still had slender hopes that a lead might be built up and weather might intervene. Hearne and Briggs knew how to exploit a soft pitch.

Druce, for the umpteenth time on the tour, failed to build on a start; and Storer held on till close of play, his stand with Mason worth a precious 43.

There was not a breath of wind on the fourth day, and the sun was scorching down. The lead was an interesting 105 with three England wickets remaining.

Howell and McLeod made sure they were valueless, and Australia after all needed only 115 to win the match and the rubber. By lunchtime Charlie McLeod and Joe Darling had made almost half of them, against an attack weakened physically and morally by Richardson's inability to bowl, although he remained on the field. He had pulled a side muscle, and his captain had been heard to murmur "We might as well pack our bags" when he heard of the problem.

Darling fell to a careless shot off Tom Hayward at 50, and a faint shiver of excitement was felt as Hill went lbw without scoring. But Gregory got on with the job, and the runs came without further damage. Australia had regained the Ashes.

It was, enthused the *Argus*, the "most brilliant page in Australian cricket literature", while another paper, with an eye on the Melbourne convention to discuss federation of the Australian colonies, stated that "we believe Harry Trott and his ten good men and true have done more for the federation of Australian hearts than all the big delegates together".

The MCG at Test match time was a social setting, and not just for the male of the species

Joy was widespread after this long-awaited triumph by Australia's cricketers. Harry Trott (another for whom the gods had dark days planned) was in fine humour at the gathering afterwards, and Stoddart manfully offered congratulations to Australia, and paid tribute to their bowling. He conceded that it was ahead of England's in technique, and that the Australian team in general was finer than any he had played against in his four tours. "My men, I am sure, all tried," he said. "The Australians are a wonderful combination, and it did not seem to matter to Mr Trott whom he put on, for each change ended in a wicket." Defeat was "a bitter pill for the people back home".

Later, in an interview with Reuters, he allowed himself to speak from the heart. He was bitterly disappointed, he said, at losing the rubber, ruminating that his side had been defeated "most horribly". His bowlers did not understand half as much as the Australians, who were such a wonderful force.

Frank Iredale, an opponent in three Ashes Test series, later recalled Stoddart's belief that no team in the world could have beaten Australia on their own pitches at this time. (Interesting view, given that England and Australia were the only Test nations in the world at that time.) Iredale's opinion of Stoddart is interesting: "We looked upon him as the beau ideal of a skipper, and as fine a sportsman as ever went into a field. Unfortunately for us he got the idea into his head that a hitting game did not pay in this country, so he pocketed his genius and gave us scientific cricket instead."

He regretted that Stoddart on this last visit took so much notice of the crowd. "I don't think he said it in any carping spirit, but he really thought he was doing good to the game by speaking as he did." It caused many to "change their opinion about his manliness". ('Andrew', incidentally, happens to mean 'manly'.) The difference, as Iredale saw it, between Stoddart and MacLaren as skippers was in the matter of temperament. Where Stoddart would coax a cricketer by playing upon his feelings, MacLaren would drive him, in the manner of W.G.Grace.

Maud Jeffries, one of "Stoddy's" more famous admirers

Stoddart lived for his team and always commanded their respect, Iredale acknowledged. MacLaren's men admired him, but feared him too. "Stoddy" was often impulsive, but MacLaren was quick-tempered, easily angered. Moody players always chafed under MacLaren, but not so under Stoddart, who generally humoured them.

Meanwhile Maud Jeffries, the famed American actress (unmarried) who was performing in Melbourne, wrote to "Mr Stoddart" from the Menzies Hotel the day after the Test to thank him for the "exquisitely beautiful flowers, your kind note, and the colours of your cricket team.

She went on to write that "I shall always value very highly your thought of me, and it will give me much pleasure to wear the ribbon which has been sent. The result of the match has been a very great surprise to many of us, but the several games that I have had time to witness will always be remembered with the greatest pride and happiness. Take all of my good wishes for success in Sydney."

The Ashes-winning Australians: left side from top – Joe Darling, Frank Iredale, Charlie McLeod; middle – Hugh Trumble, Ernie Jones, Jim Kelly; Harry Trott beside Kelly; from top right – Bill Howell, Syd Gregory, Clem Hill, Monty Noble

The *Daily Telegraph* seemed in no doubt: Mr Stoddart's Eleven were "the team of all the failures". Quotes that might have fitted well into the gloomy Kevin Pietersen saga well over 100 years later included the complaint of one of the professionals (unnamed) who said that Ranji's "airs and graces had become intolerable", and the five amateurs "were all at sixes and sevens".

"Century" (a poetess who seems to have had a gentle crush on

"Stoddy") summed up the English viewpoint:

> There are some who have said that the team's overrated,
> And many their different opinions have stated.
> Summed up in a few words their cause of defeat
> Was due to misfortune, depression and heat.

The heatwave sizzled on after the fourth Test match, keeping the Englishmen indoors, with billiards the main pursuit.

The hardships continued in Sydney, where a six-day match produced a new world record total of 1739 runs, 239 more of them to New South Wales when the last wicket fell. Druce justified his presence at long last with a century, then it was Syd Gregory's turn with a glittering 171. The star turn was Bill Howell, batting at No.11 and belting 95 with 33 strokes in an hour (four hits over the fence plus 14 fours) against tired bowlers and aching fieldsmen. The tenth-wicket stand was worth 109 and raised the Englishmen's victory target to 603. By the fifth evening they had 258 for the loss of only one man, with MacLaren and Ranji in possession. But soon both were gone, dismissed by Howell, who bowled into the rough created by Donnan's spikes. Thereafter it was a procession against the wiles of M.A.Noble and Howell.

Stoddart failed in both innings, as did young Trumper. The England captain was among those who were troubled by Noble's swerving deliveries. He spooned a catch to mid-off, Tom Garrett, who had played in the first-ever Test match twenty years earlier. Bill Storer, though, dashed to the dressing-room to inform "Stoddy" that he was not out, for some reason or other. "Stoddart, laughing over it," reported *The Referee*, "went out again. After a few more balls MA sent along a slow high full toss and Stoddart turned round to pelt it to long leg, missed as it curved in and it landed on the off stump. When the English captain returned to the dressing-room again he shook his head as he smilingly remarked to the writer [J.C.Davis], 'It is impossible to play that sort of bowling. The ball curved like a boomerang.'"

Archie MacLaren could now look back upon a gleaming string of conquests on the Sydney Cricket Ground, to be extended when he brought his own team out in 1901-02. You had only to poke your tongue out at the ball at Sydney, he claimed, and it went for four. If Wally Hammond's ashes were scattered on the pitch at Bristol, surely Sydney deserved MacLaren's.

The matches at Sydney University and at the new Gabba ground in Brisbane (against a combined Queensland and Victoria XI) were spoiled by rain, good heavy Australian rain that falls in uncompromising quantities and brooks no hopeful vigil. It finishes play for the day in decisive downpours and allows the players to go about other things. The last half-hour of a match cut down to only 57 overs before abandonment was played out in deep gloom emphasised by the gleam of street lamps. It was a dismal start to first-class cricket in Queensland.

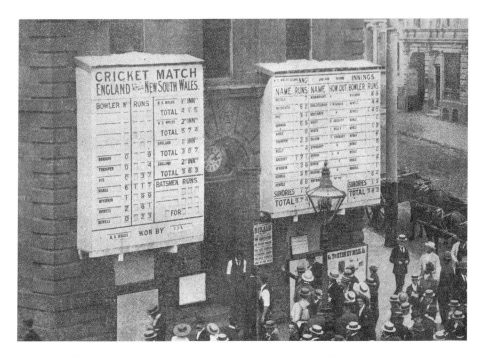

Communication was basic, but passers-by managed to keep up with the scores (NSW v Stoddart's England XI)

The Englishmen tried to be clever upon their arrival in Brisbane, alighting after their marathon train journey at Roma Street station, just outside the city. They were still seen and quickly encircled. MacLaren said a few curt words, only to be reminded that "Yes, and you've been licked three times and all!"

While the Englishmen were in this sprawling city, A.E.Stoddart announced that he would not be playing in the fifth and final Test. The events of the past three months now seem to have overwhelmed him.

His recent correspondence had included a complaint about Johnny Briggs's "Quaker" hat ("It's bad enough to be defeated but by George don't let the fellows be ridiculous"), and a poison-pen letter from Tasmania stating that his team were not wanted there, referring to an alleged slight on the previous tour when bad weather had kept the Englishmen in their hotel. (Stoddart, it may be recalled, had still managed to get a chill through batting in the rain.)

Any hurt from this unsigned note was perhaps relieved by an appeal from a man who apparently needed a pair of "Stoddy's" pants to launch him on a career as a station hand in Singleton. It isn't known whether his lower portions were clad in the England cricket captain's trousers when he presented himself to his new master.

Now, in Sydney, everyone was keen to discover whether the Australians really were so clearly superior as the post mortem on the last three Test matches seemed to conclude. H.C.A.Harrison, one of the founders of Australian Rules football, decided to ride his bike up from Melbourne. He was sixty-two. He made it in ten days, and then enjoyed the passing company of the English cricketers at the Hotel Australia during the Test match.

There were over 36,000 present at the SCG for the first day, and it looked as if England were making a contest of it when, after two innings, the home side were 96 in arrears. MacLaren had got his team away to a start of 111 with Ted Wainwright, retained in the side by Stoddart at his own expense following signs that the Yorkshireman, with his boxer's face, was nearing peak condition. His 49 was confident and completely safe. In front of a packed SCG all made runs except for Ranji, who by his own admission got out to a reckless stroke. Druce with 64 was yet another to find form frustratingly late on the tour.

Tom Richardson, fresh after the enforced relaxation, now wrote himself another page of history with a magnificent bowling display that brought him eight wickets for 94, swallowing up the cream of Australian batting with the fastest bowling by England all summer. Almost all the victims were either bowled or caught behind the wicket. That ball now survives as a mesmerising object in the author's collection.

When Archie MacLaren, again with so much depending on him, was caught at slip first ball of England's second innings – as at Melbourne in 1894 – England's lead of 96 was immediately devalued. Soon Wainwright and Ranji were out too, and as the day progressed English wickets fell regularly to Trumble and Jones. (Trumble's son mentioned in a letter to the author in 1969 that his father regarded Stoddart "very highly indeed and among the immortals of cricket".)

And so Australia were set 275, perhaps a target of some remoteness considering the diminishing totals in the match so far. Although Joe Darling flailed the bowling almost carelessly (with a bat given to him by wicketkeeper Jim Kelly, who had been given it by Archie MacLaren), McLeod and Hill went cheaply and England were in with a chance. But Jack Worrall helped swing the match. As he defended grimly, Darling got on with the job, cutting and driving all that England could offer and whipping an unruly crowd into a frenzy of excitement. They gathered 193 glorious runs that took Australia to the threshold of victory.

Darling's hundred came in a record 91 minutes, with 80 runs from boundary hits. He finished with 160 in 171 minutes (missed on 17 and 58), leaving Australia on the brink of victory. Surely his spirit lives on in Dave Warner.

During the Darling-Worrall stand a section of the crowd began screaming insults at the Englishmen and hooting every appeal. Ranji was to record his resentment at the "shower of vulgar wit", but none of the visitors was spared, least of all the outfielders. Tom Hayward's missing of Darling on 60 was attributed to it. Darling was perhaps lucky still to be in: Richardson seemed to have trapped him plumb in front of his stumps, only for umpire Bannerman to state that he was unsighted.

Worrall was out at last for 62, and when only half-a-dozen more hammer blows were needed Darling's wonderful innings ended. It was his third hundred of the series, and established him as worthy to captain Australia on their next three tours of England, where he won the series of 1899 and 1902 before running into the Honourable Francis Stanley Jackson in 1905.

Gregory and Noble gathered the remaining runs, and Australia had won this series (watched by a third of a million spectators) four Tests to one. At 4 o'clock, as Victor Cohen put it, it was all over bar the shouting, and at 5pm it was all shouting over the bar.

Hardly anyone now doubted which was the better side, and already there were rumblings that Marylebone should select and organise all future tours. The vanquished Englishmen, for their part, went off paddling and shark fishing.

The *Referee* now managed an interview with Stoddart. Deeply disturbed by crowd behaviour, for once he seemed eager to give his impressions.

"My remarks are intended for the people of this country," he told the reporter, "otherwise I would have no object in speaking. When I return home I will not mention a word on the subject. That would do no good."

Considering that the report was soon on the breakfast tables of Manchester as well as Melbourne, Sevenoaks as well as Sydney, he was displaying poor appreciation of the reach of the mass media in 1898.

"It is not my wish to interfere or speak in this matter except in the interests of cricket. I shall, in all probability, never visit this country again with a cricket team, and what I have said is purely for the good of the game, for the sake of the players in this country, and of English teams coming out here in future.

"This system of barracking, if allowed to go on, will inevitably reduce cricket to a low level, for your better-class players, with any sense of feeling, cannot keep on playing under such circumstances. The jeering by the crowd occurred on all the grounds, and in all our big matches.

"Our first experience was at Adelaide, where we were advised to take no notice of it. The same thing occurred at Melbourne, and we were similarly advised, whilst our Sydney experiences were no different. We did not take any notice of it, but when the thing is repeated in every match, and on every ground, I feel it my duty to speak, and to deplore that those in authority do not take steps to prevent it.

"I don't mean that those who jeer and hoot should be turned out of the ground. I would suggest that an appeal be made to their better feelings. If some of your influential men were to walk round the ground, speak to the people, reason with them, quietly and rationally, I am sure a great deal of good in the direction of preventing these scenes would be achieved.

"To show that moral suasion is useful in a matter of this kind, I will quote an incident in my own experience: At Brisbane, the day we played the Combined team, it was wet, and owing to a shower a cessation in play took place for a little time. The Combined team had been in the field in the morning. When they went out again in the afternoon they were hooted by a certain section.

"I saw one man who had hooted, and went up to him and said, 'Now, why did you hoot your own side?' He replied: 'Because they fielded badly.' Then I said: 'Do you consider that hooting them will make them field better?' He replied: 'I don't know.'

"I talked to him very quietly and seriously for about ten minutes during which he gazed at me and seemed to wonder what sort of person I was. At the end of that time he said he was damned if he would ever hoot them again. Every man has a generous spot in him; most of those who jeer and hoot have good points, and, if you appeal to their better nature, I am sure they will give it over."

Then came the idealistic conclusion: "If you can successfully appeal to one man, you can do so to a body of men."

The attractive Sydney Cricket Ground, where Australia wrapped up a 4-1 Ashes success in the 1897-98 series, despite fast bowler Tom Richardson's heroic performance

It was suggested to him that players and umpires as well as onlookers make mistakes.

"Quite so. In the last Test match at Melbourne our wicketkeeper appealed for a catch at the wicket, and so did the bowler. The umpire gave it not out. The crowd set to work and hooted at our wicketkeeper and bowler, whose appeal was legitimate. I was given to understand in the pavilion afterwards that the batsman admitted he was out in that stroke.

"A little later, when the Australians took to the field, their wicketkeeper appealed for a catch at the wickets, and, before the umpire had time to give his decision, he threw the ball high in the air. Mind you, I have the greatest admiration for the Australian wicketkeeper's honesty, and feel certain that he will admit having made a mistake in throwing the ball up before the umpire had given his decision. The crowd did not hoot Kelly, as they had done our wicketkeeper.

"In this last match here Hearne received a severe blow from Jones, at which the crowd, many in the pavilion, laughed. Later, Richardson was bowling, and he sent a full-toss over Darling's head, at which the crowd in the pavilion howled. There were three men who hooted in front of our dressing-room. I stood up from my seat and said they ought to be ashamed of themselves."

After all, one might ask, what were three oratorical spectators after a storming pack of tough Welsh forwards?

A final net at Sydney; then he ruled himself out

"At this stage in the game we were doing very well. Richardson told me himself that the wicket was one on which he thought he could really bowl his best. He said it would help him, and he did not think the Australians would get the runs. Of course, you know how much depended on Richardson. They hooted and howled at him to such an extent that when he came into lunch he had lost his head and had lost his bowling.

"He came to me almost with tears in his eyes and told me this. Now you see how unfair it is; not necessarily intended to be unfair, for I don't say the object of the crowd was to put Richardson off, yet they did so."

He mentioned a blind swipe by Harry Donnan, provoked by ceaseless jeering; also the shabby, impatient treatment meted out to the veteran Garrett. Stoddart was then asked about his attitude towards the cricket press.

"I am perfectly well aware that there are men in this country who write cricket as a sport, and whose notes are acceptable to all of us. It is only a certain section that do not write proper matter. They say we have had fights amongst ourselves; and when that is played out they say we drink. You can understand how repulsive this is to us. In spite of the bad luck we have had generally, and the numerous things we have had to upset us, the good fellowship existing between us has been most marked. I myself can safely say that I have never heard a cross word spoken by any member of this team to another. By writing in this way such men do great harm to the game in every way."

What of the tour overall? In spite of everything, A.E.Stoddart had enjoyed the tour very much indeed.

At the conclusion of the final Test match he had been presented by the Sydney and Melbourne cricket authorities with a gold watch in a hunting-case "as a token of their esteem and as an acknowledgement of his many services in the cause of cricket in Australia". And in Melbourne his stolen life membership badge was replaced.

But by now the barracking question was the topic on the lips of cricketers everywhere. In responding to a toast at the end of the fifth Test, Stoddart was again outspoken, and his remarks were more or less endorsed by Harry Trott, his opposite number.

The English skipper caused some straightening of backs when he got to his feet and began: "If you will excuse me, I would like to make a few remarks which may, however, not be pleasant." He felt it his duty to speak as he did: "I have a right, as an English cricketer who has been out here so often, to make reference to the insults which have been poured upon me and my team during our journey through this country."

He spoke of his deep disappointment at this treatment, and suggested that his team had been treated more like prizefighters than a band of sportsmen. "The crowd has gone out of its way to insult us and I cannot see what we have done to incur all this at their hands." He felt that the wrath of the spectators and the Press was undeserved. "This has been on my mind for some time, and I was determined to mention it. But I hope you will not think we are dissatisfied with our tour."

Harry Trott got to his feet: "I quite agree with Mr Stoddart's remarks about the crowd. They are a perfect nuisance. [Cheers]. And yet we can't do without them. [Laughter]. I think barracking should be stopped, and they can easily do it by sending a few private detectives among the crowd. They did it in Melbourne once, and three men were taken to gaol. I think they got about a week, and there was no more barracking there for about six months!"

Australia's cartoonists and lampoonists had a field day when he complained about the crowd behaviour. This one even seemed to resent his luck in the sweepstake. Ranjitsinhji was just as much a target for criticism for his comments

Still the controversy raged. Emotive letters were sent to the newspapers, and "Mid-On" (H.W.Hedley) wrote what Stoddart considered an extremely unfair article accusing him of being over-sensitive and criticising the crowds while suffering the bitterness of defeat. (He might also have mentioned the severe depth of the grief which destabilised him following the death of his mother.) In Melbourne, Stoddart, now further hurt deeply, felt compelled to respond, saying that he had lived for nothing else but cricket, and that the criticism of him was mean, contemptible, and bad as it was untrue. He had merely intended to object to the small groups of barrackers who were "no good to man or beast".

Now it was "Mid-On" who was stung, and he penned a harsh response by way of a letter to Melbourne's *Age* newspaper, quoting Ranjitsinhji as having extolled the crowds (Ranji's book had yet to be published), and passing on young Druce's remark that the team had had a "ripping good time".

The journalist concluded his judgment on "Stoddy" with condescending geniality: "As he has only made the one mistake in 10 years, and that in extenuating circumstances, I suppose it will only be considerate to treat him as a first offender and let him down lightly. Nevertheless, it must always be regretted that the English captain on his departure from Australia this time will leave a very general impression that he is a better winner than a loser." It was one of the earliest instances of a "whinging Pom" accusation.

Bill Storer was in an uncomfortable position too. The NSWCA were debating whether he should be reported to MCC at Lord's for allegedly remarking to umpire Bannerman in the last Test: "You're a cheat, and you know it!" During an interval, NSWCA secretary Percy Bowden (brother of Surrey and England's Monty) had referred Bannerman's complaint to Stoddart, whose written reply, dated March 4, was: "In the absence of both our managers, it is impossible for me to answer your letter now. I will write you from Melbourne." When informed that Storer was to be reported to MCC over in London unless he apologised, Stoddart replied by telegram from Adelaide: "Have left matter entirely to cricketer mentioned, who prefers matter should come before Marylebone Club in preference to apology." MCC later censured Storer.

"Boo hoo": an unappetising image

It had indeed been an animated tour.

Two further matches remained, an anticlimax for Stoddart and his troupe. The Victoria fixture, started on Stoddart's 35th birthday, brought the weary tourists a handsome win, Tom Richardson, free of rheumatism at last, coming into his own in the second innings. Afterwards, on March 17, the entire touring party went along to Archie MacLaren's wedding in Toorak to heiress Miss Maud Power to wish well the batsman now regarded as perhaps the greatest England had yet sent to the Antipodes. The bride was two years older than the groom, but it seems to have been true love. Arthur Priestley, who had accompanied the Englishmen on the tour, was best man. The event turned into a near-riot when hundreds of cricket fans, most of them women, descended on the church, desperate for souvenirs and behaving like the raving mobs seen at celebrity events over a century later.

A. H. Stoddart wishes he had done this before they were such fearful breeders (This refers to Mr. Stoddart's letter denying false statements.)

Some of the lampoonery was sympathetic

Soon afterwards A.E. Stoddart was donning flannels again for the South Australia match, his last ever in Australia after four tours. "With a nervous step," Ranji observed, "Stoddart went to spin the coin, but he returned with a pleasant and confident gait which betoken a successful result." It was the only toss he won from all the first-class matches that season.

Stoddart's partnership with Jack Board rallied a sinking first innings. He made a 40 full of his best cuts and some screaming hits over extra cover, and the second 'keeper hit 59. Darling and Lyons, however, made 166 before the first South Australia wicket fell, and only five cheap wickets by Mason kept the teams in sight of each other (this leading, predictably, to the charge that Stoddart hadn't used the tall Kent amateur sufficiently during the tour). The Englishmen's second effort was better. Wainwright (107) raised 187 for the first wicket with Mason, but the promise dwindled as wickets fell steadily. A final total of 399 left South Australia needing 335 to win.

Stoddart's last innings on Australian soil brought him 16 runs and was ended by a thrilling one-handed catch at cover, significantly by a Giffen, though not George, who still insisted on withholding his presence from these contests.

Significantly too it was Australia's special heroes Darling and Hill who made another heap of runs as the match ran to a draw. Darling made 96 and Hill was there at the end with 124. With Ernie Jones's 14 wickets, it was a fine show of strength with which to farewell the Englishmen.

Clem Hill, the prodigy, was presented with a silver shield and gold watch for his coming of age, and at the ceremony "Stoddy" found himself making another speech. The subject of barracking was now practically a neurosis, and once again he felt compelled to refer to it, supported this time by none other than George Giffen. These much-travelled warriors of the cricket field both felt strongly about it. But young Hill, clutching his presentations, may have been simply pondering on triumphs to come. Meanwhile, the cricket authorities looked with satisfaction at the overall match takings of £24,836 (close to £2½ million in today's money), which produced a profit of £9000 (£900,000 in today's inflation-riddled currency).

England's captain was to write a letter open for publication in which he explained that he received nothing above tour expenses. He went further: "The accounts of my two tours I have never seen, and had no right to see, but the whole of the very large profits which were made were received by the two clubs [Melbourne and Sydney] who were our hosts, and no part of them reached the hands of any member of the teams."

This led to comment about the Australian cricketers' earnings from their tours of England. Those profits were shared by the touring players. Why should not England's top players receive something above their set fees if they helped generate profits? It was something that coming generations would sort out very adequately, especially during the Kerry Packer years.

Some of the best times for England's skipper had been in the tranquillity of the bush, with "liaison" man Phil Sheridan

Finally, at Sir Edwin Smith's farewell social, Stoddart was grateful to find support from two great Australian cricketers. Jack Lyons expressed pleasure at the way England's captain had spoken out against unseemly barracking. Then when H.Y.Sparks deplored Stoddart's speech and suggested that there would always be barracking, Giffen interrupted briefly but pungently with one word: "Rubbish!" Sparks, one of the founders of Adelaide Oval, alluded to the inevitable disappointment felt by the Englishmen at their lack of success: this was doubtless behind their complaints. And Stoddart was cheered as he interjected: "I speak for the benefit of Australian cricketers as well as our own!"

At the point of departure it was the tour liaison man, Major Wardill, who faced the press, while it was noticed that the captain had about him a "conspicuously subdued air". In an attempt to puncture the rumours, Wardill stated that he had never had charge of a better group of men. There had been no dissension.

On March 24, 1898 the English team, unable to meet Perth's request for a fixture, boarded *Ormuz* at Largs Bay, and as the ship slipped out into the Bight the captain of England's cricketers must have felt vast relief in the breeze. There would be no mother to greet him, but he must have longed to see his sisters Connie, Cissie and Minnie.

The latest rumour suggested that this 35-year-old bachelor would soon be returning to Australia to marry either "a fetching Sydney girl or a smart Melbourne widow".

The one positively good thing he did take back to England was a magnificent £1350 sweepstake prize, having drawn Reaper, which ran second in the Newmarket Handicap during the final Test match. Each professional, with £25, shared his luck, and official hosts Ben Wardill and Phil Sheridan, together with the amateur cricketers, were each given a diamond scarf-pin. The skipper could not be accused of being anything less than thoughtful.

For their part, the professionals, who patently adored their captain, gave him a Mappin & Webb Coromandel tantalus with a set of three decanters as a token of their esteem. It was a poignant experience to see it sold for £850 at an auction in England in 1996.

Ranji, with his flair for timing, had penned a charming farewell letter to Australia as he headed off to his homeland for a term "to look after his endangered claim to be Jam of Nawanagar".

Tom Richardson, after much suffering, rested his weary frame. Stoddart was to write some calculations on the flyleaf of one of his *Wisdens*, musing over Richardson's bowling figures in 1894-95 and 1897-98 and during the English seasons which followed. Another comparison revealed (notwithstanding "Stoddy's" erring mathematics) that of his chief support bowlers, Bobby Peel got through much more work in 1894-95 than did Jack Hearne three years later.

The reception at Tilbury dock was much quieter than on the return of the previous expedition, but warm nonetheless. An Australian journal depicted the homecoming of Stoddart with the British Lion. A welcoming John Bull says: "I'm sorry I trusted him to you. He's looking woefully tame." To which the skipper philosophically replies: "No wonder, considering the horrible beatings he has had."

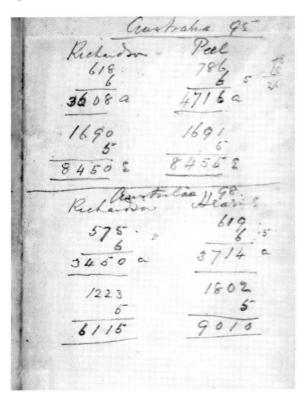

Post mortem: Drewy Stoddart does some calculations in the back of a Wisden to compare the performances of his principal bowlers on the 1894-95 tour of Australia and the more recent one in 1897-98

An Ill Star

The tour reviews went on for some time in the newspapers and in private. A letter from H.A.Tate to E.B.V.Christian reveals the feeling of at least one cricket enthusiast: "If WG had gone instead of Wainwright or Briggs, his mere <u>presence</u> would have made all the difference. I do not think Stoddart a good captain. In '96 he captained the second MCC team which opposed the Australians, & I thought managed the bowling very badly. But he is a fine fellow I believe."

As for Australia's perception of him, in his tour scrapbook he had pasted some remarks about himself by "Jingle" which surely brought him some gratification: "At first nervous, he can now speak eloquently and at length, to the surprise of Melbourne journalists, who writhe under his remarks as to themselves and the 'barracking question'. He resides at Hampstead; occasionally plays for his old love at cricket; figures at the local Conservative club; but is not twin-brother to Gregor MacGregor, although the pair are inseparable."

Wisden might well have the last say: "To speak the plain truth there has not for a very long time been anything so disappointing in connection with English cricket as the tour of Mr Stoddart's team in Australia last winter."

CHAPTER 21

Disenchantment

THE 1898 season was his last full-time with Middlesex, and statistically his best. Vice-captain in this year when the county club first had an official cap, and leading the side when A.J.Webbe was absent, Stoddart stood clearly at the head of the batting averages with 52. He missed five high-scoring matches in August, and if he had been in among this flood of runs, his best aggregate (in the rich 1893 summer) would almost certainly have been overtaken.

Yet this man already had it in his mind to finish with the game. It mattered not that he seemed to be batting as well as ever. He was tired of it all, and to the despair of his hordes of admirers he would retire before the final springtime of the 1890s welcomed yet another Australian cricket team.

"Though his record was perhaps in excess of the actual merit of his play," *Wisden* curiously said of his 1898 achievements, "there can be no doubt that Stoddart was in first-rate form. After his complete failure as a batsman in Australia during the winter, there was some reason to fear that his cricket had left him, and for this reason the pleasure felt by the public at his success was all the keener. When well set he was the same delightful batsman as ever, playing a game that in its combination of grace and power could hardly be beaten."

Again his appearances for Hampstead were curtailed, and for the first time in eight years he failed to record a century for the club. Further, for the only time in his many years with Hampstead he stood other than at the head of the batting averages, Preston and Hayman exceeding his 48.

He was president of the Stoics Cricket Club this year, the opponents who had helped make his name when he hit that 485 off them twelve years ago.

And South Shields Cricket Club wrote to him in June to offer honorary life membership to one of the town's most distinguished native sons. On an MCC letterhead with his Lithos Road address penned in, he replied to the SSCC chairman to thank him and the club, and saying that he had read an account of the club's meeting while he was on tour in Australia. "Your chairman spoke so feelingly of the loss [his mother] I had so recently sustained and I feel very grateful for it. My father always took a great interest in sports & I am glad to think that his name has not been forgotten in the club of which so far as regards my birth qualification I ought long ago to have been a member & with which now owing to your recent kind action am to be connected for life. Hoping you will convey to the club my great appreciation of their kind action. I am Yours faithfully A.E.Stoddart".

The Lithos Road house which Stoddart and MacGregor shared for a number of years

The three regular pals together, cricketers and rugby footballers all, MacGregor, Woods and AES

Middlesex's 1898 county campaign suffered a squelching beginning, and Stoddart, greeted warmly by the crowds on his reappearance after the Australian tour, made only three against Somerset. The rain continued for days; then against Gloucestershire he was bowled for a duck by the boy prodigy leg-spinner Charles Townsend (15 wickets in the match). But the Saturday crowd at Lord's saw him regain form with a masterly 70 not out on a soft surface. WG steered the visitors to a comfortable victory.

Nottinghamshire had Middlesex following on at Lord's in another rain-interrupted match. This time "Stoddy" made 138 to save the match, missed four times before reaching his half-century. It was his highest score for three years, and he probably enjoyed a chat with Arthur Shrewsbury about the recent gruelling expedition to Australia.

Cricket offered the view that "his recent successes have showed plainly that it was the style and not the man which was at fault during the last two or three seasons". Who knows?

Still at Lord's, the style and the man were sadly at fault in the Yorkshire match, when on a fast Lord's surface he rewarded his affectionate audience with an agonising graft punctuated by a few pedigree strokes and ended by George Hirst at 15. Middlesex had no Schofield Haigh to sling them down, rocking the stumps six times with yorkers. F.S.Jackson made a classy century, and there was sting in Yorkshire's tail. Young Wilfred Rhodes helped add a quick 97 with Frank Milligan (who was killed two years later during a cavalry attempt to relieve Mafeking).

Warner and Ford lit up the second Middlesex innings, but Stoddart failed again, Long John Tunnicliffe's remarkable slip catch giving Rhodes one of the more distinguished of his sensational tally of 154 wickets in his debut year. Just on seventy years later, blind but still keen of memory, Rhodes was asked by the author if he remembered the Stoddart dismissal. He didn't, but that was hardly surprising for a man who went on to take an all-time record 4187 first-class wickets.

At The Oval, Surrey piled up 468, despite the colourful addition of Albert Trott to the Middlesex attack. Stoddart, steady and deliberate on the drying surface, made 45 runs in 2¼ hours, and further resistance by Warner, Ford and Trott eventually denied Surrey.

At Old Trafford, Stoddart made 36, top score on a treacherous pitch; and after Hearne had followed up his first-innings 9 for 68 with 7 for

46 (how he could utilise bowlers' conditions) Middlesex needed 225 to win. Hayman and Warner gave them a good start, but W.B.Stoddart, leg-spinner and rugby player, had them both stumped, and the other "Stoddy" (19), together with the rest, failed to save Middlesex.

Away from the spotlight, at Aylestone Road, they played Leicestershire and Stoddart registered his highest score of the summer. The hosts piled up a praiseworthy 312 and had Middlesex smarting from early losses. But Stoddart stroked 157, with two hits over the ropes, an innings full of dash and spirit over 3¾ hours, just as in the good old days. *Cricket*, looking back, observed that "during the entire innings one was reminded of the days when nearly all Middlesex men played brilliant and attractive cricket". And this was supposedly the "Golden Age".

The Kent fixture was postponed because of the funeral of one of the pioneers and stalwarts of Middlesex cricket, I.D."Donny" Walker, who was laid to rest at Southgate churchyard, farewelled by many cricketers, all larger than life in Victorian cricket. A.E.Stoddart was now part of the middle generation.

Around this time an appeal was under way to preserve Prince George's Ground in Raynes Park as an open recreation space for overcrowded London. Most of the prominent amateurs gave the fund their support, and WG's subscription letter prompted Stoddart and MacGregor to forward an amount to *The Sportsman*, stating "We hasten to obey the great master, WG",

The Great Master's 50th birthday was coming up, and to mark the occasion the showpiece Gentlemen v Players match at Lord's was arranged to start on the big day.

Meanwhile, Middlesex, led by Stoddart, faced Sussex, for whom C.B.Fry carried his bat for 104, was no-balled again for throwing, and finally was bowled for 0 by a hostile Albert Trott, who was all form.

On July 18 the "Great Match of the Season" began, the Gentlemen's and Players' sides being regarded as – the absence of Ranjitsinhji and J.T.Tyldesley apart – the finest Elevens possible. There was general regret at Tom Richardson's absence, but the Surrey strong-man's form lately had simply been poor. The Australian trip had taken a lot out of him. Nor could room be found for young Rhodes, who became 12th man when the pitch showed true before the start.

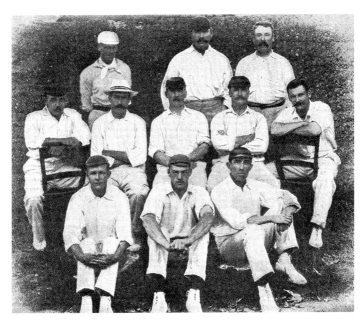

*Middlesex team in the summer of 1898 (Stoddart sometime skipper). Standing
– E.H.Bray, J.Phillips, J.T.Rawlin; seated – J.T.Hearne, A.E.Stoddart,
A.J.Webbe (captain), T.C.O'Brien, R.S.Lucas; front – P.F.Warner, R.W.Nicholls,
H.R.Bromley-Davenport*

Billy Gunn stroked 139 on the first day, when the intense heat had
cab-horses lying down helplessly between the shafts. And on Tuesday
morning, on a wicket tantalisingly enlivened by rain, Stoddart accompanied
The Champion across the Lord's turf, to waves of enthusiastic and excited
applause. WG was limping slightly from a foot injury, but scoffing at any
suggestion of a runner. And it seemed it would hardly matter when he
edged Lockwood to Lilley with only a single on the board, but the chance
slipped away and the gathering breathed in relief.

There were several close calls, but the opening pair who had
commenced so many notable innings together in two countries weathered
almost an hour of the best the professionals could show before Stoddart
was caught off Lockwood for 21.

Frank Swinnerton, who became a prolific writer and part of the
"Bloomsbury set", was there that day, an impressionable 12-year-old: "On
this wonderful occasion I saw giants of the game, and in seeing them I
entered an earthly Paradise. I sat, unluckily, next to a gross toper [drinker]

who, already full of beer before the match began, swigged at a great bottle while play was in progress, and shouted remarks which he believed to be stentorian wit for the entertainment of those whose ears he could reach. His ridicule was turned upon myself and my clothes, which were home-made and shabby; and all I remember of it was that I was filled with embarrassment. One effort, however, deserves record. When W.G.Grace (who was massive) and A.E.Stoddart (rather meagre in build) appeared together in the pavilion doorway to open the Gentlemen's innings, the wretch bawled, to the tune of a popular song:

> *I put my money on the big fat man;*
> *Doo-dah, doo-day, day!"*

The Gentlemen XI for the grand showpiece Lord's event, July 1898: standing – C.J.Kortright, J.R.Mason, A.C.MacLaren, J.A.Dixon, umpire W.A.J.West; seated – S.M.J.Woods, A.E.Stoddart, W.G.Grace, C.L.Townsend, F.S.Jackson; front – E.G.Wynyard, G.MacGregor.

If they heard the vocal offering, the batsmen no doubt smiled to each other.

W.G.Grace reached 43 before Lockwood had the privilege – for that it truly was – of dismissing him as Lilley made certain of the catch this time. "The Grand Old Man" would passionately have wanted a hundred on the day of his own half-century.

Stoddart and WG proceed to the middle, the former "meagre" in terms of physical comparison, according to young Frank Swinnerton

The battle was absorbing. Batsmen had to earn their runs by the highest ingenuity. F.S.Jackson carved 48, and the out-of-practice MacLaren fought through an hour of bedlam then made some fierce drives and hooks in a pleasing 50.

That evening, at a dinner given by The Sports Club to honour Dr W.G.Grace, Sir Richard Webster (later Lord Alverstone) proposed a warm toast to The Champion. WG got to his feet to reply, moved for once and doubting his ability to express his feelings articulately. "When I look round and see the friends and cricketers near me I wish I had Stoddart's happy knack of saying the right words in the right place. If I can't say the right words, I feel them."

He complimented his team in the current match for passing 300 on such a dubious pitch, saying: "My old friend Stoddart and myself, when we got fifty, thought we had done pretty well."

The entire gathering must have done fairly well that night, for *Cricket* remarked that "on Wednesday some of the Gentlemen seemed a little tired after their exertions on the previous day".

The Gentlemen were eventually left needing 296 to win at the rate of 100 per hour. WG's bruised hand prevented him from opening, and soon Stoddart was held at slip off Lockwood, and MacLaren succumbed to Hearne's sharp deviation. Wickets continued to crash. Sammy Woods was bowled. Wynyard was bowled. Mason and Jackson were bowled. Dixon was bowled. MacGregor was bowled. Five of these timber hits were by Jack Hearne.

Boy Townsend saved the stumps from further bruising when Tunnicliffe made an amazing slip catch, and soon only WG and Kortright were left. For seventy tense minutes they were to hold out. It was the innings of Kortright's life, and with the handicapped Doctor surviving comfortably enough, Bill Lockwood eventually came up for the final five balls.

His third ball was held back imperceptibly, as only Lockwood knew how. Kortright slashed and the catch swirled high to Schofield Haigh, who held it. The batsmen, so recently at loggerheads at Leyton, now left the field together framed in glory, WG's arm through Kortright's.

So the great traditional showpiece between amateurs and professionals had acquired another absorbing chapter. But it had lost something of value as well, for never again would it see Arthur Shrewsbury or Drewy Stoddart. What has mercifully survived is a short film sequence of the two teams walking past the "movie camera", an indescribably precious length of celluloid which captures most of the legendary names from the Golden Age smiling and chatting as they promenade past in all manner of headwear and blazers. "Stoddy" walks with confident tread and smiling countenance, pipe in hand, and wearing a striped blazer and straw boater. The regret is that the cameraman didn't splash out on a lot more film that day.

At Hove, Charles Fry, who had missed the great event at Lord's, was in the news again, registering a century in each innings against Middlesex and taking Sussex to within inches of victory. Stoddart made an attractive top-score 69 interrupted by sea mist, then a desperate 42 in an attempt to overhaul Sussex. In the end Middlesex were content to see the cool rain that ensured a draw.

It was August already in this final county season, with "Stoddy" ambling out onto Taunton's sunlit expanse. Somerset reached 221, but after Stoddart's 51, F.H.E.Cunliffe and C.M.Wells (101) whipped the tiring bowling. Trott and Hearne took five apiece in Somerset's dismal second innings, a novice named Bosanquet bowling only five overs for Middlesex in the match. The phenomenon of the googly lay a couple of years ahead.

Bristol was next, always an important call with its great bewhiskered host, whom Stoddart this time dismissed with an extraordinary catch at slip which the batsman acknowledged with a warm clasp of the hand. When "Stoddy" batted, his eye was still sharp. He stroked 70 of the best, and Middlesex fell just short of Gloucestershire's 379. The last day was washed out.

Now Middlesex entered their magnificent winning streak with success against the old enemy Surrey at Lord's, batting well when wickets were supposed to be tumbling after rain. Stoddart braved Surrey's attack with Warner, who charmingly was "not always able to make it appear that he knew all about the bowling". Jimmy Douglas made a century in the second innings on a tranquil wicket, and Stoddart made 54, the declaration apparently leaving Surrey to play out time. But only Abel (75) could withstand Trott and Hearne, and victory came to Middlesex on the bell.

Stoddart missed Leicestershire but went to Leeds to join in a creditable win when Trott (7 for 13) simply swept Yorkshire away for 45 with his unpredictable variations. This was Yorkshire's Championship year, and the monumental Tunnicliffe and Brown spent much of the remainder of the week putting on 554 together at Chesterfield. *This* was the pair that Trott and Hearne and the rain had suppressed at Headingley.

Middlesex now had to continue their glorious run without A.E.Stoddart, whose leg was injured. Not until September 5 did he return to first-class cricket. The fixture was the hotly anticipated match between his 1897-98 touring team and a Rest of England XI at Hastings. Stoddart had written to William Carless, the promoter of the festival, explaining that Druce wouldn't be playing – "finger is very bad". He had a problem of his own as well: "My leg is bad and I am very doubtful about the 2nd match. Must play in the first." He wrote that he and Jack Mason and another pal would be staying at the Dormey House for a few days before the match. Leisure was the keynote.

To disappointment all round, Ranjitsinhji was away in India. It was remarked that so long after the tour few could recall the names of all the touring team, and if a team were to be setting sail for Australia now few of Stoddart's band would qualify for selection on 1898 performances. The attraction was further diminished by the withdrawal of C.B.Fry and Jack Brown and Lockwood and Lilley. But Gilbert Jessop did his best to compensate for the missing celebrity cricketers.

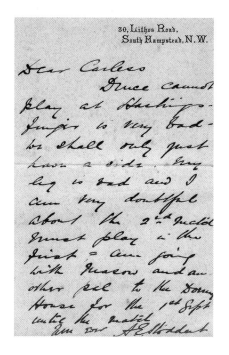

Letter of explanation

The Rest were not doing very well until Kortright and Ford lambasted 83 runs, and the Rest of England's total climbed to 236. Mr A.E.Stoddart's team bettered it mainly because of Wainwright's 75 and MacLaren's 51, an attractive hand inspired by the occasion. Stoddart himself, batting modestly down at No.7, made only seven, caught by Shrewsbury off young Rhodes.

The Rest were recovering in their second innings when Ford took a cruel blow from Richardson and couldn't continue. With WG bowled by Briggs for a duck, all was gloom for the challengers – until G.L.Jessop warmed up. He took a little more than an hour of everyone's time, but into it he packed 112 runs, and when the sound of gunfire had ceased Stoddart's XI had something to chase after all. They fetched the 182 largely through Jack Mason's skill and some dropped catches, and fittingly skipper "Stoddy" was there at the end, scoreless but well satisfied with the victory.

And so ended his final full season of first-class cricket, when his batting had shown signs of returning to the champagne class. Discounting his first two and last three first-class innings, which were of no account, he had strung together a series of first-class performances which were very pleasing in their consistency: 70 not out, 6, 138, 15, 16, 45, 36, 19, 157, 35 not out, 60, 25, 21, 4, 69, 42, 51, 70, 62, 54, 26. "He is still," J.N.Pentelow declared, "a batsman whom it is worthwhile going a hundred miles to see."

The hopes of his friends and admirers were dashed when he

declined the captaincy of Middlesex for 1899. He felt in his heart that the county, well endowed with young batsmen and with a good bowling attack, could do without him. The announcement, then, that A.J.Webbe's mantle would pass to A.E.Stoddart was wide of the mark. Gregor MacGregor was appointed captain, with Ford as his vice-captain, as the facts leaked out over a few days in March 1899.

As usual, *Cricket* had its ear close to the ground: "It is reported, and the report had good authority, that A.E.Stoddart has definitely made up his mind to give up first-class cricket. One can only express the hope, which will find a responsive echo in the hearts of cricketers of all classes and in every country where the game is played, that this decision is not irrevocable. First-class cricket can ill afford to lose a player of such infinite variety and one who has done so much by his personal influence and example to maintain the character of the game. Just now, he certainly cannot be spared."

"Stoddy" and Jack Hearne at Hastings in fashionable wing collars and watch-chains

The speculation was confirmed two days later via a telegram from Stoddart to the meticulous H.V.L.Stanton (walrus-moustached "Wanderer" of *The Sportsman*). From now on, Andrew Ernest intended to devote his energies to second-class cricket and golf. The banks of Jordan had been reached.

CHAPTER 22

Club Before County

THE cricket season of 1899 was hot, with perfect batting surfaces all over the country. W.G.Grace left Gloucestershire in May, and in July little Neville Cardus saw his first match at Old Trafford. Joe Darling's Australians were a strong all-round combination, winning the first-ever five-Test series to be staged in England by virtue of victory at Lord's.

Ranji advertised his return to England with eight centuries and became the first ever to score 3000 runs in a season. Bobby Abel (357 not out) and Surrey (811) made records that were due to stand for a long time, and Middlesex came close to taking the Championship, with Albert Trott memorably clearing the Lord's pavilion off a ball from M.A.Noble midway through this notable summer which saw the construction of the Mound Stand.

Abel and Hayward shared a stand of 448 against Yorkshire at The Oval, where the patrons lately were getting exceptional value for their money. And a Marlborough schoolboy, Reggie Spooner, whose style was to remind men of Stoddart's, was fast coming to maturity. Stoddart, as Philip Trevor pointed out, might have had himself a wonderful time in this batsman's year.

As it was, he gave the lesser numbers of club-cricket spectators much to enthuse over. It was as if the trauma of the 1897-98 Australian campaign had been washed away and he was reunited with the game he had loved for so long. He exceeded a thousand runs easily, despite a programme shortened for him by illness and an accident. He hit seven club centuries plus a 97 off Kensington Park, and a hundred at Forest Hill School. He carried his bat through the Hampstead innings for 100 not out against University College Old Boys on July 8. And there were 60 wickets too that season.

F.S.Ashley-Cooper gave his figures (in *Lillywhite*) as 17 innings for his club, 1363 runs, average 104.84, highest 163. Some time later, F.R.D'O.

Monro, Hampstead CC's historian, recalled a rich example of "Stoddy's" humour:

"Stoddart loved a joke. His friend, George Jeffery, was fond of but very shy of the opposite sex. I remember once, when I was bowling, his putting George Jeffery in a place on the boundary where I did not want him at all, and I noticed that he sidled away from that place whenever he could and each time Stoddart sent him back. I spoke to Stoddart about it and said I did not want him there, but Stoddart said 'There is a bunch of girls up there and I want to see how pink George's face will go'. He was not disappointed. George Jeffery had a large good-humoured face with a healthy glow on it, but from where I was I could see it was now of a colour to scorch everything within range."

A very strong Hampstead club side from around 1899: standing – W.R.Moon, D.J.Crump, S.S.Pawling, L.J.Moon (a Great War suicide); seated – W.S.Hale, T.S.Wheater, A.E.Stoddart, Ahsan-ul-Hak, F.R.Spofforth, H.B.Hayman; front – F.W.Orr

Jeffery, who had played rugby for England in the same team as Stoddart, evidently forgave him for the mischief. In time he stood as best man at "Stoddy's" wedding.

In Wilfred Flowers's benefit, eventually started at Lord's on Whit Monday, May 22, 1899, a bizarre match was completed in a mere 185 minutes, the time it would take a Geoff Boycott or Jonathan Trott to play himself in. (Flowers, a Notts and England cricketer, had also been on the MCC ground staff for many years.) It was a good one for "Stoddy" to have missed. Four Somerset men made "pairs" in their totals of 35 and 44, and Albert Trott, now probably the world's top all-rounder, took 11 for 31 in the match (Hearne 8 for 45).

When Somerset were eight down for 8, Cyril Foley, fielding for Middlesex, scampered to the pavilion in some agitation. A friend of his had dreamt that a cricket team had been dismissed for 10, so he offered to bet Stoddart, a spectator now, one sovereign that this would be Somerset's fate. The offer was declined. Foley, known as "The Raider" since featuring in the notorious Jameson Raid in South Africa ("very dark night – beastly ride – rather a bore"), ran over to Stoddart a second time to make a fresh offer, but again it was refused. "Stoddy" already knew of the dream, and had often been heard to say, somewhat virtuously, that "no game is worth playing at all which is not worth playing without a bet". So they kept their sovereigns in their pockets.

Sammy Woods dragged Somerset to the shabby respectability of 35, and the meagre Middlesex total of 86 remarkably was sufficient for an innings victory.

Drewy Stoddart was an unsuspecting onlooker at Lord's again early in June when George Thornton had to withdraw from the match with Sussex after having fielded throughout the first day. W.L.Murdoch sportingly permitted Stoddart to take his place, and in a match of heavy scoring he took up position at the wicket in the highest company once again, a smiling Cincinnatus whom Ernest Killick bowled for 0.

Middlesex went on to amass 466 (Ford and Trott centuries), and when Sussex went in a second time, 79 behind, Fry and Brann again opened with a century stand, a partnership dissolved when Brann edged Stoddart to slip. His duty done, he was withdrawn from the attack by MacGregor and the formidable bowling duo of Trott and Hearne got on with the job.

His appetite had not been whetted, and it was back to the stocks and shares and club cricket for him.

Later that month his 485 at last was exceeded as the highest score ever recorded, and he paid tribute to the remarkable schoolboy Arthur

Collins by presenting him with a bat for his undefeated 628. Young Collins was to die in the forthcoming Great War.

"Stoddy" was opening the innings with W.G.Grace again in the MCC v Staffordshire match at Lord's late in August and scoring a 91 to go with a neat little bowling performance of 3 for 3 (Arthur Woodcock, a future suicide, taking 5 for 33). More runs, 65 of them, followed in the MCC v Oxfordshire match.

William Carless invited Stoddart to play in the Hastings Festival in September, and was congratulated when his persuasiveness paid off. Stoddart was booked for America with Ranji's team in mid-September and must have regarded these two matches as possible further useful practice. The first was against the "old enemy". WG won the toss for the South of England and ordered the Australians to bat. It was very hot, and the Champion would have been very grateful to Jessop and Bradley for disposing of Darling, Trumper and company for a mere 148.

Now Stoddart went in sixth and made only 13. Bill Howell bowled him and finished with 7 for 57, but the South stole a lead of 35 and the match was very much alive. When finally Joe Darling declared, the South were set 318. They made 207 against a hostile Ernie Jones (7 for 101). Facing Australian bowling for the final time, "Stoddy" was bowled by Jones for eight.

For Home Counties against the Rest of England, still at Hastings, he made another 13, and when quick runs were called for, 44 in classic style before young Wilfred Rhodes had him caught. The Rest were set 311 to win, a tall order in the time remaining (150 minutes) even in the Golden Age. But Gilbert Jessop was there, and it was a mystery that WG held him back for so long. When "The Croucher" did finally appear he spent slightly longer than an hour heaving 100 not out. The draw duly arrived, the Rest still 60 short, but another half-hour of Jessop might have been more than enough.

Jessop was to write tellingly about Stoddart. His unpublished notes were perused by Gerald Brodribb when composing his Jessop biography *The Croucher*: "To me Andrew Ernest Stoddart was the beau ideal of all that a batsman should be. A crisp cutter – for cutting was not deemed unbusinesslike in those days – an adept at forcing the ball past cover, a straight-driver of considerable force, and an expert in dealing with the short rising ball. Added to which a defence which never failed to arouse my envy. The puzzle to me was that he did not make even more runs than he did . . . . Fate willed that he should play the majority of his innings on the pitches of Lord's, the sporting propensities of which are proverbial."

There is probably no more penetrative picture of "Stoddy's" near-genius than this.

Looking back on 1899, *Wisden*, somewhat irritably, had this to say: "Into the reasons that induced Stoddart to abstain from first-class cricket until the end of the season it is quite useless to enquire. One may be excused, however, for taking with a grain of salt the reasons publicly put forward, as one cannot recall a single instance of a batsman of Stoddart's rank growing tired of first-class cricket while still capable of doing himself justice."

A puzzle indeed.

CHAPTER 23

◆◆◆

American Jaunt

THE cricketers who sailed from Liverpool in September 1899 in the Cunard liner *Etruria* (a "smelly" vessel, judged by Jessop's log, and no less odorous for Sammy Woods's cigars at breakfast) were "by long odds the greatest coterie of willow handlers that has ever invaded Uncle Sam's realm", according to *The American Cricketer* magazine. Who would question the claim when such as Ranji, MacLaren, Stoddart, Townsend, Jessop, Woods, Bosanquet and the coloured South African C.B.Llewellyn prepared to unpack their flannels in the exciting new world?

Ranjitsinhji (about whom rumours were soon buzzing: he was allegedly "looking for an American lady to marry") was bothered by bronchitis for most of the short tour, and the prodigious Townsend was surprisingly far less of a force away from home. As for A.E.Stoddart, he stood clearly ahead of the rest as an all-round performer, intensifying the feelings of regret that he was now only a part-time player. He took part in all five matches, averaging 58 and taking 22 cheap wickets. Jessop came close as a star attraction.

The tour was funded by the Associated Clubs of Philadelphia, and there was a formidable round of social functions, starting in New York harbour, where the reception party's tug met them down-river. The opening fixture, against Twenty-two Colts of Philadelphia, was spoilt by poor weather and a sub-standard pitch.

At Haverford they played the first of the two first-class matches against Gentlemen of Philadelphia, and a resounding win transpired. Jessop and Woods bowled the locals out for 156, then Archie MacLaren made a sparkling 149, backed up by fifties from Ranji and "Stoddy". Jessop hit a lightning 64, 49 of them while Stoddart was adding but a single. The great J.B.King managed no better than 1 for 102 as Ranji's band piled up 435; and there was a complete collapse in the Philadelphians' second knock, Stoddart taking 4 for 18.

All aboard for America: standing – umpire, S.M.J.Woods, B.J.T.Bosanquet,
A.Priestley, unknown, umpire; seated – G.Brann, A.C.MacLaren, K.S.Ranjitsinhji,
A.E.Stoddart, C.Robson; front – G.L.Jessop, W.P.Robertson, C.B.Llewellyn,
C.L.Townsend

After a farcical exhibition match they went to play Fourteen of New York at Staten Island, where Stoddart, standing in as captain, took seven wickets; then George Brann pounded 137 not out, and Jessop flailed the attack as the tourists stretched well ahead. With two and a half hours to survive, the New Yorkers did well to lose only eleven wickets.

Now came the return match with the Gentlemen of Philadelphia, this time at Germantown. The pitch was soft, but the English combination made 363, Stoddart top-scoring with a "great" 74 (caught off the great fast bowler Bart King) and sharing a stand of 120 with Ranji. Then Bosanquet and Llewellyn bowled the opposition out twice for paltry scores, "Bosie" idly tossing about his wrong'un between the fall of wickets and drawing from fellow Middlesex player "Stoddy" a prophetic comment that if ever these mysterious balls were bowled to a good length they could be matchwinners. Within a few years B.J.T.Bosanquet was winning Ashes Tests at Sydney and

Trent Bridge with his "wrong'un" or "googly" or "Bosie".

While in Philadelphia the cricketers had been taken by their hosts to watch a game of American football at the Penn Stadium. During proceedings Drewy Stoddart whispered to Charlie Townsend that if only he could be on that field he would run rings around these footballers: they seemed so slow. One of their hosts overheard the remark and tapped "Stoddy" on the shoulder: "No doubt you would, Mr Stoddart, but once they caught you, you would never run again."

The final match was staged in Toronto, where Canada were humbled in two days, Stoddart 63 not out and 3 for 7. Here Ranjitsinhji, who moved in high places most of his adult life, was the guest of the Prime Minister, Wilfred Lauvier. Three innings wins, two draws and, as expected, no losses, fair quantities of rain and lots of amusement: this was the story of the short expedition. They had seen Niagara Falls and they had taken up Sir Thomas Lipton's invitation to watch his yacht *Shamrock* challenge for the America's Cup ("No race" was declared that turbulent day, and the cricketers returned to shore green around the gills).

By the end of October, the White Star liner *Oceanic* had them all safely back in England's cool and overcast winter setting. Kruger had declared war on Britain in South Africa as the 1890s played themselves out. An age was dying. The times were changing. On the first day of 1900, Captain Valentine Todd, off duty from the front-line perils of the Boer War, was killed by a stray shell as he was bowling in a cricket match. The ball stayed firmly in his grasp, just as the vignette of events of the past decade would remain always in the memories of the true Victorians.

There were major changes at Middlesex in 1900. A.J.Webbe became club secretary, and Plum Warner, highly sensitive to the heritage and to the responsibilities awaiting, became vice-captain of the county club.

To draw further on Warner's writings: Stoddart, whom he now knew so well and who had had such an influence on him, was "a most encouraging captain, and by his sympathy and understanding got the best out of his eleven. He realised, as many do not, that cricket is an uncertain game, and he never blamed a man for making a mistake. 'All I ask,' he used to say, 'is that everyone should try his hardest.' He was a fine judge of the game, and in Australia, as here, his popularity was immense."

Again the word "uncertain".

CHAPTER 24

Swansong

RANJI passed 3000 runs again in 1900, and Jessop also drew crowds everywhere, sending them home in lively conversation from Lord's, Worcester and Hastings after 60-70-minute centuries.

Yorkshire began their hat-trick of titles this season of the optional follow-on and six-ball over. Tom Hayward made his thousand by the end of May (it was whispered that the only safe place for him was out in the middle, since he had "got a girl into trouble"), and Albert Trott, powered by good ale, again made well over 1000 runs and exceeded 200 wickets, including four poor devils at Bristol who, facing "pairs", were "b.Trott 0" in the second knock.

Jim Phillips continued his witch-hunt with judgments against Arthur Mold, for one, and Somerset's Tyler, for another, for throwing. But a man about whose action there could be no question plucked out 261 batsmen: Wilfred Rhodes was establishing himself with emphasis.

One extraordinary statistic glittered jewel-like in the summer of 1900: Stoddart's final innings for Middlesex. There had been a knock against Sussex late in May, a few days after the relief of Mafeking had swept tumultuous joy and relief over the land. "Stoddy" came in for Roche, the two-fingered Australian off-spinner, who fell ill just before the start, and batting at No.4 he was bowled for a single by fast bowler Cyril Bland, one of so many cricketers destined for a sad and dramatic death. (At the end of a fairly long life he trussed his wrists and ankles and threw himself into a canal near Cowbridge.)

Usually going in for Hampstead after a wicket or two had fallen, Stoddart (who sometimes wore a Free Foresters cap) made a slow start to the club season. He picked up wickets by way of compensation, including six of London Scottish, whose Albert Kinross enjoyed an exquisite moment at "Stoddy's" expense: "The great and only W.G.Grace was a lumbering elephant beside him, for, like the hero of the lady novelists of his period, there was something of the Greek god about Stoddart. Any artist would have jumped at him as a model.

"Stoddart cut one hard to me at point. It hit my breastbone – an impossible catch that one couldn't shape to – and raised a lump as big as an egg. The next one – for I had at least saved the boundary, or even a single – the next one curled and curvetted above my head, a hard mishit. In an agony of suspense I watched and followed it, and when at last I had it safe, Stoddart himself said 'Well caught!' as he passed me on his way to the pavilion."

Stoddart the "Greek god"

Artist "Rip" regretted Stoddart's retirement

He stroked five centuries for Hampstead in 1900, Stoics being the first to feel the weight of his battle-axe. There was also an interesting match at Lord's when Hampstead played MCC, for whom the dreaded Albert Trott thrashed 57 and 171 and took 9 for 77 and 7 for 96, including a bewildered F.R.D'O. Monro, yorked by a fast slinger. As Monro walked back he was passed by the next batsman, A.E.Stoddart, who was chuckling at the dismissal and offering broad comfort: "You got the old man's fast one alright!" (Trott was then twenty-seven years old.)

"Stoddy" himself had quite a match: 68 not out and 33, and 8 for 50 in MCC's first innings, when surprisingly Spofforth managed only one wicket for 84. The all-Australian duel between Trott and Spofforth was full of fire and incident. "Spoff" was one of Trott's four consecutive victims in the first innings, but later, far from registering a "pair", the Demon scored 11 runs off one ball (including several overthrows) under the net boundary experiment around the ground perimeter. The exertion and humour of it all must have left old Spofforth little enough breath.

A farewell double-century to cherish in his old age

Before this unusual game there had been J.T.Hearne's benefit match, played at Lord's between Middlesex and Somerset. As a compliment to the great bowler Drewy Stoddart decided to reappear for his old county. It would be, once and for all, the last time he would play for Middlesex, and on Whit Monday, with only 12 to his name, he became one of Tyler's seven victims, having hit out against the final ball before lunch.

By the day's end Somerset, with Vernon Hill having performed a left-hander's blitz, were already ahead of the Middlesex 172. In this innings George Beldam was placed at very short slip for Trott's bowling after several senior fieldsmen had declined. "My life isn't insured!" Stoddart had chuckled. When Trott's deadly fast one found the edge of Tyler's bat and cannoned to Beldam's right ear, the youngster held a miraculous catch, while understanding his colleagues' earlier diffidence.

Next day, with 10,000 present, Middlesex went in 69 in arrears, the Hampstead pair A.E.Stoddart and H.B.Hayman opening. The day was fine but cool. The pitch was fast and firm. And on that pitch for over four hours Stoddart entertained that gathering. He raised 151 with Hayman, and after Beldam had been sleeping partner for a few overs, R.W.Nicholls helped add 152.

Stoddart's cutting and straight-batted driving were sumptuous, but even to the short rising deliveries he drew back calmly and did as he wished. Sammy Woods broke down; Len Braund was no-balled before releasing the ball (a run was added); and the Somerset fielding became ragged as Stoddart hit mercilessly, as if still in his heyday. As he passed 200 there were signs that he was starting to flag. He had been in for almost five hours. Finally, seeking his 37th boundary, he advanced to Lewis and partly from exhaustion missed the ball and was left stranded as Newton broke the wicket. If ever proof were needed that there was genius in his make-up this innings, alongside all that had gone before, provided it.

He was overheard later saying that this innings of 221 (his thirteenth first-class century at Lord's) would be "a consolation for my old age", an old age that he was to deny himself.

Cricket understandably wondered whether he would now resume first-class cricket. He was still only thirty-seven. "Cricket can ill spare a batsman of his ability. The visits to Australia spoiled him, for they made him change his style from the attractive to the commonplace, but there was nothing of the commonplace about his batting on Tuesday."

The clerk from Kilburn, the grocer from Golders Green, the cabbie from Clapham and the plumber from Perivale, they did not resent the modifications in approach and technique, may not even have noticed them. They wanted good cricket, and Andrew Ernest Stoddart usually gave it to them. Now they would have to go over to Hampstead to see him.

And it was at Hampstead in this summer of 1900 that W.G.Grace smashed a ball from Stoddart onto the roof of the Lymington Road pavilion, a huge hit in the days when the old pavilion was situated at the southern end. (The current pavilion was erected in the 1920s.) WG (65) made the highest score for his London County XI and Billy Murdoch scored 27. Hampstead had piled up 332 for six before Stoddart declared. W.S.Hale had struck 101 not out, but Stoddart was bowled for only two runs. WG's figures were a blushful 0 for 122. The match was drawn but 547 runs had been made in 6½ hours of fun.

In another Hampstead match that summer, a two-day game against MCC in June, Stoddart took a relishable 8 for 50, besides scoring 68 not out in his club's innings of 207 against a rampant Albert Trott (9 for 77).

There were more fireworks to follow. Trott opened MCC's second innings and cracked 171 (a toiling 46-year-old Spofforth 5 for 118, Stoddart 1 for 19 off 11 overs). Second time round, Hampstead managed 206 (AES 33, irresistible Trott 7 for 96, all bowled or leg-before). What a loss this man was to Australia.

"Stoddy" was back at Lord's for some MCC fixtures mid-summer. The first, not first-class, was against the touring West Indians, for whom Constantine senior made the first century for West Indies in England. Not only was his hundred made at the home of cricket but it was against a side captained by Lord Harris and containing W.G.Grace and A.E.Stoddart (who made 30 and 18, and, given a long bowl, took 7 for 92).

Then, again at Lord's, after two University games, both quite undistinguished for him, Stoddart made 45 for MCC against Minor Counties. And in the second innings, before a lamentably small gathering, he stroked his final hundred at Lord's: a glittering 136 (109 in boundaries) against an attack boasting George Thompson and R.O.Schwarz.

He also played at Lord's against the touring Haverford College team, scoring 35 before being caught by a gentleman named Justice and watching his opening partner young Warner going on to his century. "Stoddy" enjoyed a lengthy bowl: 2 for 58 off 27 overs.

At Hastings, lured back by the agreeable conditions, he turned out for South against North, who piled up 440 runs. It was a match of hurricane partnerships: 163 in 80 minutes by J.T.Brown and J.T.Tyldesley; 108 in under an hour by Tyldesley and Denton; 146 in 85 minutes by Jephson and Lockwood. But while others were enjoying themselves, this time Stoddart was left out of it. Batting at number seven, he was caught off Rhodes for one sad run.

He did better for the Rest against Sussex and Surrey, hitting 15 and 64 in a farewell to Hastings highlighted by Trott's century (in what was practically an average time of 80 minutes in those hectic festival afternoons). Abel's eyesight may have been ailing and he may have hedged at the fastest bowling, but here he made his twelfth century of the year, and Rotherhithe glowed with pride at the success of its odd little son.

So now it came to the last of "Stoddy's" first-class cricket matches, appropriately at Lord's, and appropriately beginning with a partnership of 85 with William Gilbert Grace. The younger man, as if by tradition, scored the faster. Stoddart made 51 before one of his best former batting henchmen, Jack Brown, gathered the prize of his wicket.

Now a part-time cricketer again, Mr Stoddart, immaculately attired, as ever, poses before the pavilion at Lord's

Jessop helped WG add 85 in half-an-hour, and when the Champion was dismissed at last for 126, his final century at Lord's, Wynyard and Trott pulverised the attack. Yet the 474 of the South was not far beyond the reach of the North. Most of them got runs, despite Jephson's patient lobs, which induced six conceivable catches in the direction of Stoddart. He held four, including Hirst and Rhodes, and was excused the others on

Plenty of time now to reminisce, and what better than to look at some old photographs?

account of their degree of difficulty.

He made only 11 on his final visit to the first-class crease. WG had already fallen to a wonderful catch by "Baby" Lawton at short slip ("That's the fellow I got into the side, Stoddy, and look what he does to me!") and now Lawton caught Stoddart as well.

CHAPTER 25

Who is Ethel?

A.E.STODDART was now a businessman, and still a club cricketer, an ex-Test captain of England, and once the finest rugby three-quarter ever known. He was 38 years old as the 1901 cricket season dawned, but this year he would not be one of the sun's rays. Instead, while the Wills tobacco company featured him perhaps optimistically as Number 1 in their cigarette card issue, he was once more involved with letters to the press defending his amateur status at the time of his final Australian tour.

He continued to make runs for Hampstead, although his appearances were restricted to a dozen innings in 1901, the last of them worth 109 against Surbiton, with an overall average of 50.

The Hampstead dinner at the Trocadero was, as ever, a splendid occasion with many great cricket names present. Kennerley Rumford rendered *The Old Grey Fox* and *When the Swallows Homeward Fly*, and none other than the Scottish performer Harry Lauder sang merrily.

The summer passed and soon it was grey November, when the club held its AGM in the dining-room at Lord's. Stoddart, to everyone's gratification, remained on the committee.

In 1902, that gleaming year in cricket's story, he was pleased to renew the acquaintance of some of his old Australian adversaries. He also made a century at Richmond, consecutive ducks during The Week, 92 against UCS Old Boys and 80 not out against South Hampstead in August, and was elected a life member of Hampstead Cricket Club in November.

In the 1903 season there was but one innings, ended in its infancy. Beyond that, troubled by old injuries and beset by increasing weight, he batted no more for Hampstead, the club which had given him his start and for whom he had stroked over 13,000 runs in 16 summers (best 1862 at 155.20 back in 1887).

No more, that is, until 1907, when he had a last fling during The Week. Hampstead got Old Westminsters out before lunch, and during the interval some of the senior players, Swinstead and Stoddart in particular, happened to come in for some good-natured ribbing, which prompted the skipper to put these two in first. As the afternoon wore on and the younger men watched with interest and, ultimately, dumb admiration, the opening stand amounted to 221 as both the batsmen made hundreds. A.E.Stoddart, "ageing veteran", finished 100 not out, a final flourish almost as poignant as his Middlesex farewell of 221 seven years previously. It brought his tally of centuries in minor cricket to 68.

An aged batsman enjoys a net

His career with Hampstead was now absolutely over. He had amassed almost 14,000 runs for the north London club at 70 per innings, and gathered nearly 800 wickets besides. His reign, if not as long as it might have been, was supreme while it lasted.

(As a hesitant sidelight: in 1986 the author was invited by Hampstead CC to play in a centenary match to celebrate "Stoddy's" 485. Missed three times before reaching 20, he went on to make 74. The thrill was enhanced by the presence along the boundary edge of Keith Miller, who was visiting a lady friend in the area, and "always enjoyed things to do with history". A year later came an invitation to play in another celebration match, but the thought of halving that lifetime ground average was enough to prompt a polite refusal to return.)

"Stoddy" kept a remote eye on the game. He sent a congratulatory telegram to George Hirst when the wondrous Yorkshire allrounder achieved the unique double of 2000 runs and 200 wickets in the 1906 summer. And when Middlesex decided to start a cricket "nursery" in 1908 he gave the initiative his wholehearted support and promised to help in the scheme as conducted at The Queen's Club. It was a chance for him to help mould unspoiled youth. And at the end of that season he thoughtfully wrote a letter to Plum Warner congratulating him on his fine performances for the county. It was correspondence much cherished.

An unusual postal item featuring a signed W.D.& H.O.Wills cigarette card and addressed to Stoddart's residence in Lithos Road

Stoddart for a time had been secretary of Neasden Golf Club, spending more time at the 18-hole sport now. He played frequently with members and proved successful as a coach, though on one occasion his patience was stretched by "a bounder of a fellow" who had suggested that "Stoddy" was a crisis golfer only so long as no money was at stake. But put half a sovereign on the match and the outcome might be different. This must have touched a nerve left raw from the "shamateur" allegations of his top cricket days. He broke his rule and played for the wager, beating the "bounder" out of sight 8 and 6, and placing the 10 shillings straight into the servants' Christmas box in the clubhouse.

He also sometimes had a round with writer Max Pemberton, who thought Stoddart to be "a sad man and reticent". Nonetheless he remembered him for some humour as the great batsman was leaving the Lord's pavilion "to achieve another of his beautiful centuries".

Pemberton wrote: "Pausing a minute at the top of the steps, he espied a jovial and popular Irishman who sat smoking his pipe and proudly telling his neighbours that he knew Andrew and loved him like a brother. So Stoddart hailed him. 'Are you dining anywhere tonight?' he asked jovially. Quick to snap up a free dinner, the Irishman called back: 'No, my boy, I'm not dining anywhere tonight.' 'Then how hungry you'll be,' said Stoddart, and went on to make his runs."

He had a further story concerning golf: "Stoddart took to golf in a quite astonishing way and was a scratch player within a year. The achievement aroused much jealousy, chiefly among the English, who said that his style was all wrong and that he played like a cricketer, and not like a golfer. I remember lunching with him one summer's day in a well-known club not far from Sandwich and becoming aware that a couple at the next table were taking his name in vain. Evidently they did not recognise him, but they had heard that Stoddart was out playing and were interested. Presently one of them exclaimed: 'Why there he is, driving from the last tee,' and they ran to the window to watch the great cricketer come in. 'Look at that,' cried the fellow who had first spoken, 'a cricket stroke and nothing else,' and having thus satisfied themselves that Andrew Stoddart was an impostor, they returned to the table and went on with their lunch. To the end they remained ignorant of their mistake and they continued, I suppose, to tell their friends how badly Stoddart played and how ridiculous it was that he should be at 'scratch'."

The golf club at Neasden had been established in 1893, on the north side of Neasden Lane and Dollis Hill Lane, and the course record for some years was 75, jointly held by Drewy Stoddart and a chap named Milne. The club had a limited number of female associate members (who were not allowed to play at weekends), some of whom would surely have taken an interest in the famous England cricketer and rugby star. The course had been swallowed up by housing development by 1930.

On October 27, 1906, Drewy Stoddart at last married. It was probably on his first tour, nineteen years previously, that he had met a young Australian girl, one who must seriously have caught his fancy but who was evidently tempestuous. She was Ethel von Sinnbech, soon to marry a Mr Robert

Luckham. It can only be assumed that she and Drewy rekindled their friendship whenever he went back to Australia and that eventually she followed him to England, having gone through a hushed divorce.

The wedding (about a week after Jack Hobbs's, as it happened) took place at St Stephens Church, Hampstead. The cool sportsman actually played golf that morning. He went round with the officiating clergyman the Reverend Maxwell Tracy, playing against his best man, the faithful George Jeffery, and Arthur Godfrey, the organist. And the bridegroom, wearing his Middlesex blazer and a white cap, actually lost two and one, possibly distracted by the ordeal that lay ahead.

One way to ease the nerves on the morning of a man's wedding: golf with his best pal and the minister

The church was decorated for Harvest Festival, and Ethel Elizabeth wore a white gown and held a wreath of pink roses and a shower bouquet, her face hidden by a lace veil. The congregation, which included "quite a respectable assemblage of Australian friends of the happy pair", sang

Ethel, the intriguing woman who was the love of Stoddart's life

O Perfect Love, and as the register was signed a solo was rendered by a certain Miss Luckham. Although Ranjitsinhji had once spoken highly of "Stoddy's" singing voice (and his niece many years later spoke of her uncle Drewy's pleasant crooning for the family in parlour gatherings), the local newspaper made no mention of whether he broke into song prior to or during the reception. Among the gifts for the bridal couple, Hampstead Cricket Club presented them with a fine silver tea service (which was sold at auction almost a century later, in 2004, for £1850 nett).

Up at Hampstead Town Hall a much more ostentatious wedding was in progress: Marie Lloyd, the raunchy music hall queen, had chosen Haverstock Hill as the site for her nuptials. Also that day, Miss Christabel Pankhurst presided over a Votes for Women meeting, while that night Mrs Emmeline Pethick-Lawrence, another key suffragette figure, was released from Holloway Prison seriously ill.

By then, Mr and Mrs Stoddart, illustrious sportsman and bubbling bride, were on their way to Bournemouth for a brief honeymoon.

Stoddart had just become secretary at The Queen's Club at an annual salary of £300, succeeding the eminent C.J.B.Marriott, his old rugby friend, who had departed to run the Rugby Football Union. The living would be comfortable enough for "Stoddy" and his bride. His job was something of a sinecure, with hours to fill, usually in idle conversation with members, some of whom were eminent people – such as Sir Edward Grey, who as Foreign Secretary would announce the start of the First World War, when the lamps would be going out everywhere, with no likelihood of being turned back on in the foreseeable future. Most Queen's Club members, though, had nothing on their list of achievements to compare with secretary Stoddart's sporting accomplishments.

He could tell a story very well, though if he ever told one about himself it was usually against himself. His reminiscences tended to be humorous, never unkind, and if he disliked any particular person he passed him by and went on to something else. On a winter evening, in front of a blazing fire, or on a summer twilight he would sit in on discussions often devoted to picking England cricket teams, the best of the day, the best ever, combined sides to play Mars, and so on. He took a quiet interest in proceedings, always safeguarding the claims of W.G.Grace, whom he considered to be *the* cricketer. Even then there were men with short

memories who were sinfully tempted on occasions to overlook the Grand
Old Man in favour of certain stars of the moment.

Plenty of time to chat, coach and sip whisky: Stoddart at Queen's Club,
bottom of steps, on the right

F.B.Wilson once listed "Stoddy's" choice of a Best-Ever XI, and
an interesting line-up it was: Grace, Shrewsbury, MacLaren, Ranjitsinhji,
Jackson, Hobbs, MacGregor, Lockwood, Lohmann, Peel and S.F.Barnes.
It seems likely that on some other evening Tom Richardson and J.T.Brown
might have found favour.

"Stoddy" was instrumental in the Queen's Club's adoption of the
colours his sides had worn in Australia: red, white and pale blue on dark blue.
There were occasional excitements at the club, such as the visit to Queen's
of young Prince Albert (the future King George VI), and infrequent links
with the past: cricket meetings and dinners, visits to Lord's for a net or as
a spectator, the once-in-a-while cricket matches such as those at Shillinglee
Park with Ranji, and at Hampstead during The Week, and in 1908 he led
Queen's to a low-scoring victory over Uxbridge. In his side that day was

Albert Relf of Sussex and England, who was to shoot himself in 1937.

But on the whole the activity dried up. The dust had settled, and cricket's old familiar sounds and smells were no more. The fading of his name from the sports columns of the newspapers was complete.

A future king arrives at Queen's, greeted by club president Lord Alverstone, with club secretary Stoddart half-hidden

Occasionally there were other reminders of it all. There was the Trocadero banquet to "Plum" Warner's triumphant English crew in the spring of 1904, when he was gratified to learn from Warner's speech that his own name was still held in high esteem in Australia, and then when he went to farewell Warner's talented 1911-12 combination from St Pancras to the Great South Land.

He chatted at the club with anyone who approached him, his voice apparently soothingly quiet and still faintly suggestive of a past not wholly London or public school. On occasion he confessed to feeling regret at having cut short his active sporting career, but by now he was limited to playing the occasional foursome at bowls, with whisky and soda the stake.

Learning another game: tennis at Queen's

Remembering his rugby honours

He had time enough now to drink the whiskies constantly proffered by men keen to speak to him, and his weight increased. When he and Ethel moved to their final home in Clifton Hill he was quite heavily fleshed.

After their marriage in 1906, Mr and Mrs Stoddart resided at 24 Crediton Road, alongside Hampstead's cricket ground. The club's minutes reveal that "the committee were pleased to allow Mr Stoddart to have a gate made in his fence on to the cricket ground, reserving the rights to our ground landlord." That would save the somewhat less athletic ex-cricketer a few yards.

In time he and Ethel were to move to 20 St John's Wood Road, a property just over a minute's walk down the street from Lord's Ground, but now long since demolished. The 1911 Census indicates a private house of nine rooms, occupied by Stoddart (secretary of a sports club [Queen's]) and his wife Ethel, 38, born in Melbourne; with two young servants, Ada Jenkins (cook) and Emily Forsdyke (housemaid).

The Stoddarts' final abode was soon to be 115 Clifton Hill, again within walking distance of Lord's (along Abbey Road, then Grove End

Road), where the turf and the pavilion had for so long been his spiritual home. The house, in an elite locality, was spacious, with four levels, pleasant aspects and a walled garden. And apparently it was haunted. Previous occupants had noted an unlisted maid floating about, and at times the bed bumped and levitated.

The last of the grand cricket functions, only a week before the Great War began in early August of 1914, had been the Lord's Centenary Dinner, held at the Cecil Hotel and attended by a host of distinguished people, A.E.Stoddart among them, with Lord Hawke presiding. To run the eye down the guest list is to peruse a Who's Who of amateur cricket in the Golden Age. And there were lords enough to lend credence to the illusion that this was how the ground got its name. Lord Hawke read out a greeting from Prince Ranjitsinhji, Jam Sahib of Nawanagar and went on to say that he could not prophesy what England would be like 100 years from now (mercifully for them all), but they knew that Lord's and MCC would continue to flourish and increase their popularity.

Some remarkable research by genealogist Debbie Beavis has recently uncovered much obscure detail of the mysterious Mrs Ethel Stoddart. Much about her had been smokescreened, and her biography remains quite complex. The conclusions, though, are supported by Ethel's great-niece Karen, who lives in Melbourne and was the first to identify the compelling evidence.

Ethel probably met "Stoddy" during either his first (1887-88) or second (1891-92) tour of Australia, when she was quite young. At the time of her marriage to him so many years later, in 1906, she was not a "widow". She was a divorcee.

The bombshell conclusion to Mrs Beavis's vast research web is that Drewy Stoddart and his eventual wife Ethel almost certainly had a daughter, who must have been born out of wedlock some years before the marriage. Stunning late discovery though it is, everything seems to point to the reality that England's finest sportsman did not, after all, die childless. But the girl had to be shielded in an era when illegitimate birth was considered shameful.

Ethel, the future Mrs Stoddart, had been born and baptised Emilie Elizabeth Sinnbeck in Gippsland, Victoria in 1868. Her Irish mother died two years later. Her father Peter Sinnbeck, born near the Germany/Denmark border, now having remarried, took his family up to Sydney. In due course young "Ethel" married Robert Luckham, Plymouth-born sports journalist and later advertisement manager of the best-selling *Bulletin* magazine. This was in December 1892. The match seems never to have been a truly happy one. She left him in 1898, and boarded a German passenger ship to Hamburg. It was in that city that the precious studio photograph, the long-lost and presumably one and only surviving image of her, was taken. It is thought that she then journeyed to England to pick up the threads of her spasmodic romantic relationship with Drewy Stoddart.

A telling letter from Ethel to the husband from whom she distanced herself

Copies of letters between Ethel and husband Bob Luckham (lodged with the court during the divorce proceedings) reveal the true extent of the breach. "Dear Bob," she wrote (by hand) on January 11, 1901. "You will be surprised to hear from me after such a long interval, but as I have been away from Australia now for two years & four months, & as I never mean to return or live with you again, don't you think it would be as well if we were both free. You may want to marry again & indeed I would like to see you happy with a woman who would be more suited to you than I, we were never happy together, & since you treated me so shamefully when I came to England first I can never forgive or forget. You can easily divorce me for desertion & it would be best for us both."

She went on to say that she wouldn't be in England much because the weather didn't suit her. Any letters that Luckham cared to write would be forwarded to Paris or Reims via GPO London: "wherever I may be at the time with my friends." In conclusion: "Nothing you can ever say or do will have any weight with me & nothing would ever induce me to return." Then the very firm concluding remark: "Think it over & let me hear from you soon."

Luckham's typewritten reply: "Dear Ethel – As you say, I am surprised to hear from you. When you left Sydney it was in the clear understanding that you would be back in 12 months at the outside. You speak of my treating you shamefully, but you will please to recollect that I continued to send you funds until I heard from George Rapley (in whose presence you so stated) that you did not intend to return to me."

Her desperate husband went on to explain how he had tried unsuccessfully to find a London address for her, and came to the conclusion that she had deserted him. He wrote that he would not divorce her, and poignantly closed the letter with a plea: "I am willing to receive you and forgive your desertion if you at once reply that you will return to Sydney. If I do not hear from you I can only assume that your action had been premeditated before you left Sydney. Yours in sorrow and awaiting your answer, Bob."

Ethel's reply, from Paris, July 4, presumably 1901, was not what he wanted: "Dear Bob – I received your letter about a month ago, when I was in London for a time. I can only say as I did before, that I do not intend returning to you, that is final – you offer to forgive me & take me back. I thank you, (it is more that [sic] most men would do) but I do not love you. We were badly matched, & are better apart & no power on earth can ever bring us together again. I have even forgiven you for the picture of the girl selling matches, but I have not come to that yet. I am happy & contented, & have many friends – do not expect to hear from me again, it is more than likely I shall go to America in the autumn with the lady I am living with – it is her home. With best wishes for your future happiness from Ethel".

By the time of her marriage to Stoddart in 1906, Ethel had added the "von" to her maiden name and was now claiming to be a widow – even though she must have known that Luckham was still alive. She was also prone to reducing her age on official documents. It has been verified, following a scan of papers concerning both families, that she and Bob had had no children: and such was the declaration on the papers pertaining to their acrimonious divorce.

Who, then, was that young Miss Luckham, thought to be aged about sixteen, who sang a solo at the Stoddart wedding? After intensive research a bundle of deductions converged for Mrs Beavis, and they point to one plausible conclusion: "Miss Luckham" was the bridal couple's very own natural daughter, a girl named Joan whose existence for years had needed to be hushed up. She may have been conceived during "Stoddy's" 1887-88 cricket and rugby odyssey around Australasia, or perhaps more likely during his next tour four years later.

He and a few others such as George Lohmann were the handsome pick of the bunch among cricket's known bachelors. Long before the manic and obsessive "social media" of today, women of all ages discreetly kept miniature portraits of cricketers such as these in their lockets. Drewy and Ethel must have met regularly during his subsequent Australian tours.

After Stoddart's death, Ethel would travel, and five years later, while back in her native Australia, she is known to have been accompanied by a young companion. A century ago there was nothing unconventional about this. The young lady's name was given as "Emily Johnson". Mrs Beavis is convinced that this is again Ethel's and Drewy's own daughter Joan, who could not have used her earlier given surname (Luckham) while in Sydney without the risk of attracting unwelcome attention.

It was young Joan who was now in love. She married Alex Stork, and it was Ethel Stoddart who gave her away at the wedding. But the coupling was not a success. They were together for only a short time before he went off to Samarai. Joan and Ethel went to Papua, just another middle-aged woman with her escort – or mother and daughter.

Joan was Mrs Beavis's grandmother.

And Joan told her own children in due course that when her marriage broke down all those years ago she had taken refuge in the house of the Lieutenant Governor of New Guinea. His name was J.H.P.Murray, an Australian. Long ago he happened to have been a rugby team-mate of A.E.Stoddart's in Harlequin teams.

Mrs Beavis summarises this extraordinary investigation and

conclusion: "Divorce was shocking and in those days quite unusual. Illegitimacy was a scandal. Nice girls didn't – or if they did then the evidence was swept under the carpet. The Stoddarts [i.e. his sisters and their husbands] were wealthy and influential, and would not have accepted Ethel or Joan if the truth were known. If she wanted a relationship, let alone a marriage, with Andrew Ernest Stoddart then Ethel had to keep her background hidden, and that meant that she had no option but to recreate Joan's identity too. Once the lies began, there was no going back. They were all three trapped, and none of them could ever, ever tell."

She believes that there could currently be as many as thirty blood descendants of A.E.Stoddart, hardly any of whom would be aware of it.

CHAPTER 26

The Tragedy

STODDART had read of the passing of R.E.Foster and A.G.Steel in that final spring of peacetime, and then of Albert Trott, who had made a mess of his life, touching such depths of despair that he chose to end it all with a bullet at his lodgings in Willesden. Stoddart's grief had already been stirred by news of his rancher brother Harry's death on June 28, 1914 in Rio Grande Hospital following a stroke. Buried in Fairview Cemetery, Salida, Harry was much mourned in the San Luis Valley. Drewy had also been saddened by the death of J.T.Hearne's nephew, who had worked at Queen's as a groundsman and coach, and who had shot himself this same year. "Stoddy" had been called upon to write to the coroner.

Last reunion of the brothers and sister: standing – Minnie, Drewy and Connie; seated – Harry and Cissie

Drewy Stoddart's own life was corroding quite rapidly following a severe dip in his health in February 1914. His finances appeared insecure, his marriage often seemed joyless and uninspired, and his nerves were in a ruinous state. He resigned his position at Queen's, and after partial recovery from severe influenza there were thoughts of a voyage to Australia. But he could not be bothered with it. Probably owing to financial anxiety, he had allowed his MCC membership to lapse. When he applied to renew it, he was refused. That must have stung a man who had played so often for the club and who had been elected as a member right after his splendid stand of 266 with Arthur Shrewsbury in the commemorative match at Lord's twenty-seven years previously. Memories of that performance and so much besides, on cricket and rugby fields, must have played through his mind as he gazed motionless down the silent confines of Clifton Hill.

115 Clifton Hill, where "Stoddy" drew his final breath

He was in a poor state by April of 1915, the momentous month of Jack Johnson's dethronement by giant cowboy Jess Willard for the world heavyweight title, the month of the calamitous Gallipoli landings on the 25th, of widespread fear that the Zeppelins would destroy London and much else, while trawlers were being sunk by German predators. There was much public fear and despair. Marie Lloyd was winning damages for libel from a cinematograph company in the Strand; George Joseph Smith was taken to Bow Street on charges of murdering his "brides in the bath"; Lord Rothschild's funeral procession saw Park Lane lined with a high proportion of London's Jewish population. The Russians were driving back the Germans on the East Prussian front, but sinister poison gas was being used at Ypres. Meanwhile the ill-fated Grand Duke Nicholas in Russia was announcing himself as being confident and trusting in God.

On Easter Saturday, April 3, 1915, the Stoddart household was dark with foreboding. Andrew Ernest Stoddart had been out all day. Now, in the quiet of the evening, having returned to the villa in Clifton Hill, he drew a long pistol from his pocket and placed it on the table. He told Ethel that he was tired of everything and was going to end it all. "Life is not worth living," whispered the broken man.

She pleaded with him not to speak like this. Things could be sorted out. In the morning they would talk to friends. She picked up the pistol, but he took it from her after a brief struggle. She clutched the box of cartridges, knowing the pistol to be empty.

He tucked the pistol back in his pocket and left the room, saying goodnight to his wife and her companion Isabel Dalton. Later, just before midnight, Mrs Stoddart went up to his room and switched on the light. He was in bed. There was no smell of smoke and no gunshot had been heard, but blood was trickling down his cheek.

Ethel cried out, and Mrs Dalton hurried upstairs. Police Constable Corrie, who answered the emergency call, found the revolver gripped in Stoddart's right hand. A second box of ammunition lay nearby, missing one cartridge.

"Suicide while of unsound mind": the inquest jury at Marylebone seemingly had but one verdict to return. They had been told how moody, forgetful and restless Mr Stoddart had been, how money problems had played on his mind. He was said to have "lost all his money through the war". A good-humoured husband had been reduced to a state of irritability where even the rustling of paper threatened to drive him mad. They had listened to clinically concise evidence from Dr Saunders (who years earlier had played football against him) relating to the position of the bullet wound; to the fact that the lungs had shown impending pneumonia, which always induced despondency; to the observation that the heart was enlarged, as was common in athletes. There were many among the shocked readers of the news who could testify to the man's big-heartedness in a figurative sense as well.

His total effects amounted to around £1000, a modest sum even at that time for a man of his standing. (The house in Clifton Hill, now a listed building as part of the Eyre Estate, was more probably leased rather than owned by the Stoddarts.) His will had been drawn up less than six months previously, and in the apparent absence of legitimate offspring it was in favour of "my dear wife". (This was surely the final factor in the concealment of Joan, the secret daughter.)   The document was witnessed by Laura Adams, the household cook, and B.Dalton, Ethel's companion, formally Isabel but the "B" suggesting that she was known as Bella or 'Bel. Probate was granted to Ethel Elizabeth Stoddart on May 11.

"The tragic death of Mr Stoddart has drawn a sigh from thousands," the *Pall Mall Gazette* mourned. "Could nothing have been done? Thousands remembered him and his glorious batting and rugby play; and in how many country houses is his portrait at this moment hanging with those of the other great sportsmen of our time? Had his admirers but known of his difficulties would they not gladly have ended them? Something forbade it, perhaps pride. It is all too sad for words."

The *Daily Telegraph* looked back mistily: "Stoddart, had he cared, might have held a front place among the giants of the game much longer than he did, for when he retired quietly and unostentatiously his bat was full of runs. He gave up when he could have held his own with the best of the youngsters. All said when he passed out of cricket that he was one of the greatest of all batsmen, no mere run-getter, but a batsman who had it in him to rise superior to weather and wicket conditions. He wanted no perfect-tempered pitch; rather he revelled in what is often and not inaptly described as a 'talking wicket'. He certainly, and with much frequency, conquered the bowler on the latter's wicket, and on these occasions one knew and saw the master mind.

"The votaries of the new Rugby game may say that the old was slow, but the crowds of witnesses never found football dull when Stoddart's black and red stockings were seen twinkling down the touch-line.

"And in summer how often, on the classic playing-grounds of England, at Lord's or at The Oval, at Trent Bridge or Old Trafford, within sound of the bells in the Harry Tower at Canterbury, or with the smoke from the tall Yorkshire chimneys pouring over Park-avenue or Bramall-lane, Stoddart set every pulse beating faster round the ropes, divided between joy in the bright beauty of his cricket and anxiety lest he should make too many runs and win the match. 'Slow cricket' was creeping in like a paralysis even then on some grounds and in some county teams, to threaten the future of the game and the county clubs' balances at the bank; but Stoddart gave it no countenance. He drove as hard as the elder Gunn, and while he made nearly as many centuries as Shrewsbury, he made them far more quickly. *Sit tibi terra levis.*"

According to his wish, he was cremated. Arrangements were handled by J.H.Kenyon Ltd. The assembly at Golders Green Crematorium would have been larger on April 7 if the funeral had been announced earlier than just a few hours beforehand. So many cricketers and footballers, too, were away at the war.

A.J.Webbe was there, mourning someone who had been as dear to him as a son; as was Plum Warner, in khaki, a different kind of captain now, grieving the loss of a man he had worshipped almost as a father. Tour supporter Sir Arthur Priestley, MP, was present, and former flat-mate as well as team-mate and rugby adversary Gregor MacGregor, with Stanley Scott, "Punch" Philipson, George Burton, and Jack Hearne ("In fond and grateful memory of my old captain" was prominently inscribed on that wreath), all of Middlesex. Lieutenant Gordon Inglis attended on behalf of "Sport in Australia", and several Hampstead members went, together with Bruce Renny, who had claimed his wicket at the end of the historic 485 against Stoics.

The author finds the grave around 1968

E.B.Noel, the new secretary at The Queen's Club, and other members and staff were present. MCC, Blackheath RFC, Neasden Golf Club, and the Army Rugby Football Union ("To a very great sportsman" on the wreath) were all represented, and Albert Knight, most religious of cricketers, was there; also H.V.L.Stanton, trusted journalist. A friend from "Stoddy's" very early days in South Shields, now the Reverend J.E.Hoopfell, attended, and there were many others, including *Wisden's* editor and Judy Stevens, famous racquets coach.

On the stroke of four o'clock the open hearse came into sight, the coffin almost hidden beneath the flowers and wreaths, the most conspicuous being a sheaf of white lilac to "My darling Nello, from his wife". The pet name might have taken many by surprise.

The service was conducted by the Reverend H.Trundle, and when at last the coffin slipped from view, tears were shed unashamedly.

Lengthy research was needed to establish that "Stoddy's" ashes were conveyed several days later to Coventry, where they were interred in the grave of his mother in the parish churchyard of St Nicholas, Radford. Ethel and his three sisters, two nephews and a niece were all in attendance.

The church was all but destroyed twenty-five years later, when men, women and children were killed and gravestones were shattered as one of the most horrific of Luftwaffe blitzes hit Coventry and surrounds in November 1940. Although the cross from the Stoddart memorial of pink granite was blasted away, the inscribed base survived, swathed in undergrowth when the author discovered it in 1968. Some years later the base itself was removed, vandalism in the churchyard having left the authorities little option.

Cricket-lovers know 1915 for what it was: a year of widespread and inexorable sadness. Hours after trilling "You devils!" and shaking his fist at the sinister Zeppelin in the sky, W.G.Grace was dead, following "Stoddy" and Australia's young demi-god Victor Trumper into the Great Pavilion. In 1916 *Wisden* devoted 83 pages to obituary notices, almost all the result of battlefield slaughter.

The cricket fields, the planet itself, would never again be as WG and his lesser companions had known them.

As incisive an obituary as any, and a substantial one at that, had appeared in the *Morning Post*, possibly penned by "Plum" Warner: "There have been many 'double internationals'; few, however, have so gained the eminence of A.E.Stoddart both in cricket and [rugby] football as to earn the unquestionable right to captain his country's side in each branch of sport.

"Whenever 'A.E.' walked out from the pavilion to the wicket the crowd felt confident that they were to have their full money's worth . . . the pace with which he got his runs when set was often astonishing." That 32 at Trent Bridge in 1886 which had taken him 200 minutes was cited as an example of his "bull-dog tenacity". In 1893, his most fruitful summer, the 195 not out in the first innings against Nottinghamshire at Lord's was "simply dazzling", while the 124 in the second was "equally faultless until he began to tire". Reminders of hundreds and Test match triumphs filled several column inches.

From another pen came details of the schooldays, and the story of how "Stoddy" used to take a team each summer to a school in Forest Hill, and presented a bat to the most successful young batsman. He held a spectacular catch one year, and a lad came up to him later and said, "I wish, sir, I had taken that catch you did." And the cricket hero replied: "So you will, when your hands are as big as mine."

A.E.Stoddart's widow went to New Guinea in 1924 and invested in a copra trading station in the hills, nine miles from town. She made friends and gained the confidence of the native kanakas, some of whom she employed. When a landslide closed the road she was forced to sell at a very low price. She tried to bounce back by taking out a gold-mining licence, although as an unattached woman she was not allowed into the field. She was nothing if not bold and adventurous. Next she built a bungalow, living meanwhile in a grass hut. When she returned to England in 1938 she learned that her New Guinea property had been buried by volcanic lava. By 1939, A.J.Webbe was seeking help for her through the columns of *The Cricketer*. Middlesex CCC minutes show that A.E.Stoddart's old county club were continuing to pay her a weekly allowance.

During the Second World War, Ethel worked in a munitions factory, and she finished her days in a flat, 1c Grove End House, overlooking Lord's ground. Her companion, Isabel Dalton, who had been with her on that terrible night in 1915, had lived at Grove End House since 1930. The author, in the late 1960s, managed to trace Ethel's doctor, who described her as being quite sprightly, and remembered her as much as anything for her reddish hair, obviously dyed. "She knew she was dying," he wrote, "and accepted it calmly." He recalled suggesting to her that she must enjoy living alongside Lord's in view of her husband's long association with the ground. Her reply took him by surprise: "I can't bear the ruddy [or it may have been 'bloody'] place." He vaguely remembered Ethel referring to Drewy's death: "She seemed to speak with a little bitterness."

In 1948 she had been tracked down by a journalist and quizzed about her life and her husband. She declared that she had not been to a cricket match since 1915. Across the street Don Bradman's 40th birthday was being celebrated during the Australians' match at Lord's against the Gentlemen (Bill Brown 120, Bradman 150, Lindsay Hassett 200: total 610 for 5 declared). Ethel confessed to a slight desire to see The Don bat. Then, probably eyeing the presentation silver rose bowl and tobacco jar on the sideboard, she loyally remarked: "But Bradman can't play rugby!"

She died in the St John and St Elizabeth Hospital on October 19, 1950, just as the street in South Shields where her late husband had been born – Wellington Terrace – was undergoing a change of name. Cause of death was given as leukaemia and liver cancer. In her will, she left the silver rose bowl to a certain Hugh Waldron Dallas, £50 to a friend named Miss Meta Drieden, a silver salver to the lady associates of Neasden Golf Club, and a silver pocket flash to Sir Samuel Wilks, who was one of her late husband's relations.

Andrew Ernest Stoddart was idolised for years, but overshadowed so soon after his passing. Cricket's massive library is laced with praise and anecdote concerning players who made more runs, stayed longer in the limelight, or created thin and momentary sensation. Any random search will attest that Stoddart has been paid less than his due honour. In cricket's library wherever he is mentioned it is usually for the briefest and often inaccurate reference. He was a hero whose name has faded, and the manner of his death may be to blame.

> Stoddart, you need never mind them,
> Play with freedom fine and true,
> Get your bat just well behind them,
> Give the 'fields' some work to do.
>   When at length you leave the wickets
>   Midst a large admiring throng,
>   You will feel yourself a hero,
>   Stormed with cheerings loud and long.

"Century"

We can cast our gaze across the fields where "Stoddy" spent his sporting life, Lord's ground more apt than most. The concrete needs to be stripped away, yet the great pavilion stands for everything. Built while Victoria lived, it has been the backdrop for so long to the deeds of great and small.

Picture the shapes, however dim and ghostly, of the Victorian cricketers as they go about their pleasure on a warm afternoon. Half-close the eyes, wait for the jet airliner to pass over, listen to the age-old cries of "Wait!" and "Come on!" and the timeless click as the man in pads persuades the little ball towards the onlookers.

There is the champion, back from cricket combat on the other side of the globe. The smile is gentle, half-hidden by the flowing moustache, as the audience shows its appreciation. The cap is set dead centre, immaculate shirt carefully creased, sleeves rolled just clear of the wrists. The feet settle and the bat taps expectantly. Muscular shoulders, strong forearms and wrists, and keen eyes await the ball; firm thighs and eager calves are ready to spring. The blade flashes and the ball flies to the distant grassy outfield. Paid men pick up their pens to write. Idle men clap their hands.

This motion isn't timeless or even immortal. It dies within weeks if not days, just as tomorrow's sweet strokes will thrill and satisfy and then wilt like flowers. Some of the personalities will live on through a cumulative, composite process, in varying degrees of remembrance. That callous old man with the long beard and scythe and hour-glass will always be setting aside some of the day's bright stars for the sullen twilight of the sportsmen's limbo.

Philip Trevor was perceptive enough to feel that, for whatever reason, Stoddart's name in the years ahead "may not perchance appear in big print". It may well have been that an underlying sense of revulsion at the circumstances of his death harmed his glorious reputation. But Andrew Ernest Stoddart, most popular and accomplished of cricketers and rugby footballers, earned a giant niche in the history of English sport and Australia too remains indebted to him.

His voice whispers through the night: Why did they forget me?

Drewy Stoddart lives on in bronze: Neale Andrew's fine modern sculpture for Hampstead Cricket Club

A.E.STODDART: The Statistics

Test matches (all against Australia)

	M	Ins	NO	Runs	HS	Av	100s	50s	Catches
1887-88	1	2	0	33	17	16.50	0	0	1
1891-92	3	5	0	265	134	53.00	1	1	1
1893	3	5	0	162	83	32.40	0	1	0
1894-95	5	10	1	352	173	39.11	1	1	2
1896	2	4	1	103	41	34.33	0	0	1
1897-98	2	4	0	81	25	20.25	0	0	1
	16	**30**	**2**	**996**	**173**	**35.57**	**2**	**3**	**6**

* He captained England in eight Test matches (seven in Australia), winning the toss only twice. Three of these matches were won, four lost, and one drawn.
* Stoddart was the first captain to declare a Test innings closed (Lord's 1893).
* The 173 (at Melbourne) remained the highest score in Australia by an England captain for the next 80 years.
* He was the first England captain to put the opposition in (Sydney 1895).
* He took two Test wickets for 94 runs, bowling in four Tests, and he held six catches.

First-class matches

	M	Ins	NO	Runs	HS	Av	100s	50s	Catches
1885	4	8	0	149	79	18.62	0	1	1
1886	13	24	1	640	116	27.82	1	2	11
1887	17	28	0	799	151	28.53	2	2	12
1887-88(A)	9	15	0	450	94	30.00	0	4	8
1889	18	35	2	817	78*	24.75	0	6	10
1890	24	45	1	845	115	19.20	1	4	12
1891	20	32	1	857	215*	27.64	1	3	22
1891-92(A)	8	12	0	450	134	37.50	1	2	5
1892	26	47	2	1403	130	31.17	1	7	17
1893	28	50	1	2072	195*	42.28	4	13	17
1894	24	39	0	1174	148	30.10	1	5	20
1894-95(A)	10	18	1	870	173	51.17	2	5	7
1895	25	43	0	1622	150	37.72	2	11	28
1896	28	50	2	1671	127	34.81	4	7	35

	M	Ins	NO	Runs	HS	Av	100s	50s	Catches
1896-97(WI)	9	15	0	416	143	27.73	2	0	10
1897	12	21	0	650	109	30.95	1	3	14
1897-98(A)	7	11	0	205	40	18.63	0	0	3
1898	15	26	4	1038	157	47.18	2	7	16
1899	3	5	0	78	44	15.60	0	0	1
1899(USA)	2	2	0	130	74	65.00	0	2	1
1900	7	11	1	402	221	40.20	1	2	7
Totals	**309**	**527**	**16**	**16738**	**221**	**32.76**	**26**	**86**	**257**

Stoddart took 278 wickets in first-class cricket at 23.63 apiece: best figures 7 for 67 for A.Priestley's XI against Jamaica, Sabina Park, Kingston, 1897.

BIBLIOGRAPHY

A Country Vicar	***Cricket Memories*** (Methuen, 1930)
Alcock, C.W.	***Cricket Stories*** (Arrowsmith, 1901)
Altham, H.S. & Swanton, E.W.	***A History of Cricket*** (Allen & Unwin, 1949)
Alverstone, Lord & Alcock, C.W. (ed)	***Surrey Cricket – Its History and Associations*** (Longmans, Green, 1904)
Ashley-Cooper, F.S.	***Edward Mills Grace*** (Chatto & Windus, 1916)
Binns, Richard	***Cricket in Firelight*** (Selwyn & Blount, 1935)
	Blackheath RFC Records 1875-1898
Caffyn, William	***71 Not Out*** (Blackwood, 1899)
'Century'	***Cricket Rhymes*** (Cricket Press, 1899)
	Christie's Directory 1871-2
Delaney, Trevor	***Rugby Disunion: Volume One – Broken Time*** (Delaney, 1993)
Derriman, Philip	***Grassy Pitches and Glory Years – Grand Visions of the Sydney Cricket Ground*** (Playright, 1998)
	Dictionary of National Biography
Dunstan, Keith	***The Paddock That Grew*** (Cassell, 1962)
Fagan, Sean	***The First Lions of Rugby*** (Slattery Media, 2013)
Farjeon, Herbert	***Cricket Bag*** (Macdonald, 1946)
Foley, C.P.	***Autumn Foliage*** (Methuen, 1935)
Frith, David	***"My Dear Victorious Stod"*** (Lutterworth, 1977)
Frith, David	***Stoddy's Mission*** (Allen & Unwin, 1994)
Furniss, Milliken & Christian	***How's That?*** (Arrowsmith, 1895)
Gale, Norman	***Cricket Songs*** (Methuen, 1894)
Gordon, Home	***Background of Cricket*** (Arthur Barker, 1939)
Grace, W.G.	***'WG': Cricketing Reminiscences & Personal Recollections*** (James Bowden, 1899)
Hadfield, John	***A Wisden Century 1850-1950*** (Sporting Handbooks, 1950)
Harris, John & Wust, Ken	***Bendigo District Cricket 1853-1990*** (Crown Castleton, 1991)
Harris, Lord & Ashley-Cooper, F.S.	***Lord's and the MCC*** (London & Counties Press Association, 1914)
Hawke, Lord	***Recollections and Reminiscences*** (Williams & Norgate, 1924)
Iredale, F.A.	***Thirty-three Years of Cricket*** (Beatty, Richardson-Sydney, 1920)
Jessop. Gilbert	***A Cricketer's Log*** (Hodder & Stoughton, 1923)
Kinross, Albert	***An Unconventional Cricketer*** (Shaylor, 1930)
Laughton, Tony	***Captain of the Crowd: Albert Craig, Cricket and Football Rhymester 1849-1909*** (Boundary Books, 2008)

Lawton, A.E.	*My WG* (unpublished manuscript, 1947)
Lazenby, John	*Test of Time: Travels in Search of a Cricketing Legend* (John Murray, 2005)
Leveson Gower, H.D.G.	*Off and On the Field* (Stanley Paul, 1953)
Lucas, E.V.	*Cricket All His Life* (Hart-Davis, 1950)
MacLaren, A.C.	*A.C.MacLaren on Cricket* (Treherne, 1909)
Marshall, Revd F.	*Football – the Rugby Game* (Cassell, 1892)
McCarthy, Winston	*Haka! The All Blacks Story* (Pelham, 1968)
McKelvie, Roy	*The Queen's Club Story 1886-1986* (Stanley Paul, 1986)
Meynell, Laurence	*Plum Warner* (Phoenix, 1951)
Moffat, Douglas	*Crickety Cricket* (Longmans, Green, 1898)
Monro, F.R.D'O.	*The History of the Hampstead CC* (Home and Van Thal, 1949)
Moyes, A.G.	*Australian Batsmen* (Angus & Robertson, 1954)
Moyes, A.G.	*Australian Bowlers* (Angus & Robertson, 1953)
Moyes, A.G.	*Australian Cricket: a History* (Angus & Robertson, 1959)
Owen, O.L.	*History of the Rugby Football Union* (Playfair, 1955)
Pemberton, Max	*Sixty Years Ago and After* (Hutchinson, 1936)
Pollock, William	*The Cream of Cricket* (Methuen, 1934)
Price, A.B.	*English Cricketers at Barbados. January, February, and March, 1897* (West Indian Guardian,1897)
Pullin, A.W.	*Alfred Shaw – Cricketer* (Cassell, 1902)
Rae, Simon	*W.G.Grace: a Life* (Faber, 1998)
Richard, Huw	*The Reds and Whites* (Aurum, 2014)
Ronayne, Michael	*Test Cricket Tours No.1 England 1876-7 to 1939* (Ronayne, 1984)
Sewell, E.H.D.	*The Log of a Sportsman* (Fisher Unwin, 1923)
Smith-Turberville, H.	*Reprints* (privately printed, 1929)
Standing, Percy Cross	*Anglo-Australian Cricket 1862-1926* (Faber & Gwyer, 1926)
Standing, Percy Cross	*Cricket of Today & Yesterday* (Caxton, 1902)
Standing, Percy Cross	*The Hon.F.S.Jackson* (Cassell, 1906)
	The Stock Exchange in 1900
Swinnerton, Frank	*Reflections from a Village* (Hamish Hamilton, 1978)
Thomas, J.B.G.	*Great Rugger Matches* (Stanley Paul, 1959)
Thomson, A.A.	*Rugger My Pleasure* (Museum, 1961)
Trevor, Capt.Philip	*The Lighter Side of Cricket* (Methuen, 1901)
Wakelam, H.B.T.	*Harlequin Story* (Phoenix, 1954)
Warner, P.F.	*The Book of Cricket* (Dent, 1922)
Warner, P.F. (ed)	*Cricket (Badminton Library)* (Longmans, Green, 1920)
Warner, P.F.	*Cricket Reminiscences* (Grant Richards, 1920)
Warner, P.F.	*Gentlemen v Players 1806-1949* (Harrap, 1950)
Warner, P.F.	*Lord's 1787-1945* (Harrap, 1946)
Warner, P.F.	*My Cricketing Life* (Hodder & Stoughton, 1921)

Webster, Ray & Miller, Allan	***First-Class Cricket in Australia Volume 1 1850-51 to 1941-42*** (Webster, 1991)
Whimpress, Bernard & Hart, Nigel	***Adelaide Oval Test Cricket 1884-1984*** (Wakefield, 1984)
Williamson, John	***Football's Forgotten Tour: the Story of the British Australian Rules Venture of 1888*** (Williamson, 2003)
Wilson, F.B.	***Sporting Pie*** (Chapman & Hall, 1922)
Woods, S.M.J.	***My Reminiscences*** (Chapman & Hall, 1925)
Yeoman, James	***History in South Shields Street Names*** (Shields Gazette, 1962)

NEWSPAPERS AND PERIODICALS

The American Cricketer; The Australasian; Baily's Magazine; Bell's Life in London; The Bulletin; C.B.Fry's Magazine; Coventry Herald; Cricket: A Weekly Record of the Game; The Cricketer; The Cricket Field; Daily Graphic; Daily Telegraph; Evening Standard; The Golden Penny; Hampstead and Highgate Express; Melbourne newspapers *The Age, The Argus, The Herald, and Punch; The Morning Leader; The Pall Mall Gazette; Shields Daily Gazette; Sporting Celebrities; Sporting Sketches; The Sportsman; The Star; The Strand Magazine; The Sydney Mail; The Sydney Referee; The Times; The Windsor Magazine*

INDEX